CARNIVAL GAMES

THE COMPLETE PROFESSIONAL DEALER'S HANDBOOK

Edward F. Cervinski

Copyright © 2025 by Edward F. Cervinski

All Rights Reserved. No part of this book shall be reproduced, stored in a retrieval system, transmitted by any means--graphic, electronic, or mechanical, including photocopying, taping, and recording--screen played, dramatized, or copied by any other means without prior written permission from the author.

Visit the author online at: www.cervinski.com

Published in the United States by

Stellaberry Press

Las Vegas, NV

First Edition

Library of Congress Control Number: 2024901823

Publisher's Cataloging-in-Publication data

Names: Cervinski, Edward F., author.
Title: Carnival games : the complete professional dealer's handbook / Edward F. Cervinski.
Description: Includes bibliographical references and index. | Las Vegas, NV: Stellaberry Press, 2025.
Identifiers: LCCN: 2024901823 | ISBN: 978-0-9770100-2-8 (spiral bound) | 978-0-9770100-7-3 (paperback)
Subjects: LCSH Carnival games--Handbooks, manuals, etc. | BISAC GAMES & ACTIVITIES / Gambling / Table
Classification: LCC GV1835.2 .C47 2024 | DDC 791/.1--dc23

Quantity discounts are available on bulk purchases of this book for educational, gift purposes, or as premiums. If you do not find this book in your favorite bookstore, or you'd like more information on this book or any of our other titles, you may place single or bulk book order copies online by visiting: www.stellaberrypress.com.

Author's notes: 1) Baccarat and Pai Gow Poker are included in this book, although some may argue they are not true Carnival Games. Instead of writing two separate smaller books for Baccarat and Pai Gow Poker, the author decided to include both of these games, along with the other Carnival Games, here in one book. 2) Carnival Games are ever-evolving. Rules change periodically. Each casino has its own house rules and payouts, and new games or variations are occasionally introduced. This book aims to be up-to-date on common dealing practices at the time of printing, while future editions will incorporate industry-standard updates. Keep in mind, casinos are free to implement their own rules, dealing preferences, and payouts, which may differ from those presented in this book. For suggestions or inclusion of new games, contact the publisher.

Throughout this book, words of he/him/man/men or any other male-dominated reference is not meant to exclude, subdue, or lessen the value or equality of the female gender or sex, most specifically female dealers, players, and staff members. The author's intent is to include both genders and allow for quicker reading without having to specifically name them both by shortening the terminology to just the male gender.

Periodic use of slang, non-standard words, phrases, double entendres, and other descriptive content may be offensive or derogatory. It is crucial for dealers to be aware and recognize the meanings behind such language and innuendos. This awareness is not only helpful but unfortunately necessary.

®Registered Trademarks and ©Copyrighted materials of each Carnival Game are owned by their respective entities and are included here under the Fair Use Doctrine (codified in Section 107 of the U.S. Copyright Act) for teaching purposes.

CONTENTS

Introduction	4
General Expectations and Conduct of Dealers	6
Casino Personnel and Duties	9
Dealer Responsibilities	10
Carnival Games Equipment	15
Financial Transactions	22
Properly Cutting and Handling Cheques	24
Skillful Card Shuffling	26
3 Shot Poker	30
Baccarat	31
Big Wheel	46
Caribbean Stud Poker	48
Casino War	49
Crazy 4 Poker	50
DJ Wild	52
High Card Flush/I Love Suits	54
Let It Ride	56
Mississippi Stud	58
Pai Gow Poker	60
Texas Hold'em Bonus Poker	65
Three Card Poker	66
Ultimate Texas Holdem	68
Proper Carnival Games Etiquette	70
Callouts: Alert versus Approval	71
Carnival Games Employment	72
Gambling Addiction	75
Closing	76
Acknowledgments	78
Carnival Games Quotes	79
Glossary	80
Footnotes	124
Notes	125
Index	126
Poker Hand Rankings and Payouts	128
Carnival Games Comparison Table	130

INTRODUCTION

Stepping into a casino is like stepping into another world—a world full of dreams, hopes, and often, frustration and despair. Casinos appeal to all five human senses. Players see the flashing lights of slot machines, spotlights on each table, and progressive jackpots climbing to new heights. They hear the ringing of slot machines, the shouts and cheers of players winning, and the agony of losing. Establishments fill the air with inviting scents, offering beverages—and often food—that are consistently delicious. Players buy-in with their cash, bet their cheques, hold their drinks, sit at the tables, lean into the armrests, and perhaps pick up the cards or toss the dice from their hands. They appreciate the soft carpet, comfortable chairs, and high fives when they or another player win. Occasionally, someone bumps into another, spilling drinks, and there exists a tolerance between players literally rubbing shoulders with each other.

Players engage for many reasons: to make money, make enough to cover rent, pass time, get a thrill, hope for a jackpot, meet family/friends, play with strangers, curb boredom, feed an addiction, for any other reason, or no reason at all.

While casinos aim to profit, they excel in providing guests with a great experience. One way is by offering a variety of table games within players' budgets, allowing them reasonable hope of winning against the house, enjoying the play, and encouraging players to return, whether they win or lose. Nowhere are these varieties more plentiful than in the Carnival Games section.

To start, let's rule out what this book does not cover: non-casino games found at amusement parks, carnivals, circuses, fairs, festivals, or similar venues. Games like ball, bean bag, or ring toss, balloon, bottle or plate breaking, fishing holes, potato sack, or squirt gun races that can be played by anyone, at any age, including children, to win, most commonly, a stuffed animal. There are over 100 of these "fun" games. Players there won't get rich, but they won't go broke either.

Let's dive into the adult-type, casino Carnival Games.

Carnival Games in this book encompass all the other casino table games not classified under Blackjack, Craps, Poker, or Roulette. Although there are many more Carnival Games than are presented in this book, the fourteen most popular games featured here include:

3 Shot Poker	Crazy 4 Poker	Pai Gow Poker
Baccarat	DJ Wild	Texas Hold'em Bonus Poker
Big Wheel	High Card Flush/I Love Suits	Three-Card Poker
Caribbean Stud	Let It Ride	Ultimate Texas Hold'em
Casino War	Mississippi Stud	

No other casino table game type showcases such variety and inventiveness as Carnival Games. Dozens of Carnival Games exist, with new games introduced yearly at trade shows and expos worldwide.

These games are licensed to casinos for their players, and a casino's profitability from each Carnival Game determines whether they keep or eliminate it. Games like Baccarat, Pai Gow Poker, and Ultimate Texas Hold'em are often offered on multiple tables, alongside other staples.

Other than slot machines, Carnival Games offer the potential for the highest "longshot" odds in the casino. Stratospheric Progressive payouts, sometimes exceeding $1 million USD, are unheard of in any other main casino table games. The allure is that for a small wager of $1 to $5, and patient luck, any player has the possibility for a substantial jackpot. Games like Baccarat and Pai Gow Poker have among the lowest house edges, under 1.5%. On the other hand, the Big Wheel heavily favors the house with upwards of a 23% house edge.

While players need games to be fun, simple, and give the impression they are easy to win, the early success of a new Carnival Game is largely due to competent and knowledgeable dealers who can correctly, efficiently, and professionally deal and explain the game. These games must be professionally taught to dealers.

This book focuses on explaining the current most popular Carnival Games (as listed above), while future editions aim to incorporate new games that casinos offer their guests.

Written from a seasoned professional dealer's and gaming instructor's perspective, this book's purpose is to teach and enable aspiring students to become professional Carnival Games dealers. When used by top-notch instructor(s) in classroom demonstrations, this educational material will serve to acclimate how each game is properly dealt.

This book covers how to deal, rules, payouts, techniques, proper procedures, requirements, equipment, player options, common house policies, etiquette, dealer responsibilities, history, and so much more. It also acknowledges the importance of responsible gaming and addresses gambling addiction. Readers of this book can't miss the 125-plus photos, illustrations, and tables, along with a generous Glossary of proper (and slang) terminology to use when communicating with players, other dealers, and staff members. Ambitious students have all the tools to learn, deal, audition, work, and excel as a Professional Carnival Games Dealer.

If you're ready to deal among the most versatile of casino dealers, step up to the table, clear your hands, greet your players, and announce...

Place Your Bets!

GENERAL EXPECTATIONS and CONDUCT of DEALERS

Casinos, legalized gambling, horseracing, poker rooms, and sports betting all face stiff competition when competing for the gambler's dollar. Successful properties take great care in the location, design, and amenities offered. Many casinos design their floor space, atmosphere, and architecture, and even patent vent-pumped scents, to entice customers to visit and stay at their property. These customers are often gamblers, but they are also diners, convention/conference/seminar attendees, concert/show viewers, swimming pool relaxers/partiers, and hotel guests. These same customers often have a myriad of choices (especially in Las Vegas, Nevada), of where to stay, eat, and play. Hotels and casinos know the value of having customers return for another visit. They also know the most important part of these hospitality businesses are the customer service employees, most specifically the front-line people. From the bartender who makes drinks, the server who brings food, to the hotel check-in specialist who assigns a room, and yes, to the dealers who deal the games, all these people have one goal: make the guest's stay enjoyable, memorable, and repeatable. Front-line employees spend the most time with each guest and have the largest personal influence to meet and exceed guests' expectations, from whether they enjoy their current visit to whether they return.

In any casino, a dealer's biggest responsibility is to enhance guests' experience while they visit the property. From the moment he greets guests with a friendly "hello" and a big smile to the end of the interaction, a knowledgeable and personable dealer not only delivers excellent guest service but also tends to earn higher tips or tokes, even from players enduring a tough losing streak. This positive attitude will improve the dealer's reputation and credibility with casino management to potentially obtain better shifts, more scheduled hours, preferential treatment, and advancement in the company. A casino employee should recognize that it is expected of him to treat all people he encounters as VIPs; everyone is important and should be treated well.

At a minimum without specific order, dealers need to follow these expected standards of conduct:

DO's

1. Be nice, friendly, polite, and professional to everyone, always. (Worth repeating.) Be nice, friendly, polite, and professional to everyone, always. They are the reason the casino exists, and dealers have a job.
2. Greet all new players with a smile, eye contact, and a simple "Hello." Address them as "Sir," "Ma'am," or "Miss."
3. Make periodic eye contact with each player.
4. Thank players for playing as they leave the table, or every time they toke/tip the dealer.
5. Say "Please" and more often "Thank You." They both go a long way.
6. When making change for a player, wish him "Good Luck" or "Play Well."
7. Engage in light, friendly, even fun conversation between rounds of gameplay, so long as it doesn't slow down the game or distract the dealer from properly dealing the game.
8. Know the carnival game assigned. If unfamiliar with how to deal a particular game, inform management. They can often switch dealers so that every dealer knows the game at his table. But be open to learning a new game as it will add to the repertoire of known games.
9. Be punctual, which means a dealer arrives at least 15 minutes early to punch in. Be on time when returning from breaks for the next dealer's rotation or push, otherwise the next dealer is robbed of his full break. If unable to push to the next table timely, (i.e., emergency restroom break, nosebleed, runny nose, etc.), alert a supervisor, as he can fill in temporarily so that the string of pushes does not get interrupted or delayed.
10. Be neatly groomed.
    a. Hair should be clean, trimmed, styled well, and free of unnatural color(s).
    b. Fingernails should be short, neatly trimmed or manicured, and minimally polished.

    c. Not all casinos allow beards, mustaches, sideburns, and goatees. When they are allowed, they should be neatly trimmed and maintained.
    d. Uniforms should be clean, freshly ironed, and all accessories worn (name tag, vest, apron, etc.).
    e. Shoes should be free of dirt, comfortable, new looking, and polished if necessary.
    f. Smell nice. Shower and use deodorant. Avoid strong perfumes and colognes.
    g. Brush and floss teeth for fresh breath before arriving at work. Use breath mints while on break.
    h. Makeup should not be excessive but applied minimally only to enhance beauty.
    i. Jewelry should be tasteful, non-offensive, and kept to a minimum.

11. Keep the cheque rack/house bank neat at all times. Use clear spacers when necessary. Remove cheques from the right side of the bank. Work from the outside-in.
12. Know the casino and the location of its restaurants, bars, shops, showrooms, hotel front desk, hotel elevators, player's card desk, cashier, ATMs, pool, parking garage, security desk, restrooms, ballrooms, valet, bell desk, and so much more. Dealers are often asked for directions to any of these or some other outside property/venue.
13. Keep the pace of the game moving along. Alert inattentive players when they can bet, but don't rush them. Remember, the more hands a dealer can deal, the more chances for that next toke. Be efficient but not sloppy.
14. Use the correct callouts when necessary.
15. Clap/shake hands out front of self to show surveillance every time a dealer first arrives at each table and before leaving the table. Do this also before and after every time there is a need to touch/scratch any part of the body, to adjust clothes, go into a pocket, or to touch any chips/cheques from a player or the chip rack.
16. Take breaks/eat/drink/smoke in designated areas at the back of the house away from guests, not on the casino floor.
17. Act like a mature adult when dealing with management. Floor decisions are always final and rarely overruled. Right or wrong, do what is asked or told by management and comply.
18. Apologize if a mistake is made. We are all human; we all make mistakes. Casinos are aware of this inevitability and have resolutions in place to fix errors. Call the floorman if necessary, fix the issue, then move on. Don't keep the topic fresh for continued discussion, or so that players can expect repeated apologies.
19. Beware of theft, cheating, angle shooting, player collusion, and anything unordinary that compromises the integrity of the game. Call the floorman immediately and alert him of the issue. He'll handle it.
20. PAY ATTENTION! A dealer is hired to deal the game. Reread that last sentence again. A dealer is hired to deal the game. Attentiveness is key. Do not people-watch or engage in conversation that distracts the full attention away from the game. Inattentiveness causes as much as 90 percent or more of dealer errors.
21. Adhere to the house rule regarding players showing or discussing their cards during the hand. This may be permitted at some casinos, but if not allowed, it could void the hand.
22. Adhere to house preferences on dealing each game, multi-hand wagers, order of dealing, card placements, take and pay procedures, discards, shuffle, and registering bonus bets.
23. Use the correct hand when revealing player's cards, taking bets, or issuing payouts. The dealer's right hand is used for these procedures for players on his right two-thirds of the table. Use the left hand for the first two player spots. Don't cross arms to take/pay bets.
24. Be aware of player collusion. Some casinos permit players to share information about the cards they hold, others strictly prohibit it. In such casinos, on certain games, signs may be posted, and any player found sharing information may have their hands voided or be forced off the table. Always know the house rules regarding player collusion.

DON'Ts

1. Never argue with a player. A dealer can explain a rule once if the player is in the wrong, and oftentimes that resolves the issue. But, if a mistake or error is made, or the player is still upset, alert the floorman. Let him settle all disputes.
2. Never call for Security. Call the floorman over urgently. Alert him of the situation. He will make the determination if Security and/or Surveillance is needed to review a hand or any other situation. In rare cases when the supervisor is unable to respond, it might be ok.
3. Never throw anything towards any player. This includes his ID card, player's card, or cheques when making payouts.
4. Never hustle tokes. It sounds desperate, is severely frowned upon by every casino, and will cause the dealer to receive a written warning or be terminated.
5. Never refuse a toke/tip/gratuity from any player, regardless of the amount. Always accept it and thank the player.
6. Don't loiter in the casino, especially in uniform. When the shift is over, leave.
7. Never make decisions for a player. A dealer can explain the rules briefly and tell the player what his options are, but nothing further. Dealers are often called upon to educate players of all skill levels. Be patient with them.
8. Never chew gum, smoke, text, or make a phone call while on the casino floor. Do not wear headphones/earpieces to listen to music.
9. Don't bring any personal items into the pit area. Sometimes female employees are allowed an area in the pit podium to store a purse, but don't count on it. Ask beforehand.
10. A dealer should discourage friends/relatives from playing at his table. This creates a conflict of interest and possibly shows favoritism that other players and management can easily detect. It is often not allowed, per house policy.
11. Don't whine/complain to the manager/floorman/supervisor in front of guests. Discuss in the back of the house.
12. Don't pick up any item off the floor while seated or standing for active dealing. This includes cards, chips/cheques, tokes, dice, roulette balls, or any other item. Call the floorman; it is his job to fetch and inspect these items.
13. Do not compromise accuracy and completeness for the sake of speed. Speed will come with experience. Always focus on accuracy and completeness. This is not a race.
14. Do not compare one's dealing skill set to those of another dealer. Every dealer should strive to be the best dealer he can be. Always be open to learn more.
15. Never let one's attitude be negatively affected by one or more belligerent players such that the dealer's skill, attitude, integrity, style, etc., becomes compromised or substandard. If there is an issue at the table, inform a supervisor.

A dealer's appearance, attitude, courtesy, people interaction, amount and level of service, gaming knowledge, pride in self and in his work, ALL reflect on his success and continuation of employment at a casino. Never underestimate the influence dealers have, positive or negative, upon their guests.

REMINDERS:
- Always know and adhere to the specific house shuffle, dealing, and payout procedures.
- Report every dealer error, no matter how minor, to the floorman. DO NOT "self-correct."
- Payouts to all players on the dealer's right two-thirds are paid with the right hand.
- The first two betting spots on the left side of the table are paid with the left hand.
- House procedure may require a burn card and have the dealer stack or spread apart his cards—face down—after all players have received their cards.
- A cut card may or may not be used.
- A 6-Card and/or Progressive bonus bet may be offered.

CASINO PERSONNEL and DUTIES

HIERARCHY of CASINO STAFF

Following is a general list of Casino Personnel and can vary from each casino. Below are their overall roles and some of their primary responsibilities to the casino. (See illustration 1.)

Illustration 1

Owner – Company or person who is the possessor, proprietor, or shareholder. Holds the licenses (gaming, food, alcohol, hotel, etc.).

Security – Team of trained individuals who protect the casino's money, property, staff, and patrons from violent crime, theft, cheating, inappropriate behavior, and trespassers. Escorts people off the premises and can detain people who have committed a crime until police arrive. Also oversees the count team while on the floor collecting money from the table drop boxes and slot machines. Brings fill orders to tables.

President/VP/Board of Directors – Executives who maintain/improve operations for the whole casino property.

Surveillance – Video cameras constantly record nearly every square inch of the casino property, except where prohibited by law (restrooms, inside hotel rooms). Also refers to the highly trained technical (IT) team who watches, monitors, suspects, flags, and investigates any problem, individual, or situation. Works alongside Security.

Casino Manager – Oversees the gaming part of the casino and its enforcement of policies.

Assistant Casino Manager – Assists Casino Manager.

Shift Manager – Runs day-to-day operations. Monitors staffing and resolves disputes.

Pencil Person – Part of management team responsible for maintaining adequate staffing levels of dealers, assigning dealers to tables, opening/closing tables, and the EO list.

Floor Supervisor – Assists Shift Manager, resolves disputes, verify cash transactions/large payouts, and makes floor rulings.

Cashier – Cage employee who exchanges or dispenses cash or cheques. May handle markers or casino credit.

Dealer – Trained professional who deals the game, maintains integrity, and spends the most time with players.

Player – Customer who plays for profit and enjoyment. It is this playing that makes the casino money, so the casino stays open, expands operations, pays its employees, and shares profits with shareholders.

DEALER RESPONSIBILITIES

Carnival Games Dealers have many responsibilities at the table, away from the table, and while transitioning between tables. They must remember a plethora of checklists. From gaming rules and house rules to standards of conduct, knowing the correct payout for each bet, using the correct left/right payout hand, and constantly watching for card/bet tampering or switching, among other duties, the dealer's attention is profuse.

Of all the responsibilities and expectations of a dealer, three stand out as critically important:

> 1. Integrity – The dealer must be honest in all his actions and keep the game honest and fair for all players. This includes "Game Protection."
> 2. Knowledge – The dealer must be properly trained in the game(s) he deals from opening to closing the table.
> 3. Calling the Floorman – The dealer must alert the floorman when a mistake is made by either the dealer or player, when any equipment malfunction happens, or when suspecting cheating occurs. Dealers should NEVER fix any mistake.

TABLE ASSIGNMENT

When a dealer arrives for work and punches in, he'll receive a table number assignment. This states which table(s) the dealer will deal. The dealer will either need to tap/push the current dealer out of that assigned table once he's finished dealing that hand and start dealing, or he will need to open that table. Dealers are expected to deal for approximately one hour until the next dealer comes along to push him out, the table closes, or it is time for a break. New dealers to a casino are often unsure of "how things go" and this is a great time to ask (and ask often) other dealers or the floorman.

OPENING the TABLE

When a dealer opens a table, the first thing to happen is the cheque bank cover must be unlocked, removed, and stored elsewhere (sometimes under the table or in a special place for the table covers). New dealers should take direction from the supervisor and other dealers during this time. Supplies, such as cards and lammers, will need to be brought out. Bank verification will also need to happen.

DEALER CHANGES (PUSH) ♠ ENTRANCE ♥ EXIT ♦ DEALER ROTATION

Carnival Games dealers normally spend 60 minutes at a table before they are pushed to go on break for 20 minutes. While there is no actual rough physical "pushing" of the dealer, it is the process of a dealer rotation. The existing dealer must finish dealing the current hand before exiting his position from the table. No push should ever occur during the hand or payouts. Base dealers need to clap their hands and exit. (See photo 1.) Incoming dealers should also clap their hands face up before touching anything.

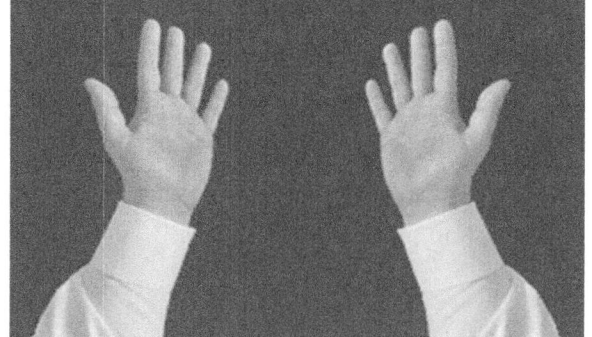

Photo 1

KNOW the GAME BEING DEALT

Nothing substitutes a good solid education or trade school instruction in Carnival Games. Many dealers start as players and think they know a lot about dealing. Sad truth is while many of them know various rules, they haven't a clue on house rules, correct payouts, correct payout order, correct use of left/right hands, or many of the other common (and need-to-know) aspects of the game. Over time, these games evolve, change, and new bets are introduced.

There are no stupid questions. If a dealer is unfamiliar with the game, he should ask and learn. If a dealer lacks confidence or needs a review of the rules, additional training or a refresher course should be taken. A professional dealer will, at a minimum, know how to deal several games presented in this book and use correct payouts, callouts, correct payout order, proper cheque and card handling, and so much more. Like the old saying: "No one is ever too old to learn."

CHEQUE BANK MAINTENANCE ⚬ CASH HANDLING ⚬ FILL ORDERS

Cheque bank maintenance refers to the organization of cheques. A dealer should always work from the outside-in when taking cheques from the bank. Every bank has rows of cheques that are of different denominations and different colors. Two things remain constant—higher value cheques are always towards the center of the bank, and every full column contains 20 cheques. Any stack less than 20 cheques should have lammers separating the smaller groupings of cheques. A properly organized bank can be counted quickly, allows for accurate disbursement of cheques, and looks more professional. Only work out of one row per color of cheques. Work from the outside-in, keeping the larger denominations in the center and smaller toward the outside edges.

When handling cash, separate and **layer the bills face down on the left side of the table** directly in front of the cheque rack. (See photo 2.) Watch for counterfeit bills! No more than 25 bills should be verified at one time. Next, bring out cheques from the bank, an amount equal to the cash and place the **cheques to the right of the cash**. Break these cheques down with drop-cutting and sizing-in methods. (See photo 3.) Re-verify and state the amount, "Changing $1200," for example. Stack the cheques, push/slide them to the player, and wish him good luck. Place the cash onto the slit and plunge it with the paddle into the dropbox below. (See photo 4.) Occasionally, an eager player will reach out to grab the cheques before the dealer slides them to him. As soon as this happens, the dealer needs to warn the player, "Stop. Let me push the cheques to you properly, please." All cheques need to be proven. Check with house policy. See the sections on **Proper Cheque Cutting** and **Financial Transactions**.

Photo 2

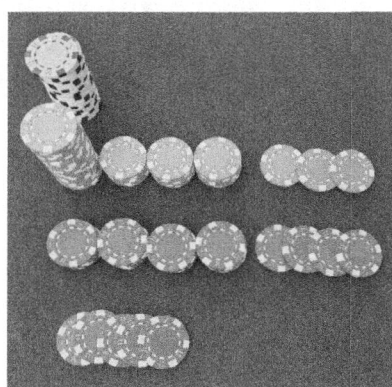

Photo 3

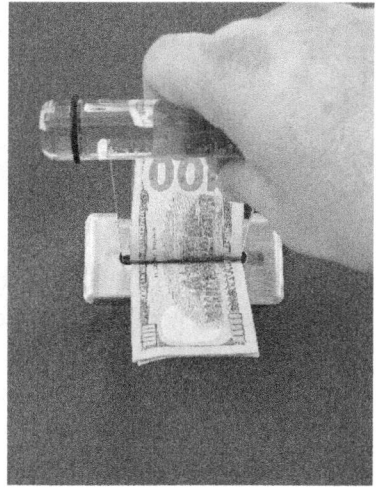

Photo 4

Fill orders are the request for more cheques to be brought to the table because cheques in the bank are being depleted. A full bank makes it easy to make change and looks more professional. A security person will bring cheques based on a fill order receipt to show the transfer of cheques (a fill) from the main cage to the table. When instructed, tip the chip tray (See photo 5 next page,) and slide the chips upright onto the table. Repeat for multiple trays. (See photo 6 next page.) Organize the cheque value from largest (closest to the dealer in neat rows) to the smallest (furthest away from the dealer). Finger-verify all columns are the same height and run down the largest denomination stack of 20 cheques. (See photo 7 next page.) Fill orders, like all table transactions, follow specific procedures. If security arrives during a hand already in progress, they will need to wait until the entire hand is completed. Players should hold off from placing new bets. Both the dealer and floorman verify/sign off the fill slip before dropping it into the drop box (See photo 8.) Inform the supervisor of any discrepancies.

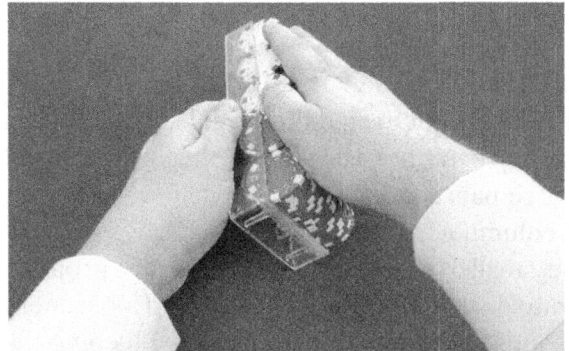

Photo 5

Photo 6

Photo 7

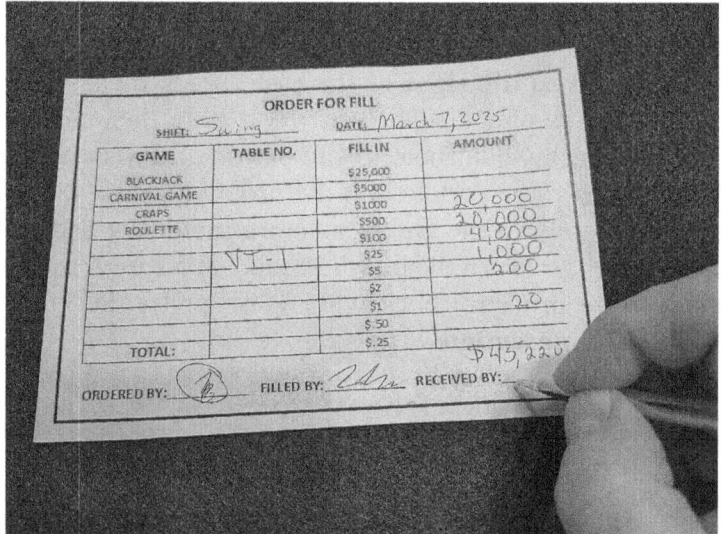

Photo 8

LOGGING IN of PLAYERS' CARDS ▪ LOBBY STATUS 💰 LOGGING OUT

Welcome all new players to the table. Ask for his player's card and give it to the supervisor. Normally, the floorman will handle tracking a player's play. If the player does not have a player's card, ask if they'd like one made. This tracks a player's time and average wagered amount, among other things, while at the table and earns the player tier/reward points for card level and comps. As players move positions, the pit boss will move him digitally on the table screen. When a player ends his session, the supervisor logs that player out. Be mindful of how much a player abruptly walks away with as the floorman will ask the dealer before closing out the player tracking.

AGE VERIFICATION ♠ CHECK for IDENTIFICATION

Every staff member of the casino has an obligation to ensure that each person who walks into or is anywhere near a gaming area is of legal age. Local, state, and/or federal laws dictate the minimum age requirement to gamble in a casino or poker room. If someone looks under 25 years old, card that person. **Dealers have been terminated** on the spot **for allowing underage players to play or for failing to check identification for an active underage player.**

This is a SERIOUS OFFENSE!

The casino, supervisory staff, and dealer's failure to identify those who are underage and/or who have allowed them to play face stiff penalties and fines. A supervisor should be called for any person who refuses to show a legal and valid, government-issued identification, or if the identification is suspected to be fraudulent. **DO NOT make change to or allow a bet from any suspected underage player until his age has been verified.**

DEALING ▪ CONTROLLING the GAME

A dealer's complete attention is needed from the moment the dealer watches the previous dealer exit until the next dealer arrives. All equipment at the table, including cheques, cash, cards, shoes, table sign, and lammers are the responsibility of the current dealer to be accurate, complete, and in working order. These are some, but not all things a watchful dealer needs to control the game.

The pace of Carnival Games varies widely. Verify bets by counting the amount, quickly yet efficiently. Repeat bets back to the player to match their intention. Be conversational with players but don't chitchat so much that it distracts their focus off the game. Watch the players, especially their hands, other dealers, and even supervisors. Watch everyone! Make use of peripheral vision. Use correct lammers throughout the game when necessary, as this protects the dealer in case of disputes. Ensure bets meet the minimum/maximum requirements. Disallow late bets, especially after cards have been dealt to other players. Run the game. Collect losing bets. Pay winning bets properly. Watch for cheating. Use proper callouts and call the supervisor when necessary. Be helpful to players. Keep an orderly cheque rack. Thank players who offer a toke. Always remain professional.

GAME PROTECTION: WATCH for THEFT, CHEATING, and COLLUSION

Cheating has existed for as long as gambling games have been played. Most people like to win and will do so honestly. These same players will also take defeat in stride as part of the game. However, there are those who figure if they can't win or make their gains honestly, they'll cheat, deceive, or thieve. Fortunately, for a casino, security cameras, sharp dealers, and ever watchful players have resulted in a vast reduction in cheating. The penalties are severe, and the disdain is enduring for those who attempt to undermine an honest game. Still, the need and requirement for game protection will always exist.

Dealers must keep a good eye out for ANY and ALL irregularities that happen within his time at the table including while he pushes and leaves the table. Dealers can suspect, but never accuse players, other dealers, or staff of cheating. Always bring the suspicion of irregularity to the attention of a floorman, supervisor, or shift manager and let him handle it from there. Have proof and be concise when relaying this information. Intentionally or not, players cannot be allowed to compromise the integrity of the game by cheating.

Common things to watch for while dealing:

- Players showing signs of capping, dragging, past posting, or pinching.
- Players throwing the cards harshly, even dangerously.
- Players sending signals or gestures.
- Players working together to have one distract the dealer while another cheats.
- Players using a device to hide, mark, switch, or otherwise tamper with any equipment.
- Players reaching into the dealer's bank or working stack, or touching any part of a fill order.
- Players criticizing another player's play or the dealer.
- Players causing delays that hold up the game, including verbally abusing others to antagonize or aggravate another player.
- Players touching a winning bet before a payout is issued, or a losing bet before it is taken.
- Players being rude to anyone else at or near the table.

CALLING the FLOORMAN for CLARIFICATIONS or HELP

Dealers should not make resolutions to problems concerning play. A floorman's assistance is needed for player disagreement with the rules, actions, or another player's attitude; with mechanical issues such as damaged equipment; with suspected cheating or theft; or to attend to any player's need.

The management staff's list of responsibilities for the casino is endless. Their complex jobs have one goal in mind, keep the casino running as smoothly as possible, which includes resolving issues promptly when they arise.

While a dealer shouldn't "cry wolf" with trivial issues within his power to resolve, he should always feel comfortable in asking for assistance from a boxman, floorman, or manager.

DEALER BREAK

After dealing for a full hour, the dealer gets pushed off the table, and it's time for a break! Dealers are not expected, nor permitted by law, to work a continuous eight-hour shift without a break.

Fortunately, dealer breaks are worked seamlessly into the dealer rotation. The dealer on break should go to the designated break area or employee dining room (EDR). Before leaving the table, he should make a mental note of what time he needs to return from break. Don't arrive early and definitely don't arrive late for the next push.

DEAD SPREAD ♠ ♥ ♦ ♣ CLOSING the TABLE

Once an active game ceases to exist—that is, all the players leave the table—the game is now a dead spread. The table may close for the time being or remain open for any new players to join. When a table is empty, dealers have several tasks to complete:

- Ensure all cheques are neatly organized in stacks of 20 separated by a clear spacer.
- Keep themselves looking neat.

A closing table refers to a table without players or a game in process, where a secure bank cover is about to be installed.. The dealer will need to rely on instructions from the floorman. Gather all equipment (lammers, cut cards, etc.) and secure it within the bank cover. Once the cover is locked, the dealer is now "homeless." He may receive a new table assignment, be assigned to go on break, or be sent home for the shift.

ENDING the SHIFT

A dealer's shift will end for various reasons:

- They have completed a full shift.
- The scheduled shift is going into overtime (OT).
- There is no longer a need for the rest of the scheduled shift.
- Too many dealers are assigned.
- The table has broken.
- The dealer asked for and received approval for an early out (EO).
- The dealer has become sick during his shift.
- There has been an emergency.
- The room closed for the time being.
- The dealer has received disciplinary action.

Never miss or be late for a shift or leave a shift early without supervisory approval. If a dealer gets sick during his shift, he should notify his supervisor or shift manager immediately. The dealer should always check with the pencil person to confirm his shift has finished early and he can clock out/go home. Never rely on another dealer's assumption or say-so.

CARNIVAL GAMES EQUIPMENT

General equipment is examined here. Specific equipment is discussed in that game's section.

TABLES

There are many different table designs to list, but all will have a dealing area on the layout, a dealer standing or sitting area, a cheque bank, a place to discard cards, a layout for that particular game, armrest rail, drink cup holders, and seating areas for the players. (See illustrations 2 and 3.)

Illustration 2   Illustration 3

CHIPS versus CHEQUES ◉ COLORS & VALUES

Chips and cheques are often spoken of interchangeably; however, they are not the same. A chip has no cash value and is used at the roulette table, in poker tournaments, or as promotional chips. A cheque does have cash value and will always have the monetary value printed on it. A standard casino chip or cheque measures 39mm in diameter, is 3.5mm thick and weighs 11.5 to 14 grams. There are also larger chips/cheques, approximately 47mm and even oversized rectangular gaming plaques for very large denominations. Professional casino chips/cheques are made from clay, ceramic, plastic resin, or a combination thereof. Often the casino logo, colors, and dollar values are all embedded into the chip/cheque. To prevent counterfeiting, some casinos have radio frequency identification (RFID) microchips inside the chips/cheques. These microchips use electromagnetic fields (wires and sensors built under the table felt) to track player action/betting amounts, and dealer performance.

Cheques come in various colors, but U.S. casinos have largely assigned (though not standardized) the same colors to certain denominations. Check with each casino. For the most part, denominations are:

$1 – White or Blue	$500 – Lavender or Light Purple or Pink
$5 – Red	$1,000 – Yellow/Canary
$25 – Green	$5,000 – White or Brown (Chocolate) or Orange or Grey
$100 – Black	$25,000 – Cranberry or Pumpkin
	$100,000 and higher are all individualized.

CHEQUE RACK

The cheque rack "bank" or "well" holds all the cheques as part of the table's bank used to make change for players. It also holds many different lammers. The cheque rack (see photo 9) is much wider and holds twice as much than its poker counterpart. When the table is closed, everything fits into the cheque rack and is

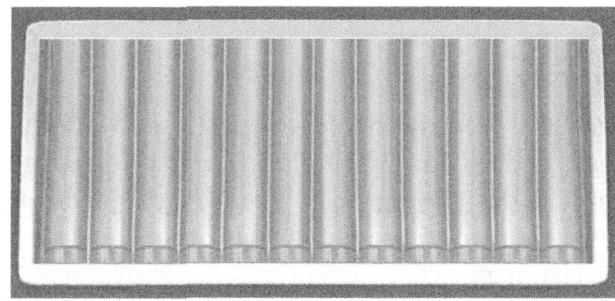

Photo 9

The Complete Professional Dealer's Handbook 15

covered by a see-through locked rack cover. Unlike poker cheque racks that never change in value, a Carnival Game's cheque rack will constantly change in value—and there is no way for a dealer to determine how much should be in the bank. Players come and go, win and lose, and color up, all affecting the cheque bank's value and number of cheques in each denomination. As the dealer works with a rack, cheque tubes are depleted from the outside inward. Each chip column is a full stack of 20, separated by a clear spacer. Once the full column is less than 20 cheques, a clear spacer is used to break down every $25 in red, every $100 in green, every $500 in black, every $2000 in lavender/purple, and every $5000 in yellow. Always work out of the right side of the rack. Keep the rack looking organized and make use of clear spacers when required.

TABLE MIN & MAX SIGN

Every casino table is required to show the minimum/maximum betting amounts for the game being played. Limits can change based on player traffic or by player request to increase/decrease (See illustration 4.)

CARDS

Casino table games use paper cards coated with a smooth, shiny finish. These are usually two sheets of paper glued together and measure 2.5 inches x 3.5 inches. A paper deck can cost the casino 10 to 25 cents per deck, and is replaced several times daily. Playing cards are the standard 52-card deck, split into two colors: black and red. (See illustration 5.) Each black set of cards is divided into two suits, spades and clubs. The red set of cards is divided into two groups as well, hearts and diamonds. Within these four suits, each suit has 13 different cards in Rank: A-K-Q-J-T-9-8-7-6-5-4-3-2. (Ace can be high or low but low when setting the deck). There are 12 court or face cards.

Illustration 5

JOKER

Jokers are bonus, extras, or wild cards used in several games (Pai Gow Poker, DJ Wild). A joker often substitutes for another card to complete a hand. But depending on the game, one or both jokers may be used. (See illustration 6.)

Illustration 6

CUT CARDS

Cut cards (see photo 10) are plastic, metal, or other thin material cut in the same dimensions as the playing cards. They are used to hide the bottom card in the playing deck, to cover the dealt dealer's hand prior to its revelation, or, to protect the stub once the dealer has finished dealing the current hand.

Photo 10

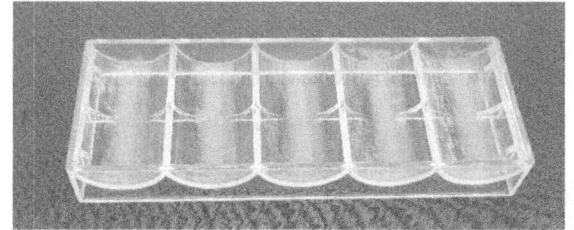

CHIP TRAY

A chip tray (see photo 11) is used to portably transport large amounts of chips from one table to another or to/from the cashier. Each tray can hold up to 100 chips/cheques (five rows of 20) and full trays can be safely stacked up to five high.

Photo 11

MACHINE SHUFFLER

Shuffle machines can be programmed for various trademarked games. They hold multiple decks, shuffle a second deck using RNGs while the first is dealt, and dispense the correct number of cards. These machines track each card, signal errors if one is missing or flipped—potentially voiding the current hand—and can also sort decks by suit and rank. (See illustration 7.)

Illustration 7

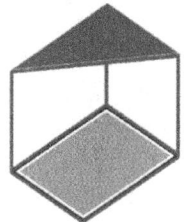

DISCARD TRAY

These trays hold used cards before re-shuffling and are always found on the dealer's right side of the table. (See illustration 8.)

Illustration 8

MINI-FAN

Some casinos provide a cooling fan for the dealer. No longer common (See photo 12.)

Photo 12

LAMMERS

Lammers, solid-colored discs used by dealers to signify specific situations, are common at nearly all casino tables. For Carnival Games, several varieties exist, though each casino decides whether their use is mandatory or optional. Common lammers are illustrated (see photo 13.)

Banker – This button indicates who the Banker is.

Clear Spacer – A clear disc separates full or incomplete stacks of 20 in the house rack for easier rack counting.

Dealer – This button informs everyone where the current action is, or it may protect the dealer's cards.

Envy – This lammer shows a player has made a bonus or side bet, paying out if another player at the table achieves a specific winning hand during the same hand. It allows players to benefit from others' successes.

House Way – This lammer is used when the dealer sets a player's hand according to the casino's rules, known as the "House Way," such as in Pai Gow Poker.

Numbered Lammers – These lammers are used when a commission is accumulated and owed by a player, or anytime a marker or credit is taken out.

Player – (uncommon) This button indicates the Player.

Tie – A lammer to indicate a Tie in the game.

Photo 13

The Complete Professional Dealer's Handbook

LAMMER RACK

Usually, lammers are stored in the cheque rack, but in the case of a Baccarat table, they often have their own lammer rack, which is placed outside the cheque bank, behind the commission boxes. (See photo 14.)

Photo 14

CHAIRS

Dealer's Chair – When a dealer sits to deal a game, he sits in a chair usually more comfortable than those afforded to players. These chairs often have more padding in the seats, and they swivel so the dealer can turn and pivot to reach, collect and pay each player's bets, without staying stagnantly straight. A dealer's chair is usually higher than a player's chair, allowing for greater arm reach, and often has several adjustable axles, quickly customizable to each incoming dealer. These combined features are designed to help dealers have better posture during long hours of dealing.

The player's chair shares similar features with the dealer's chair, though its height may differ and it might not swivel, or only minimally compared to the dealer's chair. In recent years, casinos have upgraded player's chairs, making them significantly more comfortable for extended periods of play.

DIGITAL DISPLAY BOARD

Progressive Digital Display Boards generally show the payouts for a Progressive or other type of bonus bet. Every bonus wager adds to the running tally, fueling player interest and excitement. Some bonus bets can pay as little as a few dollars, while the most difficult to obtain jackpots can run into the millions of dollars. Payouts of any significant amounts require approval from the floorman before being made. Players may be taxed on their winnings. (See illustration 9.)

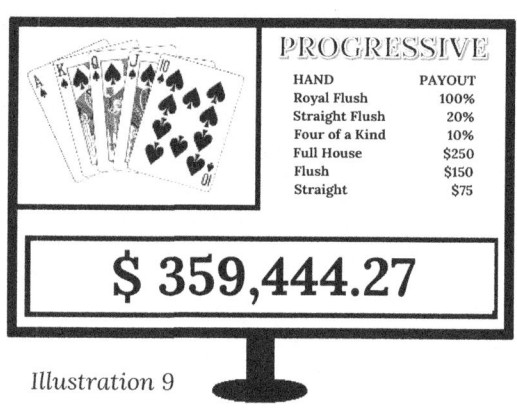

Illustration 9

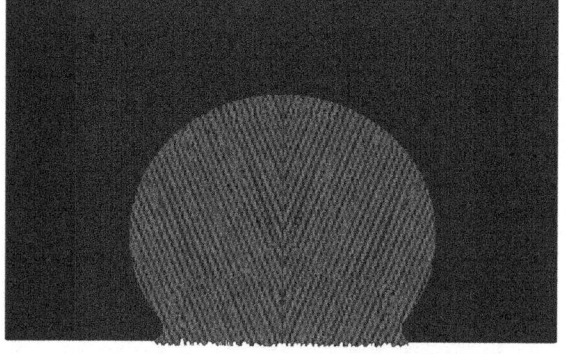

Photo 15

SHOE ACCESS PLATE

This plate covers the front of the dealing shoe where cards are dispensed. The brush-like bristles keep the cards hidden until they need to be dealt. A dealer's middle finger reaches in between and past the bristles to extract a card. (See photo 15.)

BRUSH

A cleaning object with a handle and bristles is used to consolidate dust or dirt from a table. (See photo 16.)

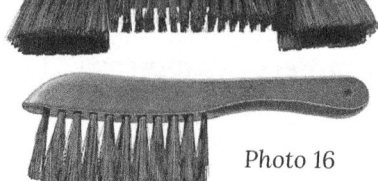

Photo 16

ARMREST RAIL

While playing, standing players often rest their elbows on this foamy outer top of the table.

TOKE BOX

Illustration 10

This container, where used, is attached to the edge of the table to one side of the dealer. Whenever a dealer receives a toke/token/tip/gratuity/zuke, the dealer thanks the player, picks up the monetary amount, taps the table, and drops the toke into the top opening of the toke box. Some casinos prefer that dealers color up—exchanging a larger number of low-denomination chips for a smaller number of higher-denomination chips—before dropping the tokes. (See illustration 10.)

PLAYOVER BOX

This clear plastic box can be used to cover and protect an absent player's chip stack. It also prevents anyone else playing in that player's spot. Other covers such as a towel or casino-printed rags are also used. (See illustration 11.)

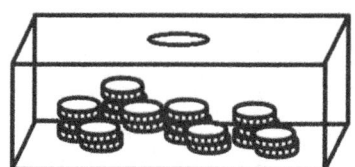

Illustration 11

DROP BOX 🔒 SLIT ▮ PADDLE

Located to the right or left side of the dealer, there is a slit opening and a paddle to plunge every player's paper currency buy-in, fill order receipts, and markers to the drop box below the table. (See photos 17-19.)

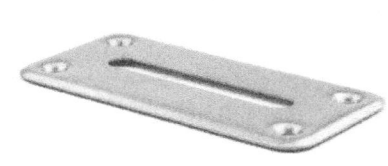
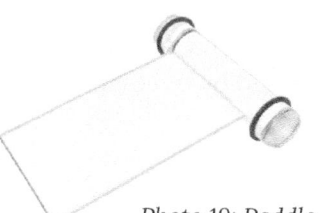

Photo 17: Drop box *Photo 18: Slit* *Photo 19: Paddle*

CHIP CARRYING CASE

Security will use this protective case to transport up to 10 chip trays full of cheques along with matching fill order paperwork for any number of tables. The sight of this case in a security person's hand standing behind a dealer alerts that a fill has arrived at his table. (See illustration 12.)

Illustration 12

FILL ORDER ▮ FILL SLIP

A receipt showing the transfer of cheques (a fill) from the main cage to the table bank is known as a fill order or fill slip. Both the dealer and supervisor verify/sign off on this before dropping into the drop box. (See illustration 13 on the following page.)

CREDIT ORDER 🔒 CREDIT SLIP

This is the exact opposite of a Fill Order or Fill Slip. It is used when high denomination or an abundance of cheques need to be removed from the table's bank. Fill orders are discussed in **Dealer Responsibilities**.

The Complete Professional Dealer's Handbook 19

ORDER FOR FILL

SHIFT:_____ DATE:_____

GAME	TABLE NO.	FILL IN	AMOUNT
BLACKJACK		$25,000	
CARNIVAL GAME		$5000	
CRAPS		$1000	
ROULETTE		$500	
		$100	
		$25	
		$5	
		$2	
		$1	
		$.50	
		$.25	
TOTAL:			

ORDERED BY:_____ FILLED BY:_____ RECEIVED BY:_____

Illustration 13

GAME-CLOSING CARD – A game-closing card is an official written document completed by the table-closing supervisor and dealer. The rack count verifies the amount of cheques in that table's bank, sorted by denomination. (See illustration 14.)

ABC CASINO

Game   *Date*   *Shift*

$25,000 _____

$5,000 _____

$1,000 _____

$500 _____

$100 _____

$25 _____

$5 _____

$2 _____

$1 _____

TOTAL: _____

DEALER: _____

FLOORMAN: _____

GAME-CLOSING CARD

Illustration 14

CUP HOLDER

A circular cutout portion of the table (See illustration 15), whether in the rail or racetrack, serves to secure drink glasses, so they are less likely to tip over and spill onto the felt. Some tables instead use a plastic or metal container with an extended lip to tuck under the table (See illustration 16.)

Illustration 15

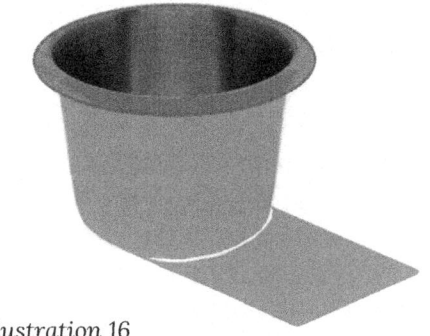

Illustration 16

LIGHTING ♠ ♥ ♦ ♣ ATMOSPHERE

Gone (sadly) are the days when men dressed up in suits and tuxedos with their significant others "dressed to the nines" for a formal evening at the casino. These scenes mostly exist in older movies. Most casinos have casual dress codes, which can be lax. However, casinos do their best to maintain their premises and have flashy decorations, chandeliers, pictures on the walls, new equipment, the bling of nearby slot machines, and some sort of spotlight on each gaming table. Some casinos pump in a pleasant scent to heighten the overall experience. A player's budget, the casino's location, the staff, parking options, current player promotions, the clientele who play, and so much more, all factor into where a player chooses to play.

AMENITIES

Aside from modern designs and a casino's location, there are other reasons a particular casino might entice a player: Amenities.

Today's casinos offer a wide range of amenities to attract, keep, and heighten a player's gaming experience. Not all casinos have every item on this list, but the more a casino can provide, the better for pleasing the player.

- ⬨ Free Wi-Fi
- ⬨ Check cashing
- ⬨ Currency exchanges
- ⬨ Padded chairs
- ⬨ Tableside food service
- ⬨ Nearby restrooms
- ⬨ Numerous televisions
- ⬨ Non-smoking tables
- ⬨ Private games booking
- ⬨ Seated chair massages
- ⬨ Sports wagering window or kiosk nearby
- ⬨ Professional dealers and management staff
- ⬨ Individual USB charging ports at each seat
- ⬨ Player comps earned through a player's rewards program
- ⬨ Strong signal strength for reliable cell phone reception
- ⬨ Cocktail service/Self-service beverage station
- ⬨ RV parking with electricity hook-up
- ⬨ Valet or free parking
- ⬨ Discounted hotel rates

FINANCIAL TRANSACTIONS

Most gaming establishments require cash to be converted into the casino's proprietary cheque equivalent. Handling cheques is faster, ensures the amount has been verified, and is often less bulky. Use the following procedures when handling financial transactions:

CHANGING CASH for CHEQUES

Properly exchanging cash for cheques is a crucial part of a dealer's role at every casino table game. When a player arrives at the table with little or no cheques for betting, they need to place the cash on the table. **A dealer can never take anything directly from a player's hand.** Arrange the cash in a layered fashion on the left side of the table, with the highest denomination on the left. The required amount of cheques is cut out on the right side. Downsizing cheques follows the same method. Always remember: Money (cash or cheques) coming in is on the left, money going out is on the right. Ensure all change transactions are handled accurately and appear professional. Use proper callouts for large amounts, slide the cheques to the player, and drop the cash into the dropbox.

FOREIGN CHEQUES

A foreign cheque is one from another casino. Many casino parent companies own more than one casino, and in that case the cashier/cage may allow a player to exchange a "foreign" cheque from one of their other casinos. However, gaming rules generally prohibit betting with a foreign cheque not issued by that casino's parent company. If the circumstances allow for an exchange, a player may receive cash or an equal exchange in gaming cheques. Some casinos will do the latter right at the gaming table. And some will take competitor's cheques if the casino is located nearby. Players are encouraged to cash out their cheques at the issuing casino's cashier to avoid problems.

CASH & MONEY PLAYS

There was a time when players could bring cash to the table and actively bet with it. The dealer would count the money, shout "Money plays," wait for approval by the pit boss, and proceed with the game. If the bet lost, the cash would go into the drop box; if it won, the player would be paid in casino cheques. Nowadays, gaming rules prohibit playing with cash due to concerns over money laundering and tax evasion. Still, cash is most likely used in private or home games.

TABLE STAKES

Any player running out of money at any time may reach into his pocket and pull out more money/cheques to play. This includes borrowing from others at the table or going to the ATM/cashier to obtain additional funds. Some casinos have mobile ATMs at the table. Ask/anticipate if the player is re-buying for more cheques in between gameplay. A current player may buy in for more cheques during a game to complete a bet. Make change for new players after the current game.

TOKES & TIPS

Where gratuities are allowed, dealers rely heavily on players' tips or tokes for the majority of their income. These offerings of gratuity should always be accepted with a "thank you."

Tap the toke lightly once on the cheque rack's corner (See photo 20.) Place it either directly into the toke box, or if they are small amounts such as $1, these tokes may be placed off to the side for coloring up later. Tapping every toke shows surveillance that the money in the dealer's hand is a toke, for the dealer, and not the house's money. And it signifies that it is not being stolen. Never "hustle" tokes or ask any

Photo 20

22 CARNIVAL GAMES

player for a tip. Not only is it unprofessional, but it will also likely result in a verbal or written warning. Tips are always a "bonus" and are never required by a player. Avoid discussions of "Georges" and "Toms" behind the scenes and remain professional. Over a long period of time, dealers will have good and bad toke days but it all averages out. All tokes/tips should be treated with the same gratitude. A $1 tip is a big deal to some players while a $5 tip may not be from other players.

Tokes that are given to dealers fall into one of two categories:

SHARED
Most casino table game dealers pool/combine their tokes over a 24-hour period, and the toke rate is calculated either per eight-hour shift or hourly. This daily toke rate fluctuates and is generally paid out on the employee's next paycheck.

NON-SHARED
However, some casino table games and cash game poker dealers operate under a "keep your own" (KYO) tips structure, allowing them to go home with real cash at the end of each shift. At tables that permit non-shared tips, dealers typically place the cheques into a toke box attached to the table and cash out later.

Some casinos will combine these two types, resulting in a certain percentage of tokes being a KYO, and the remainder as shared.

TOKE COMMITTEE
For shared/pooled tokes, a small group of elected dealers go around the entire casino floor daily to collect all the tokes from each toke box. They then rack up the cheques, count them, report, and turn in the total amount to the employee cage. This can happen each shift or, more commonly, every 24-hour period. The previous day's toke rate (total) is posted for the dealers to see, and they can get a fairly good idea what their paycheck will be. Committee members are compensated for their time and responsibility before or after their scheduled shift.

CASINO CREDIT & MARKER
A line of credit/marker is money made available interest-free by the casino to creditworthy players. It eliminates ATM fees and the need for players to bring in large amounts of cash. Players with good credit scores and verifiable assets (sufficient bank funds) can be approved for a certain amount from which a player can draw upon. This feature allows players to arrive at a casino without cash, draw upon their available credit, play, then pay back the marker either during their visit or within a short period (a month or so). Winnings and payment can also be electronically transferred appropriately. When a player wishes to access his line of credit, he will inform the dealer.

The supervisor is notified of the dollar amount. Wait for further instructions. A lammer is usually placed on the table for the amount. When told, cut out the proper amount of cheques, verify, then hand it off to the player. A player will have a document to sign, and a dealer's signature may/may not be required.

PROMOTIONAL CHIPS
Casinos have promotional chips from time to time to reward their players. Ask a supervisor how a player can redeem free/match play bets in place of real money and how payouts are handled.

PROPERLY CUTTING AND HANDLING CHEQUES

Cutting cheques (or chips) professionally is the efficient method for the dealer to quickly verify and count all the different denominations of a player's total chip/cheque stack. The two-step process, when performed correctly, is not only standard in a casino, but also visually appealing. A standard column of cheques is always counted 20 high. Over time, a dealer will know how many 20 cheques in his hand will feel like. Since hand sizes vary greatly, each dealer will need to find a comfortable way to hold a stack of 20 cheques in his hand. A dealer will then need to have his hand "memorize" what 19, 20, and 21 cheques feel like. When a tall column of 30 or more cheques are pushed forward to him, it is impressive to see a dealer reach and pick exactly 20 cheques from the top to verify. A good dealer can do this with each of his hands. This takes practice. **NEVER "thumb cut" cheques**. Run down the stack of chips if ever unsure of its total count. Then size-in the remaining stacks to the proven stack.

DROP CUTTING

To drop cut a stack of cheques, first pick up a column stack of cheques. The dealer then places the top cheque in his palm and the bottom cheque at the middle finger's fingertip. (See photos 21 and 22.)

Now, with the index finger, cut/section off the bottom five cheques. Ease the grip of the thumb and middle finger and drop (place) these five cheques as a group onto the table. (See photo 23.) For practice, pick these cheques back up and repeat over and over to get comfortable with this process.

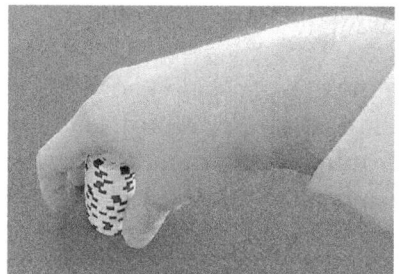
Photo 21

Photo 22

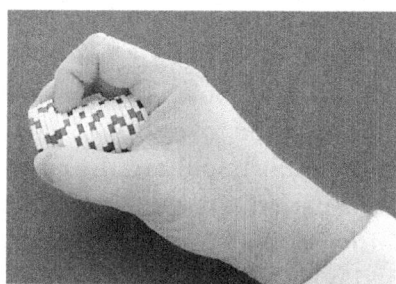
Photo 23

SIZING-IN

The next step is to "size in" the remaining chips in the dealer's hand (which is more manageable and comfortable). Sizing-in cheques means to evenly match the cheques remaining in the dealer's hand with the stack of cheques already on the table. For this example, a common $20 will be broken down using $1 cheques in four small but even piles. With the first set of five cheques already on the table, controllably drop the remaining 15 cheques in hand next to the first stack of five. Hook the index finger (see photo 24) and pull away the remaining cheques in hand.

Repeat to empty the hand and all cheques are in neat piles of five next to each other. (See photo 25.)

Once the dealer has sized-in a stack of cheques, lightly run the same hand's index fingernail to verify to surveillance that these four piles are indeed even. (See photo 26.)

Photo 24

Photo 25

Photo 26

Casinos often specify one of three accepted finishes to the sizing-in process: Horizontal fanning out, vertical fanning out, or bridging. (See photo 27 on the following page.)

Photo 27

When finished, reverse the order, stack up the cheques and slide them to the correct player. If $200 was needed in $5 red cheques, run down one stack properly and verify it, restack it, then size-in the second column to the verified first one. Count out loud if needed when verifying large denominations or amounts. Make no mistakes. Accuracy counts! If the dealer is ever unsure, he should recount everything in front of him again. **Always give the exact amount of cheques to the player, no more, no less.**

Use proper callouts. When changing cash: "Changing two hundred!" or "Changing two large!" When changing cheques: "Cheque change, two hundred, two black in!" Slide the player's cheques to him first, then drop the cash into the drop box/put the cheques into the cheque rack.

Note: A proficient dealer can drop cut and size-in cheques with either hand efficiently and professionally. Practice with BOTH HANDS!

PINCHING and PLUCKING CHEQUES

Pinching and plucking cheques are two professional—and eye-appealing—methods to remove cheques quickly from the rack. **PINCH** one cheque away from a column of cheques using the thumb and index finger. (See photo 28.)

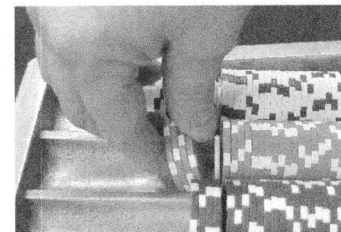

Photo 28

Photo 29

PLUCK (and **SNAP**) each additional cheque using the middle finger. (See photo 29.) Then layer each additional cheque on top of the previous cheque(s) as the index finger absorbs each new cheque. Repeat as needed.

CHUNKING CHEQUES

When multiple and successive players lose their bets, the dealer must quickly collect the cheques. The quickest method is by chunking or stacking one losing bet on top of the other, forming a column, in one swift motion. (See photo 30.) Put the losing bets into the cheque rack immediately (even if it is a dirty stack). This secures the money and prevents a player from grabbing their own losing bet, or the dealer incorrectly pushing a losing bet. Once the hand is complete, reorganize the rack properly by denomination (cheque color) before dealing the next hand.

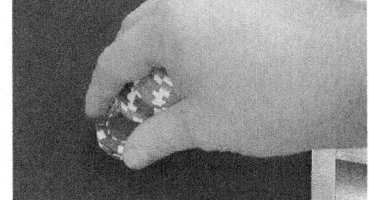

Photo 30

RACK MAINTENANCE and PAYOUTS

As previously discussed in **Dealer Responsibilities**, the cheque rack will undergo many visual changes during a dealer's shift. A rack can be full to half-empty and back. **EACH DEALER IS RESPONSIBLE FOR KEEPING A NEAT AND ORDERLY RACK.** When working out of a cheque rack, a) work from the outside-in, b) take and replenish cheques from the right side of the rack, c) do not pay left-handed directly from the left side of the rack, (instead bring out the cheques from the right side with the right hand, then pick up and pay with the left hand), and d) use clear spacers to divide 20 cheque columns or less into groups of 4 or 5 cheques. (See photos 31 and 32.)

Photo 31

Photo 32

SKILLFUL CARD SHUFFLING

Shuffling cards ensures players receive random cards and verifies that the table is using house-issued, approved cards after a deck inspection. From inspecting a new deck to cutting the cards, the entire procedure should take no more than 20 to 25 seconds. A professionally executed single-deck hand shuffle should take about 10 seconds. While speed and visual mastery improve with practice, they are always secondary to proper technique and thoroughness. Depending on the casino or specific Carnival Game, some or all of the following steps may be required of the dealer:

DECK INSPECTIONS ♠ ♥ ▓ ♦ ♣ SPREADING the DECK

A Carnival Game that uses cards will require the dealer to properly inspect, spread, scramble, and shuffle all new decks before dealing any game. Games may require one or more decks for play. Most Carnival Games will have a shuffle machine. The game may require one or more decks. When setting up a table, start with one deck. Fan the deck of cards face up from left to right. (See photo 33.) Be quick but professional looking when spreading the deck. This is another opportunity for the dealer to subtly shine! Inspect each card visually but quickly, making sure that all 52 (or 53) different cards are present and there are no missing or duplicate cards. In one sweep, pick up the cards in reverse order by "un-fanning" them left to right. Turn the deck over face down and again fan the deck left to right. (See photo 34.) This time, singly spread each card away from the card beneath it so the dealer can quickly examine each full card from the next. The dealer is looking for two things. First, look for markings, blemishes, rips, tears, printing/manufacturing errors, or anything out of the ordinary. Second, ensure all cards in the deck are of the same color/identical backing.

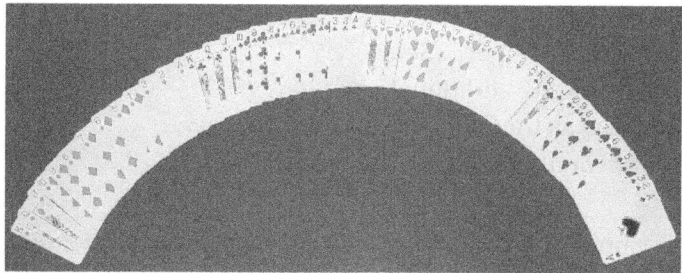

Photo 33

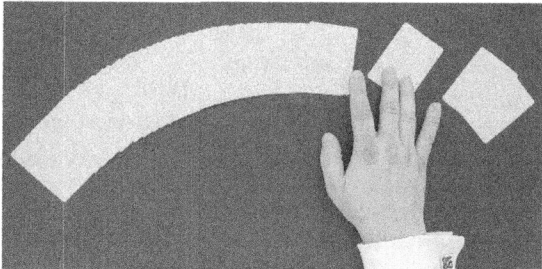

Photo 34

If the table has a shuffle machine, load the first deck into it and then repeat the above steps for the second deck. Alert the supervisor of any deck inspection issues.

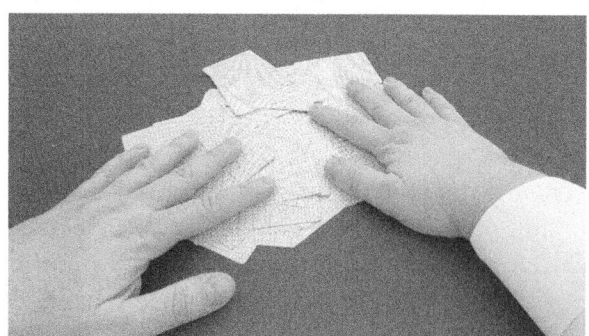

SCRAMBLING the CARDS

Once the dealer is satisfied with the deck, it is time to mix (wash) them up by scrambling them. This is the first process of randomizing the cards. Since the deck is already face down from the previous step, using both hands, mix the cards well by using a circular motion with each hand for three to five seconds. (See photo 35.)

Photo 35

SQUARING UP the DECK

Gather the spread-out, scrambled pile of cards into a small concise pile and pick up the cards so they face in, away from the players. (See photo 36.)

Photo 36

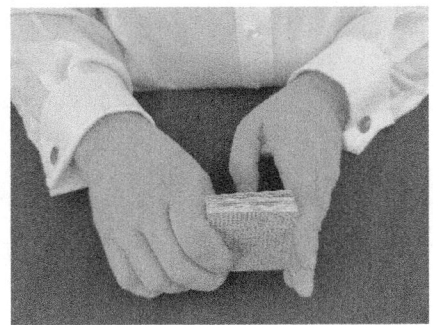

Lightly shake and turn the cards so they fall into an L-Shape. Then, turn with one motion to obtain a neat pile face down. (See photos 37-38.)

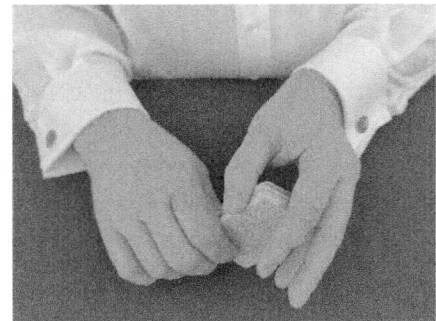

Photo 37

Photo 38

Finally, square the deck by making it into one neat pile, then pinch opposite or bottom corners. (See photos 39 and 40.)

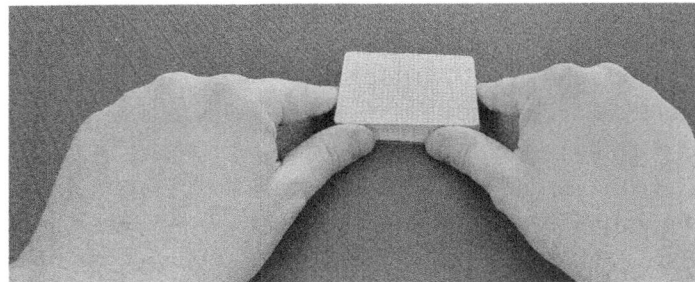

Photo 39

Photo 40

HAND and FINGER PLACEMENT

Now that the deck is in one neat pile facing down, it is time to shuffle the deck professionally. Two absolutely **WRONG** ways to shuffle come from playing home games, and while they're okay at home, they're never acceptable in a casino or professional setting. (See photos 41 and 42.)

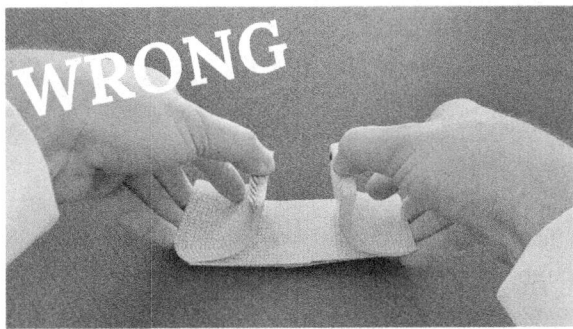

Photo 41: Overhand Shuffle

Photo 42: Bridge/Cascade Shuffle

The correct way is to start with the deck lengthwise in front of the dealer. Split the deck into two equal piles by gripping the top of the deck with the middle finger and thumb with one hand. Slide, but don't lift, the top half of the deck over to the side. (See photos 43 and 44.)

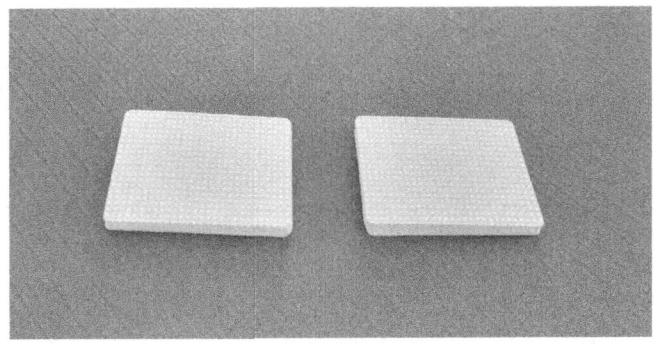

Photo 43

Photo 44

TURN

After splitting the deck, the dealer may need to rotate the right half a half-turn. Using the right index finger, **push the bottom-left corner and rotate the deck clockwise** until the corner reaches the upper-right. This ensures a more balanced corner exposure during the riffle. (See photo 45.)

Photo 45

SHUFFLE TYPES

Next, the dealer places his hands flat on top of the decks and slightly turns the deck outwards so that there is a "V" shape between the two halves. (See photo 46.) The middle and ring fingers can extend over the top of the deck to touch the table surface.

RIFFLE

Lift and release both inside corners where the two thumbs meet. Layer/integrate the two corners. Release a card or two from each side much like gears working to fit together. The riffle should be effortless, with little pressure placed on the entire deck of cards. Practice this step independently with each hand. Do not release too many (clumps of) unshuffled cards from either half. (See photo 47.)

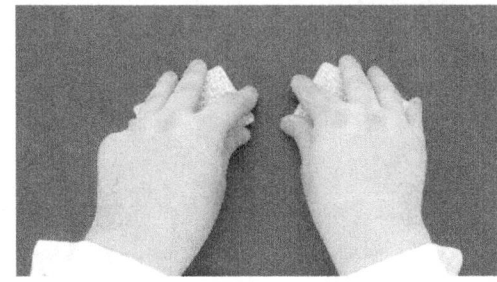

Photo 46

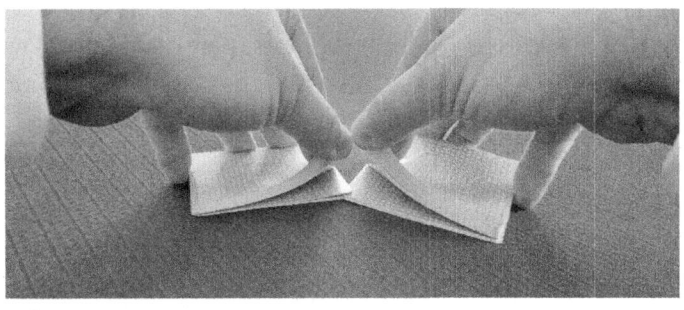

Photo 47

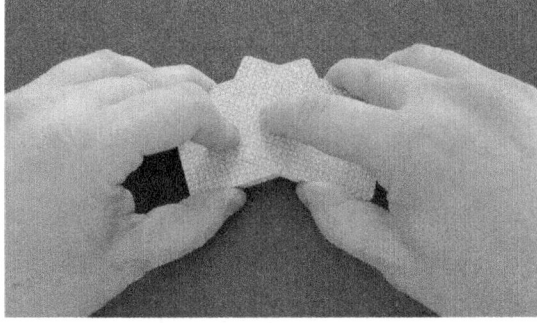

Photo 48

When finished, crisscross push the cards inward together forming kitty cat "ears" away from the dealer. (See photo 48).

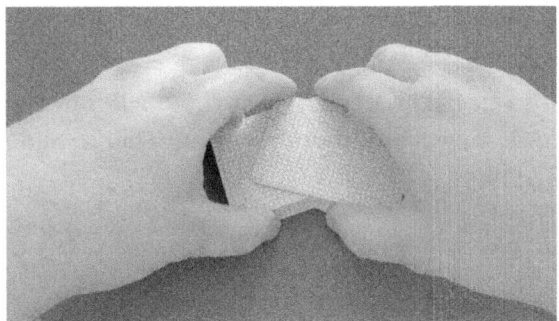

Photo 49

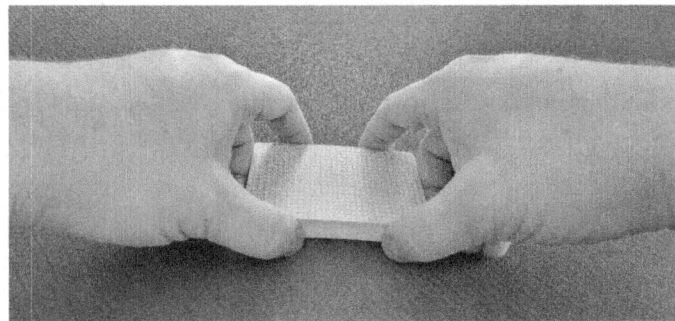

Photo 50

Next, the dealer will use his index fingers and pull these "ears" toward himself. (See photo 49.)

Finally, push these two deck halves toward each other using the outward fingers while maintaining control of the deck. The two halves will now become a single pile once again. (See photo 50.)

The dealer has successfully completed one full riffle. **REPEAT** as many riffles as required by the casino.

STRIP

Another step in the shuffle process is to strip the cards. Lift the single deck no more than an inch off the table. (See photo 51.)

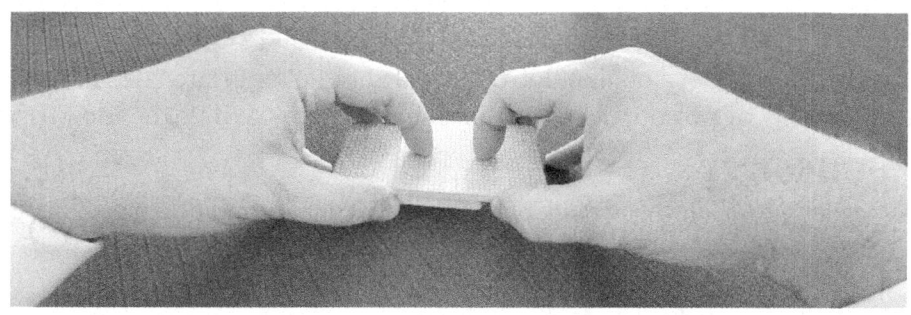
Photo 51

Take roughly 25 percent of the top cards and slide them discreetly onto the table. (See photo 52.) Notice the finger placements of both hands. Strip three times. Some casinos require up to five strips. Place the remaining cards on top of the stripped pile. DO NOT EVER strip cards from the middle or bottom of the deck.

Photo 52

Place the last section on top of the three to five stripped sections.

Repeat the riffle step once more. When completed, the dealer will have performed a riffle, riffle, strip, riffle shuffle sequence. (**Note:** Every casino specifies their own house shuffle, including **Marrying** or **Butterflying** decks.)

"Know thy house shuffle."

BOX

To box the cards, some casinos will have the dealer **take one-third of the top of the deck and put it on the bottom of the deck**. Or some require the bottom third of the deck to be placed onto the top.

CUT CARD PLACEMENT ♥ CUTTING the DECK

With the deck already inspected and properly shuffled, it is time to cut the cards. Place the cut card in the center of the table past the deck of cards. (See photo 53.)

Photo 53

WAIT! Before a dealer cuts the cards, make sure there aren't other items left to do BEFORE cutting the deck.

Note: Most Carnival Games where the dealer hand shuffles and a cut is required, the dealer will cut the deck himself.

To cut the deck, use only ONE hand. Move the top half of the deck forward and away from the dealer and place it on top of the cut card. (See photo 54.) Release it. Go back for the bottom half and with the same hand, place it on top of the first half. (See photo 55.) It is important for the dealer to do a second full release! (See photo 56.) Square the deck up once again. All players are entitled to see that the entire deck has been verified on both sides, scrambled, riffled and stripped correctly, then cut and viewable in between all steps. Once the deck is cut, square it up. The deck is now ready for play.

Photo 54

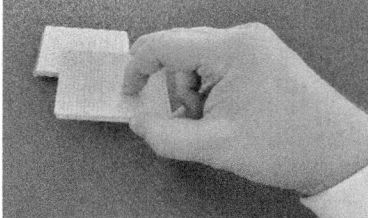
Photo 55

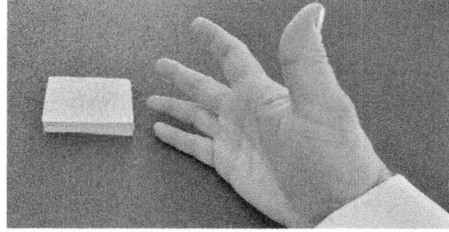
Photo 56

The Complete Professional Dealer's Handbook 29

3 SHOT POKER

Casino Gaming Development introduced 3 Shot Poker in late 2023 in Las Vegas, NV.[1] This game blends components of two popular Carnival Games: Three Card Poker and Mississippi Stud.

EQUIPMENT

Table, layout, chairs, one deck of cards, discard tray, and cheques. (See illustration 17.)

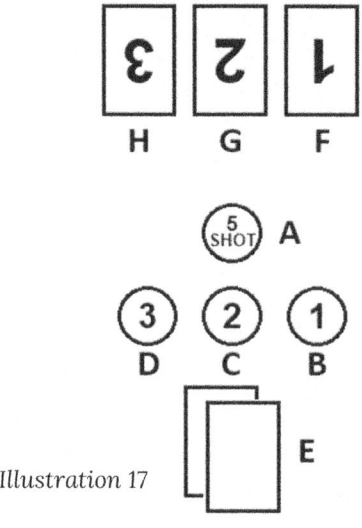

Illustration Key

- A – 5 Shot
- B – 3 Shot #1
- C – 3 Shot #2
- D – 3 Shot #3
- E – Player's 2 Cards
- F – Community Card #1
- G – Community Card #2
- H – Community Card #3

(Note: not all layouts will have all features shown.)

DEALER QUALIFYING HAND

None. Dealer does not receive a hand.

Illustration 17

SHUFFLE

See the section on **Skillful Card Shuffling**.

TYPES of BETS and PAYOUTS

- **3 Shot** – Each player's two cards are compared with each separate community card (#1, #2, and #3). The bet wins if the player's hand forms a Pair or better with the corresponding community card number.
  - Royal Flush 50:1
  - Straight Flush 30:1
  - Three of a Kind 20:1
  - Straight 4:1
  - Flush 2:1
  - Pair 1:1

- **5 Shot** – Optional bonus bet combines the player's two cards with the three community cards. Any pair 10s or higher wins.
  - Royal Flush 500:1
  - Straight Flush 200:1
  - Four of a Kind 50:1
  - Full House 40:1
  - Flush 30:1
  - Straight 20:1
  - Three of a Kind 10:1
  - Two Pair 2:1
  - Pair of 10s or better 1:1

DEALING AND PAY PROCEDURES

1. Player must minimally wager spot #1. The optional 5 Shot wager is only available at this time.
2. Dealing order: The dealer deals each player one card face down, and deals himself one card face down at community spot 1. Then, deal the players their second card face down, the dealer deals himself two cards face down, for community spots 2 and 3. Discard remaining cards.
3. Each player examines his own cards. They can play or fold. (Players may choose to play blind.)
4. If the player folds, he forfeits his bet in spot #1. The 5 Shot bet will still be active. Leave this player's hand if this wager exists. Otherwise, remove and discard the player's hand.
5. If the player plays, he wagers on spot #2 and #3, bets equal to or double his spot #1 bet.
6. After players act, the dealer reveals the three community cards. Begin hand comparison and take/pay procedures counterclockwise starting with the dealer's right. Push slightly forward, community card #1. Visually combine this card with the player's two cards. If the three cards form a pair or higher, spot #1 wins. Pull back this card. Repeat for community cards 2 and 3.
7. For the 5 Shot hand, visually combine the player's two cards with the three community cards. If this forms a pair of 10s or better, it wins.
8. Collect the cards, shuffle, and deal the next game.

BACCARAT

Baccarat, or *baccara* in Italian (pronounced bah-ka-rah), meaning "zero," is fittingly named for a card game where all face cards and tens are worth zero points. Primarily played in casinos and, although widely considered a French game, its history spans centuries, originating in Italy.[2],[3] Soldiers returning from the Italian Wars in 1494 introduced it to France, where it was extensively developed, promoted, and played. The game involves comparing two hands, the Player's Hand and the Banker's Hand. Each round of Baccarat, referred to as a '*coup*,' offers three possible outcomes: a Player win, a Banker win, or a Tie. The hand with a point total closest to, or exactly 9, wins. In the event of a tie, Player and Banker bets push, and only Tie bets are paid. Charles Van-Tenac published the first comprehensive discussion of Baccarat in his 1847 *Album des jeux*. Las Vegas didn't see its first Baccarat table until 1959, but it has since become a casino mainstay after a sluggish start in popularity. A Baccarat dealer, in more opulent or European settings, is preferably referred to as a 'croupier'—a term typically reserved for roulette dealers.

Three main and most popular variants of the game are: *punto banco*, *Baccarat chemin de fer*, and *Baccarat banque* (or *à deux tableaux*). In *punto banco*, players are restricted by a set of rules that dictate which side, the Player or Banker should receive a card, if any. By contrast, *Baccarat chemin de fer* and *Baccarat banque* allow players to make these choices. In every version, **it is important to note that each casino or card room is free to enact and enforce their own house rules,** although standard norms of playing will most likely always be followed, such as commission and drawing/standing rules.

Number of Players:	Mini Baccarat table: Up to 7 players. Midi Baccarat: Up to 12 players. Punto Banco (Big Game) Baccarat: Up to 14 players.
Number of Decks Used:	Mini Baccarat: 6 Midi Baccarat: 8 Punto Banco: 8 Chemin de Fer: 6 Baccarat Banque: 3
Also Known As:	Punto Banco, Chemin de Fer, Baccarat Banque (*a deux tableaux*), Mini Baccarat, Midi Baccarat, No Commission Baccarat, European Baccarat, EZ Baccarat.
Object:	Player wagers on one of two sides, Player, or Banker, to win. Each Player and Banker hand receives two alternating cards (Player, Banker, Player, Banker). The Player hand is usually turned up first, then the Banker's. Both hands are compared and totaled. Hands may stand on two cards or draw one card, depending on the game/rules. Hand closest to 9 wins. Players may tie. A two-card total of 8 or 9 is a Natural and immediately ends the game.
Payouts:	Remove losing bets. Some casinos require the dealer to stack them at the table's center before paying winners, then secure them in the rack.
Betting Structure:	Main bet, optional side bets.

PUNTO BANCO

In the United States, *punto banco* is the most popular version of Baccarat. The terms Player (*punto*) and Banker (*banco*) are designations for the two hands dealt in each coup, and bettors can wager either outcome. The casino always banks and plays both hands using established drawing and standing rules, unlike other Baccarat games where a player can make drawing decisions, the Player hand isn't associated with any player, nor is the Banker hand with the casino.

Dealt from a shoe with 6 or 8 shuffled decks, a cut card is positioned 14 cards from the end. Drawing the cut card signals the dealer to finish dealing that coup then deal one more coup from the shoe.

The dealer burns the first card face up. Matching the numerical value of this card, an equivalent number of cards face down are extracted from the shoe. Aces count as 1, cards two through nine are valued at face value, and face cards are valued at 10. Ten-valued cards are ONLY worth 10 points while burning cards, and NOT during gameplay when they are worth 0 points.

In every coup, two cards are dealt face down alternating one card for the Player, one to the Banker, and repeat for a second dealt card. Then both two-card sets are totaled. If either hand totals an 8 or 9, also known as a Natural, neither side draws a card, the coup has ended, and the result is announced, Player win, Banker win, or Tie. However, should neither Player or Banker hands result in a Natural, set drawing rules (known as a *tableau*, or table) are strictly followed to determine if the Player should receive a third card. Subsequently, the Banker may either receive a third card depending on the Player's third card or stand. The coup is then finished, the outcome is announced, winning cards are pushed slightly forward, losing bets are collected, and the Player or Banker winning bets are paid out 1:1 (see the **Commission** section if required.) Four to six cards are only ever revealed in each coup.

There are two versions of *Punto Banco*:

1. **Mini-Baccarat** is played on the smallest of the Baccarat tables with smaller minimums/maximums. It is popular with casual players and smaller bankrolls. The dealer handles all the cards. Banker commission is charged according to house rule. A mini-Baccarat variation where even money is paid on winning banker bets (rather than 95%), unless the banker wins with a 6, which pays only 50% of the bet, goes under various names including *Super* 6 and *Punto* 2000. Similarly, EZ-Baccarat offers no commission on Banker bets, popular Dragon 7, and Panda 8 bets, but all Banker bets will push on a winning three-card 7 outcome.

2. **Midi-Baccarat** is the other version of *punto banco*. Instead of the dealer handling the cards in its entirety, the dealer slides the Player or Banker cards to the player who generally has the largest amount of money on that corresponding bet, and that player gets to reveal the two cards. **Expect players to mutilate the cards badly** because they will. They cannot switch the cards, but once they've looked at both cards, they will turn them face up and give them back to the dealer. The dealer will resume play and determine if a third card needs to be drawn or not.

CHEMIN de FER

[Fr. iron way or railway] Six shuffled decks of cards are dealt from a Baccarat-style shoe. Players sit at a large oval table. One player is designated as the Banker, who also deals the cards. Play opens to the right of the dealer and the next Banker position proceeds counterclockwise. The remaining players are known as punters. Each Banker announces the amount of money he is prepared to risk.

The Banker's position rotates counterclockwise throughout the game. In each round, the Banker stakes the amount they are prepared to risk. Subsequently, each player, in turn, decides whether to "go bank," challenging the entire current bank with an equivalent bet. Only one player may "go bank." If no player opts to "go bank," wagers are placed sequentially. Should the collective wagers of the players fall short of the bank, spectators may also bet up to the bank's total. Conversely, if the players' total wagers exceed the bank, the banker has the option to match the higher stake; if not, the surplus bets are removed in the reverse order of play.

The Banker deals two cards face down to himself and two face down shared among the other players. The Player with the highest individual bet, or the first in the play order in case of a tie, represents the non-banker players. Both the Banker and the Player examine their cards. If either holds an 8 or a 9, they announce it, and both hands are revealed, compared, and bets changes hands. If not, the player may choose to accept or decline a third card; if accepted, it is dealt face-up. A combination of guts, experience, great guesswork, strategy, and social expectations of the other stakeholders, suggests that one should always accept a card when one's hand totals between 0 and 4, and always decline when it totals 6 or 7.

After the Player's decision, the Banker then decides whether to take another card using his own methods. Following both parties' decisions, the hands are exposed, totaled, and a winner is determined. Discarded cards are then placed in the center discard can.

If the player's hand exceeds the Banker's hand when they are compared, each wagering player receives back their wager and a matching amount from the bank, and the position of banker passes to the next player in order. If the Banker's hand exceeds the player's hand, all wagers are forfeit and placed into the bank—and the Banker position does not change. If there is a tie, wagers remain as they are for the next hand.

If the current Banker wishes to withdraw, a new Banker is the first player in order willing to stake an amount equal to the current bank total. If no one is willing to stake this amount, the new Banker is instead the next player in order, and the bank resets to whatever they wish to stake.

When the Player's hand wins, each betting player retrieves their wager along with an equal amount from the bank. The Banker role moves to the next player in sequence. Conversely, if the Banker's hand is higher, all bets are lost to the bank, and the Banker retains their position. In the event of a tie, the wagers stay put for the following hand.

Any player may "go bank." If two players from opposite sides wish to do so, they can go *à cheval*, or split half the bank. A player may continue to go bank as often as desired until a loss occurs, or they may "go bank *à cheval*," meaning on two separate hands with half the stake on each. Should a player go bank and lose, they have the option to go bank again until they lose three times.

Should the Banker opt to step down, the next Banker is the first player ready to bet an amount equivalent to the Bank's total. If no player is prepared to bet this sum, the next player in order becomes the Banker, and the bank amount is reset to whatever that new Banker bets. Typically, games have a predetermined minimum for the bank or bet amounts.

BACCARAT BANQUE

In Baccarat Banque, the shoe contains three shuffled decks. The Banker role is initially auctioned to the player willing to risk the largest amount, then follows house order. Otherwise, the first person to sign up on the list of players has the privilege of the first bank. The Banker's position is more permanent than in Chemin de fer and he retains his role until a) the complete shoe of cards have been dealt, b) he chooses to retire from the game, or c) he has insufficient funds to gamble.

A Banker sits across from the croupier/dealer with the discard area in between. Flanking the Banker are the punters. Onlooking players are not allowed to sit directly at the table and can only place bets if the active players' wagers do not meet the Banker's stakes.

The dealer shuffles the cards and then asks a punter from his right, one from his left, and the banker to reshuffle. Next, a random player is selected to cut the deck. Once all players have placed their bets, the banker deals one card to a punter on the right, another to a punter on the left, and a third to himself. This process is repeated, resulting in three, two-card hands. Each side's victory or defeat is determined solely by the cards dealt. The rules for exposing a Natural 8 or 9 immediately and, offering and accepting cards, are identical to those in *Chemin de fer*. Each punter holds the cards as he continues to win or tie. Once he loses, the next punter in rotation receives the next hand.

Like *Chemin de fer*, any player on either side may also "go bank." If two players from opposite sides wish to do so, they can go *à cheval*, or split half the bank. A player may continue to go bank as often as desired until a loss occurs, or they may go bank *à cheval*. Should a player go bank and lose, they have the option to go bank again until they lose three times.

A Banker must fully play one hand but may resign at any point after that. Upon retiring, they are required to announce the amount of their retirement funds. Following this, the opportunity to take over the bank is available to any other player—according to the rotation order—starting with the same amount of stake and using the remaining cards that have not been dealt. The outgoing Banker then takes the place of their successor. If the bank's funds run out, the Banker can replenish the stake with additional funds without losing his banking privileges.

If the sum of all punters' bets exceeds the bank's stake, the Banker is not obliged to add more funds. In the event of the banker's loss, the croupier will pay the punters sequentially until the bank's funds run out. Any leftover funds are then returned. However, the banker may choose to accept the bets and increase their stake. This action makes the bank unlimited, and the banker is then required to cover all the players' bets or give up the bank.

In Macao, shuffle two decks of cards. Punters wager pre-set limits against the banker. The Banker deals one card face down to each player clockwise. The highest card value wins. If two hands tie, the Player with the same value but fewer cards prevails. If there's a tie in point values and the number of cards, the Banker wins. A punter who draws a Natural 9 wins 3x their bet, provided the Banker doesn't also have a Natural 9. A Natural 8 doubles the winnings, while a 7 or less pays out only the bet amount. A punter may request extra cards, dealt face up. If he draws a ten or face card, he can refuse it and ask for another.

Later versions of this game, like all Baccarat games, adopt the *modulo* 10 arithmetic for calculating hand point values. Defeating the Banker with a Pair results in a payout equal to the bet. Once the deck is depleted, the Player on the Banker's left takes over as the new Banker.

NOTE: Baccarat is a game of much higher stakes and the casino monitors it closely. Dealers can expect to see a dedicated floorman overseeing and recording every aspect of the game, from betting to dealing, and payouts. Only the most skilled dealers are assigned to the high limit tables.

EQUIPMENT

Baccarat uses standard equipment found in other Carnival Games and can be found in the **Equipment** section of this book. They are: Layout, chairs, decks of cards, and cheques. In addition, these special tools of the trade are used:

TABLES

Baccarat tables commonly measure 30-inches high, much lower than a barstool-height blackjack table. There are three main types of Baccarat tables: Mini-Baccarat, Midi-Baccarat, and Big/Maxi Baccarat (see photos on the following page.)

Mini-Baccarat are most often played on a semi-circular tabletop that measures 84-inches wide x 46-inches deep and usually accommodates up to seven players. (See illustration 18 on the following page.)

Midi-Baccarat tables measure slightly wider and seats up to nine players. (See illustration 19 on the following page.)

However, the Big Baccarat table measures 12 to 16 feet long, 5 feet wide, and can seat up to fourteen players, (seven players on each side), making it as long as the longest craps table in the casino. Two (sometimes three) dealers are seated at this table. (See illustration 20 on the following page.) Generally, an assigned floor supervisor is also exclusive to this table and oversees all action.

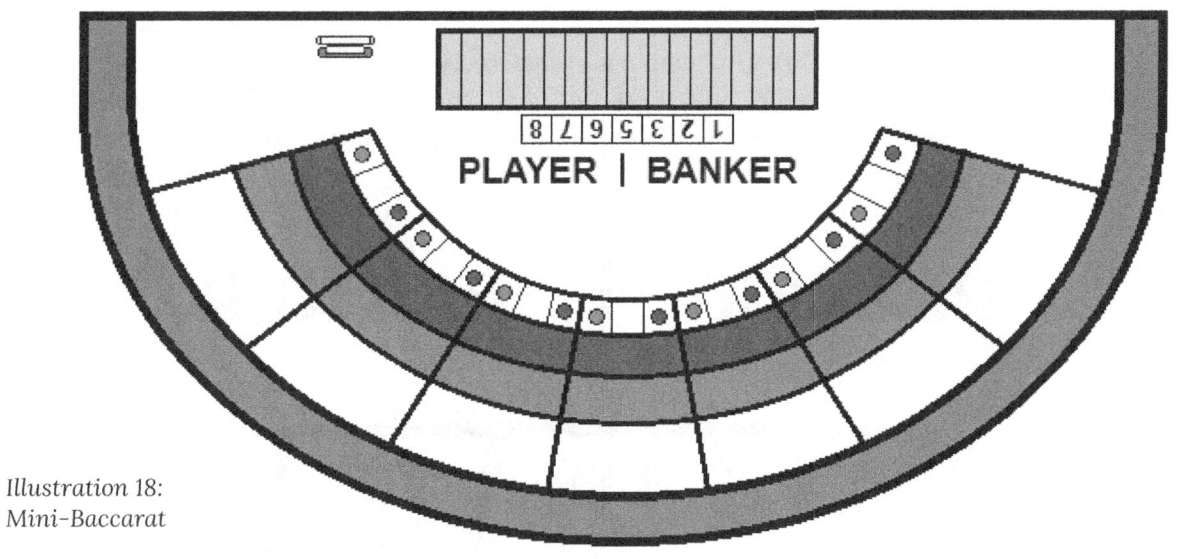

Illustration 18:
Mini-Baccarat

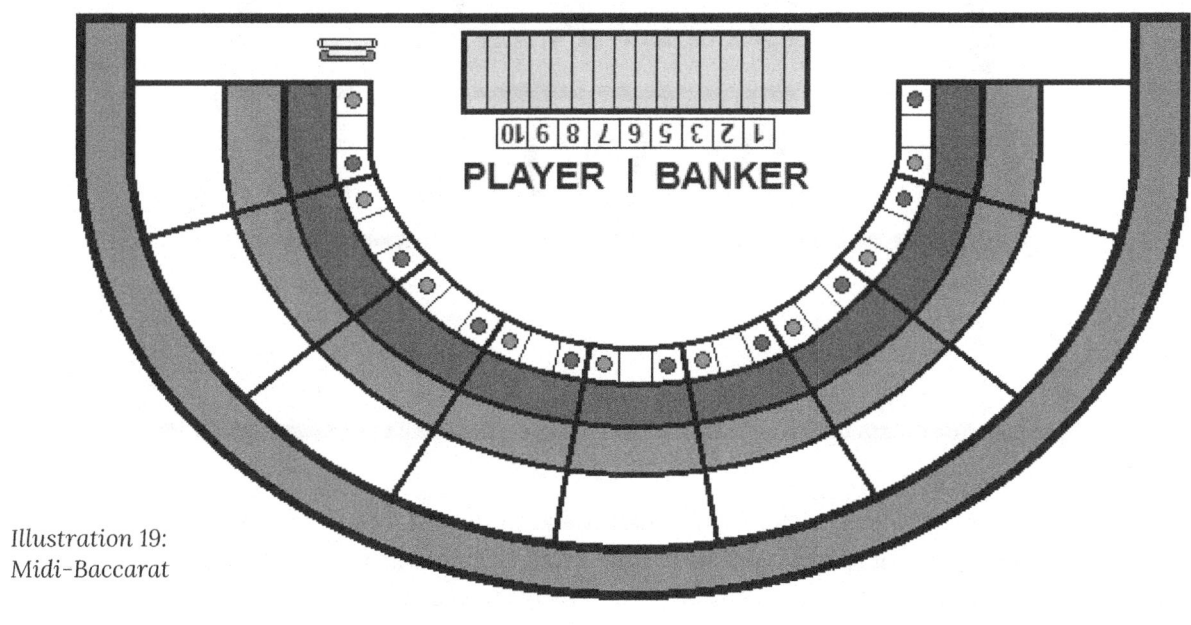

Illustration 19:
Midi-Baccarat

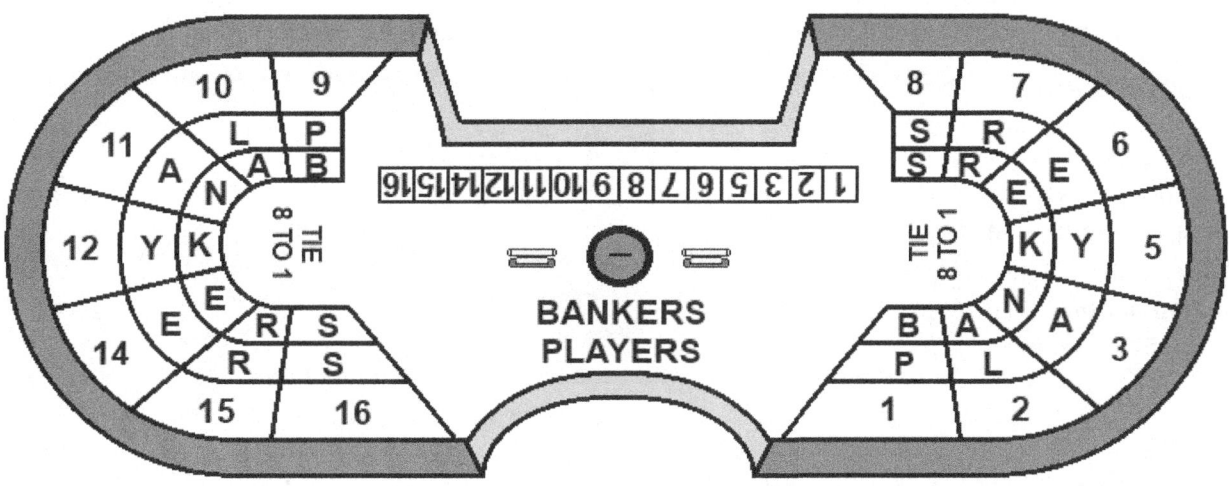

Illustration 20:
Big Baccarat

The Complete Professional Dealer's Handbook 35

LAYOUT

In certain East Asian cultures, particularly China, Japan, Korea, and Taiwan, the pronunciation of the word "four" sounds like the word for "death," which is associated with bad luck. Tetraphobia, the fear or avoidance of the number 4, is common in these cultures. Thus, the number 4 is almost always absent from Baccarat tables due to this superstition. Similarly, Big Baccarat tables will not show the number 13 due to triskaidekaphobia, the fear of the number 13, as players and casinos fear it will bring bad luck or misfortune. (See illustration 21.) Most Baccarat layouts will offer side bets to the players.

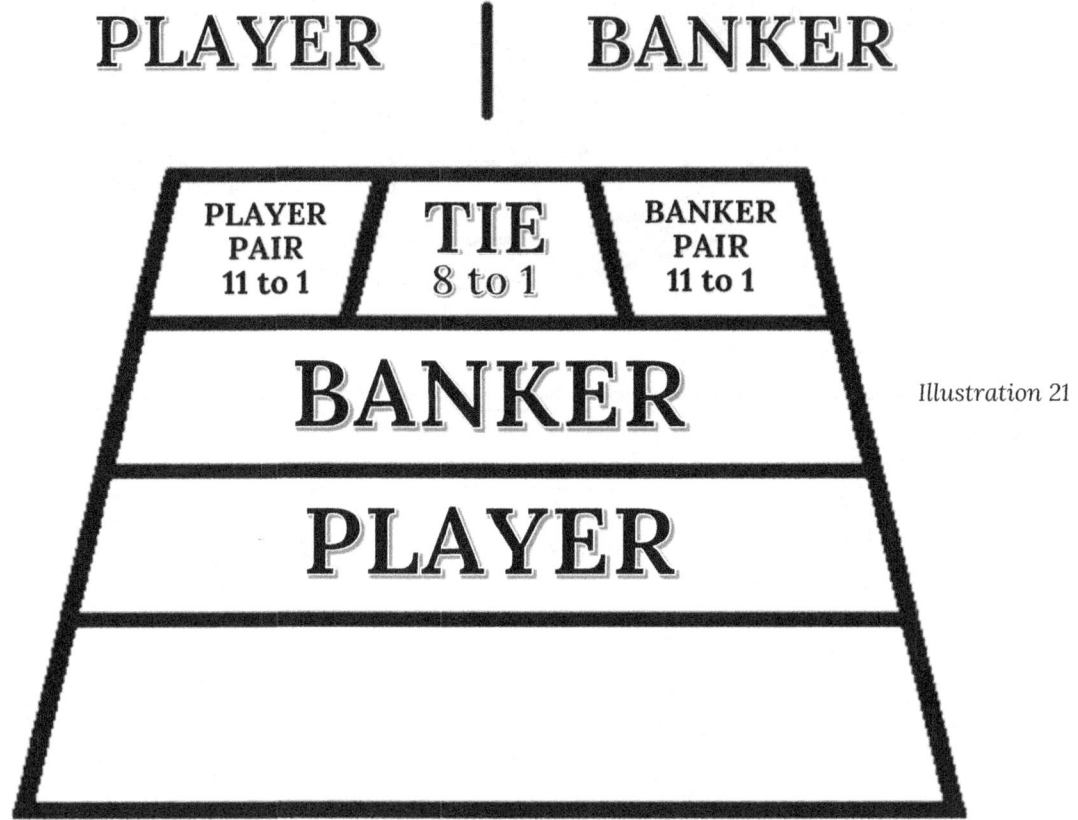

Illustration 21

CHEQUES

A round disc or token slightly larger than a U.S. half dollar coin, weighing around 11.5 to 14 grams is used in the casino for all table games played with real money. Cheques are sometimes used alongside real money but are mostly used in place of it. Cheques always have a cash value printed on both sides. Each denomination has its own color and monetary value. The use of tokens speeds up the game considerably as dealers/players can quickly count an entire stack of chips without the burden or repeated cumbersome process of counting paper bills—or checking for counterfeit ones.

CHEQUE RACK

Cheque racks are much wider in the Baccarat games, holding additional rows of higher denomination. (See photo 57.)

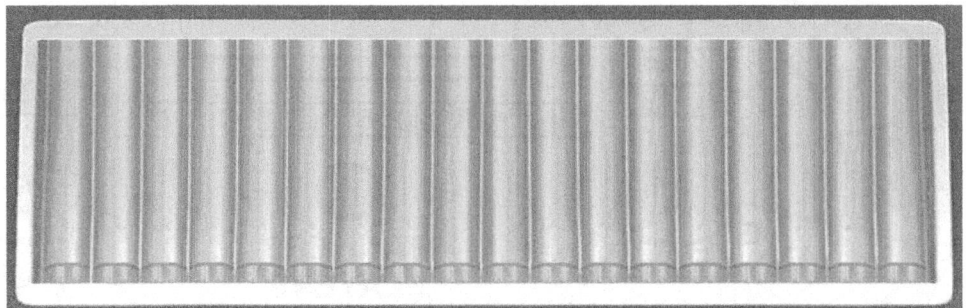

Photo 57

CARDS

Six, up to eight, decks of playing cards are shuffled and put into the shoe. Cards are organized by rank and suit. Suits are irrelevant in Baccarat; only card ranks matter, and jokers are excluded.

COMMISSION BOXES

On games that require a 5% commission, these printed boxes on the felt have numbers corresponding to each player's position. They are used as a placeholder to designate money owed to the house. Based on the number of betting spots on a table, the number of commission boxes could be higher or lower.

| 1 | 2 | 3 | 5 | 6 | 7 | 8 | 9 | 10 | 11 | 12 | 14 | 15 | 16 |

DEALING SHOE, LID, and ROLLER

Placed on the table's left side, a Baccarat dealing shoe stores all the undealt remaining playing cards. A top lid covers the entire shoe, which has a weighted roller device to push the cards forward. Tables that display an electronic grid are usually hooked up to the shoe. Dealt cards are "seen" and verified by the internal camera, which relays information about the winning hand and winning side bets to the grid. (See illustration 22.)

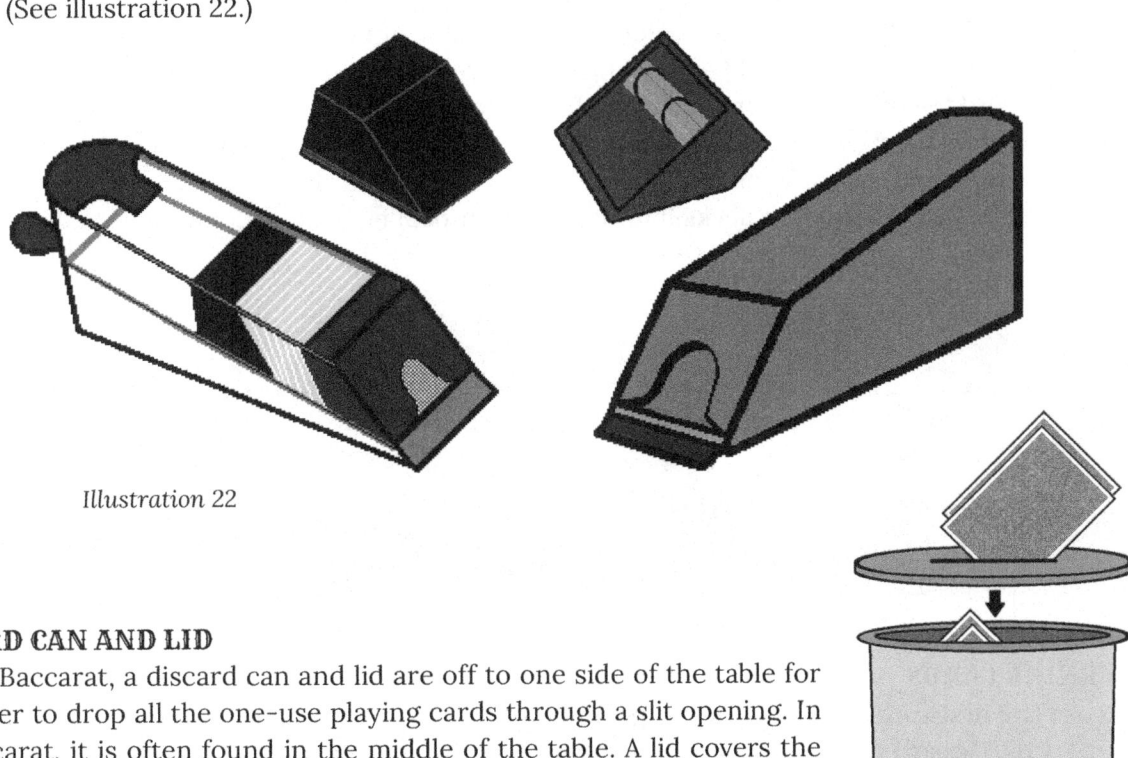

Illustration 22

DISCARD CAN AND LID

In Midi-Baccarat, a discard can and lid are off to one side of the table for the dealer to drop all the one-use playing cards through a slit opening. In Big Baccarat, it is often found in the middle of the table. A lid covers the can and at the end of the shoe, the dealer dumps the can's cards onto the table and sorts them into a neat pile to be removed from the game permanently. (See illustration 23.)

Illustration 23

PLAYER / BANKER BUTTONS

A winning Player or Banker button—often labeled in Chinese or another Asian language—is used after the hand is over to indicate which hand won. Some casinos require it, others think it slows the game down and don't use it. (See illustration 24.)

Illustration 24

DISCARD TRAY

For Mini-Baccarat, placed on the right side of the table, this upright card storage collector stores all the used cards for that shoe, until it is time to reshuffle.

LAMMER RACK

The rack (usually made of wood) that holds lammers for the Baccarat table. Stored directly in between the commission boxes and the cheque rack.

BATON/DEALER PADDLE

An important dealing tool used by the dealer/croupier in the *Chemin de Fer* game to slide cards, cash, and chips to/from players and dealers. Made of wood, plastic, or acrylic. It measures around 4.25 inches wide x 22 inches long. (See Illustration 25.)

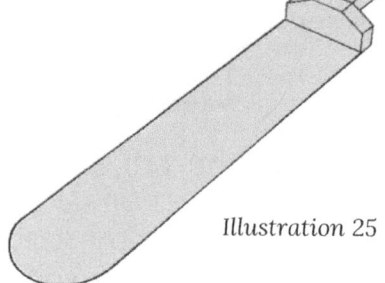

Illustration 25

DEALING PROCEDURES

CUTTING CARDS

The dealer will shuffle a six- or eight-deck shoe as needed, or the pit boss may provide a fresh box of pre-shuffled cards for Midi- and Big Baccarat games (refer to the section on **Skillful Card Shuffling**). Use a cut card to cut the deck and move the front section to the back. (See photo 58.) Once shuffled and cut, section off approximately 20 cards from the back of the decks, laying them flat on the table. Count 14 cards from the back, inserting the cut card between the 14th and 15th cards to mark the shoe's end. (See photo 59.) Place the decks into the Baccarat dealing shoe and reattach the lid if present. (See photo 60.)

Photo 58

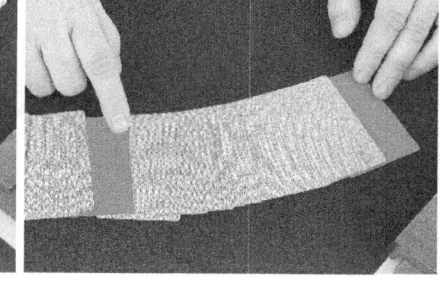

Photo 59

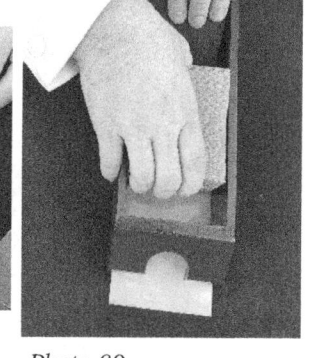

Photo 60

BURNING CARDS

Expose the first card of the new shoe. (See photo 61.) This card's value determines the number of burn cards. Discard the corresponding number of cards face down, announcing the card value and the total cards burned. Aces are worth one, and all 10s and face cards are worth 10. For example, "Six! Burning seven cards." (See photo 62.) Do not reveal the burned cards. Flip the first card face down, scoop all remaining burn cards, and discard into the discard can or tray.

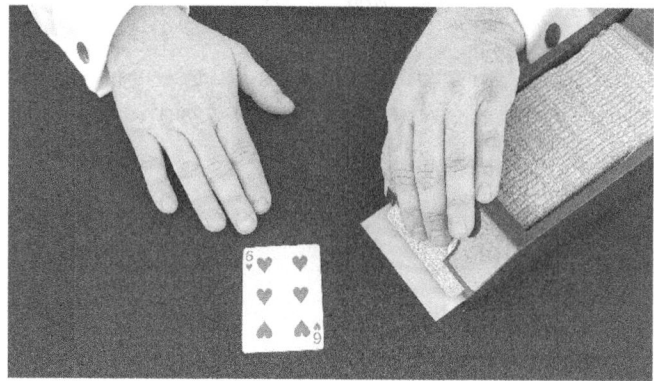

Photo 61

Photo 62

DEALING CARDS FROM THE SHOE

After the shuffle and burns, it is time to deal the game. Once players make wagers on one of three different bets Player, Banker, or Tie, cards are dealt in alternate order. Using the six- or eight-deck special Baccarat shoe, pull out one card with the left hand and slide it to the right hand face down. (See photo 63.) Pull out a second card and tuck it under the corner of the shoe momentarily (See photo 64.) Slide a third card face down to the right hand (See photo 65.) Then slide a fourth card out and combine it with the card tucked under shoe (See photo 66.) No jokers are used, but all thirteen ranks and all four suits are used. **Note**: Players may see free hands dealt without wagering any money.

Photo 63

Photo 64

Photo 65

Photo 66

The right hand contains the Player's two cards while the left hand contains the two Banker cards. Each hand consist of a total of two or three cards. Either both sides stand, only one side takes a card, or both Player and Banker each takes a card.

In Midi Baccarat, the player with the largest bet on Player or Banker physically handles the cards. Slide the two cards from the dealer's hand that corresponds to their bet (if they bet Player, slide them the two Player cards; if they bet Banker, slide them the two Banker cards). A player who has cards in his hand can bend and heavily damage the cards as cards from this shoe are used only one time. The player will direct the dealer to turn over one or both cards in front of the dealer. The player will then expose both of his cards. Once both sets of cards are in the dealer's possession and turned face-up, the dealer needs to add the totals of the cards on each side (Player and Banker) to determine if either has a Natural 8 or 9, as it will immediately end the game and neither side draws.

ADDING POINT TOTALS

In Mini-Baccarat, the dealer handles all the cards and will turn over the Player's two cards and Banker's two cards. In Baccarat, suits don't' matter, only the card ranks. The 2s through 9s are worth face value and are added as points. Kings, Queens, Jacks, and 10s, are worth zero points. Aces are worth one point. **When adding two or three card totals, only look at the total's LAST DIGIT TO THE RIGHT, the one's column.** (See illustration 26.) For example, a Player hand of 8 and 4 and draws a 10 adds up to 22, but only the last digit, 2 is the number is used as the point total. A Banker hand of 5 and 9 has a hand value of 4, not 14). The ten's column is ignored.

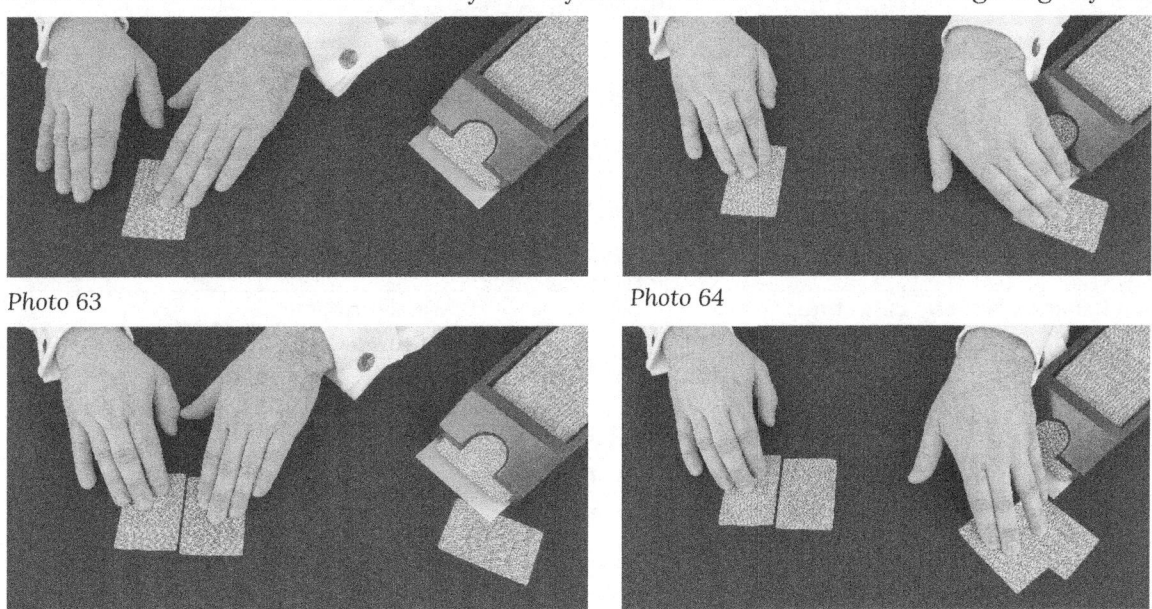

Illustration 26

PUNTO BANCO RULES for DRAWING CARDS and STANDING

Third Card Rule: The 3rd card drawing rule determines whether a third card is dealt to the Player and/or Banker hands. Both two-card hands are turned face up to determine if either Player or Banker cards have a Natural 8 or 9, which ends the hand immediately for both bets—or a third card needs to be drawn. Absent a Natural 8 or 9, the dealer looks at the total point value of the Player's hand first and uses this table to determine if the Player needs to draw one additional card or to stand.

PLAYER RULES	
Player's first two cards total:	Dealer Action:
0, 1, 2, 3, 4, or 5	Draw a Card
6 or 7	Stand
8 or 9	Natural – Neither hand draws

If the player does not have a Natural 8 or 9 total, then the Banker will follow these rules:

BANKER RULES		
When Banker's first two cards total:	Dealer Action:	
0, 1, or 2	Draw a Card	
Banker's first two cards total:	Draw when Player's third card is:	Does not draw when the Player's third card is:
3	1, 2, 3, 4, 5, 6, 7, 9, or 10	8
4	2, 3, 4, 5, 6, or 7	1, 8, 9, or 10
5	4, 5, 6, or 7	1, 2, 3, 8, 9, or 10
6	6 or 7	1, 2, 3, 4, 5, 8, 9, or 10
7	Stand	
8 or 9	Natural – Neither hand draws	

Note: When the Player stands on a two-card total of 6 or 7, the Banker assumes the Player's rules. (Banker draws on two-card totals of 0, 1, 2, 3, 4, or 5 and stands on two-card totals of 6, 7, 8, or 9).

Every dealer needs to **memorize BOTH Player and Banker rules** of when to draw cards or stand.

Again: no Natural 8 or 9, a Banker draws on two cards totaling 0, 1, or 2 points, and stands on 7, 8, and 9 point totals. Follow the two-card Banker rules for 3, 4, 5, and 6.

Reveal the third card sideways, place it to the right of the Player cards, and left of the Banker cards.

The hand with a higher point value closest to 9 wins. Either the Player wins and is paid 1:1, the Banker wins and is paid 1:1 (minus 5% commission, if required, unless a "No Commission" sign is posted), or, both hand values results in a Tie, which would pay 8:1, if wagered.

TIE HANDS
On a TIE, both Player and Banker bets push, and the dealer needs to use a hand motion similar to a hand "cutting" a piece of wood, or a loaf of bread. (See photo 67.)

Photo 67

Push the winning hand forward several inches. Remove losing bets from the right side, working counterclockwise, and place them between the two hands. Begin payouts from the right side, continuing counterclockwise. Take any applicable commission directly from a Banker payout, from the player after the hand, or from the cheque rack, and place it in the player's Commission Box. Finally, put losing cheques into the rack and discard the cards into the discard can or tray.

END of SHOE
Once the shoe reaches the cut card, finish dealing that hand, then deal **ONE MORE** complete hand. Unlike Blackjack where the current hand is completed and no new hands are dealt, Baccarat dealers must deal one more complete hand. Don't worry, the shoe will not run out of cards for the final hand. Follow house procedures how to remove the remaining cards, gather the used discards, and to begin a new shoe. On Mini-Baccarat games, the cards are most likely to be reshuffled. In Midi- and Big-Baccarat games, the players have marked, bent, and compromised the cards and those cards will automatically be replaced with new cards from the floorman.

COMMISSION
To calculate a required 5% commission on a Banker bet, divide the winning payout in half then move the decimal place one position to the left. (For example: a $25 bet has a commission of $1.25, $100 is $5 commission, $275 is $13.75 commission, and $485 is $24.25 commission).

Players have several options for paying the commission. Commissions can be:
- A. subtracted from the payout, or
- B. collected directly from the player immediately after the payout, or
- C. added by the dealer to any player's outstanding running total of commissions in the Commission Box to be collected at the end of the shoe.

Some casinos offer a "No Commission Baccarat" and sometimes it's true to that end. Otherwise, there is a popularly rising Nepal variant that charges no commission on a winning Banker hand. However, a payout on a winning Banker hand of 6 will only receive half the original bet, or a 1:2 payout.

SIDE BETS
Players have many optional side bets to choose from. Most side bets require a main wager on Player, Banker, or Tie as a prerequisite and are resolved in a single round—they either win or lose. Below are some commonly offered side bets, listed by their trademark names:

1. **3-Card Six** – Player or Banker point total 6, pays 8:1. Player and Banker each total 6, pays 100:1.
2. **3 Giving 8** – Player draws a third card; it is an 8. The Banker's stands on 3 points. Pays 200:1.
3. **4-5-6** – Players bet one of three wagers if the total number of cards between Player and Banker is four (pays 3:2), five (pays 2:1), or six (2:1).
4. **5 Treasures** – One bet that covers four different side bets: Blazing 7s, Fortune 7 (must win hand), Golden 8 (must win hand), and Heavenly 9. Pays 6:1.
5. **All Red/All Black** – Initial four Banker and Player cards are all Red, pays 22:1. Black, pays 24:1.
6. **Any 8 vs. Any 6** – A point total of 8 beats a point total of 6. Pays 25:1.
7. **Banker Natural 8/9** – (obsolete) Two separate bets that the Banker's point total is a Natural 8 or 9. Pays 9:1.
8. **Banker Pair** – Banker cards Pair result pays 9:1. Third drawn card Three of a Kind pays 68:1.
9. **Blazing 7s** – (two ways to win) Player and Banker both have a three-card total of 7, Pays 200:1; Player and Banker both have a two-card total of 7, Pays 50:1.
10. **Chan Chu 6** – (two ways to win) Banker wins with a three-card total of 6, Pays 50:1; Banker wins with a two-card total of 6, Pays 22:1.
11. **Doble Duck** – (two ways to win) Both Player and Banker have a three-card 6-6-6, pays 100:1; Either Player or Banker has a three-card 6-6-6, pays 8:1.
12. **Dragon 7** – Banker has a three-card total of 7. Pays 40:1.
13. **Dragon Bonus** – Player or Banker must win by four or more points, or a Natural 8 or 9 win. Payout varies.
14. **Either Pair** – First two cards of Player or Banker results in an unsuited Pair, pays 5:1.
15. **Fortune 7** – Banker has a three-card total of 7. Pays 40:1. (Same as Dragon 7.)
16. **Golden 8** – Player has a three-card total of 8. Pays 25:1. (Same as Panda 8.)
17. **Golden Frog** – One bet that covers four different side bets: Any 8 vs. Any 6, Natural 9 vs. Natural 7, Three-card 9 vs. Three-card 1, and Three-card 9 vs. Three-card 7. Payout varies.

18. **Heavenly 9** – (two ways to win) Both Player and Banker have a three-card total of 9, pays 75:1; Either Player or Banker has a three-card total of 9, pays 10:1.
19. **Kill** – Banker loses or ties with a three-card total of 7, OR Player loses or ties with a three-card 6. Pays 30:1.
20. **Kirin** – Player has a three-card total of 8. Pays 24:1.
21. **Lucky 6** – Two-card winning Banker 6, pays 12:1. Three-card winning Banker 6, pays 23:1.
22. **Lucky 7** – Wins if the Player and/or Banker hand has two 7s in the first two cards. Pays 77:1.
23. **Lucky 8** - Two separate bets based on a Player or Banker total of 8. Payout varies.
24. **Lucky 99** – Player and Banker each have a Natural 9 pays 25:1. Banker Natural 9 pays 5:1. Player Natural 9 pays 2:1.
25. **Lucky Bonus** – Banker wins on a point total of 6. Wager limited to 10% of Banker bet. Pays 18:1.
26. **Lucky Nines** – First four cards dealt to Player and Banker. One to four cards with a rank of 9 (same or mixed suit) wins. Payout varies on number of 9s initially dealt.
27. **Matching Dragon** – 13 different side bets a player can make to pick the number of times his chosen card rank will appear. Bet wins if that rank appears one or more times. Payout varies.
28. **Natural 9 vs. Natural 7** – Natural 9 beats a two-card 7. Pays 50:1.
29. **Ox 6** – Player wins on a three-card total of 6. Pays 40:1.
30. **Panda 8** – Player has a three-card total of 8. Pays 25:1.
31. **Perfect Pair** – First two cards of Player or Banker results in a suited Pair, pays 25:1.
32. **Phoenix** – Banker has a three-card total of 7. Pays 37:1.
33. **Phoenix Bonus** – Player or Banker must win by four or more points. A Natural 8 or 9 win. Payout varies.
34. **Player Pair** – Player cards Pair result pays 9:1. Third drawn card Three of a Kind pays 75:1.
35. **Power 8's** – Player bets on the number of times an 8-rank card appears, two up to four 8s, extra for suited cards. Payout varies.
36. **Rabbit Play** – Bet on the Player or Banker's cards to show a Pair, or if a third card is drawn, a Three of a Kind. Unsuited Pair pays 7:1, suited pays 15:1. Three of a Kind unsuited pays 50:1, suited pays 500:1.
37. **Royal 9** – Progressive bet that pays when Player and/Banker cards match different Kings and 9s that are pre-printed in front of the player. Payout varies.
38. **Royal Match** – A Player or Banker achieving a King and Queen in the first two cards. Suited pays 75:1, unsuited pays 30:1.
39. **Spread Bets** – Six different bets a player can make on Player or Banker to win with a winning point total of 1 to 3 (pays 30:1), 5 to 6 (pays 8:1), or 8 to 9 (pays 3:1).
40. **Super 6** – Winning Banker point total of 6 pays 12:1, or as high as 15:1.
41. **Three-card 9 vs. Three-card 1** – A three-card 9 beats a three-card 1. Pays 150:1.
42. **Three-card 9 vs. Three-card 7** – A three-card 9 beats a three-card 7. Pays 200:1.
43. **Tie Max (Lucky Max)** – (two ways to win) In the event of a tie between Player and Banker, the High Tie Max bet pays 10:1 if the highest point value card in a tie is 6 to 9. The Low Tie Max bet pays 55:1 highest point value card is 0 to 5.
44. **Tiger 7** – Banker wins on a three-card total of 7. Pays 40:1.
45. **Tiger Bets** – Player and/or Banker achieves a point total of 6. Payout varies.
46. **COVER ALL** – If any of the 4 listed bets wins, this bet Pays 8:1. (See illustration 27.)

Baccarat Cover All Bet

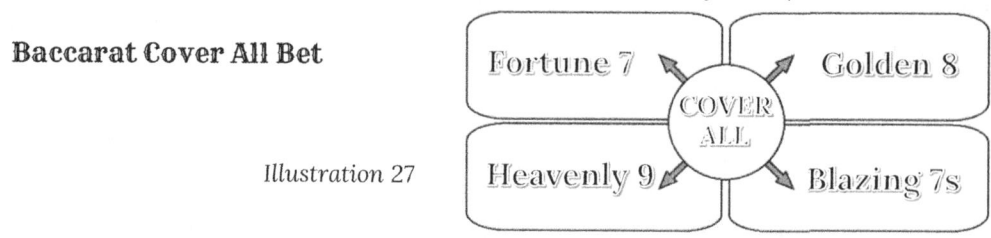

Illustration 27

BACCARAT GRIDS

Paper scorecards are almost always available to Baccarat players. These long, heavy cardstock paper have rows of empty squares players write on with the Red/Blue pen (also supplied) allows players to track, by hand, the current game's result. (See illustration 28.)

Illustration 28

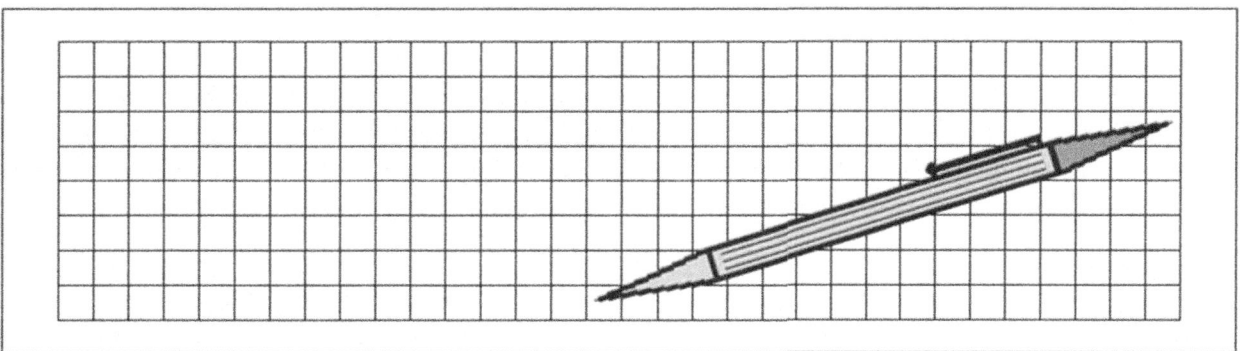

Digital Display Board Technology used in Baccarat helps players keep track of past round outcomes and discern patterns or trends. It has brought a simple card game of Baccarat into an era of electronic dealing shoes (embedded with a camera to see the next dealt card) hooked up to a digital TV-size grid towering over the table to show the players the current shoe's card history. Many players rely on this game board on whether to wager, which bets, and how much. Beware!, while past results can indicate future cards to come, it won't predict which order, or which hand will get the cards. These types of forecasting fall under the Gambler's Fallacy. (See illustration 29.)

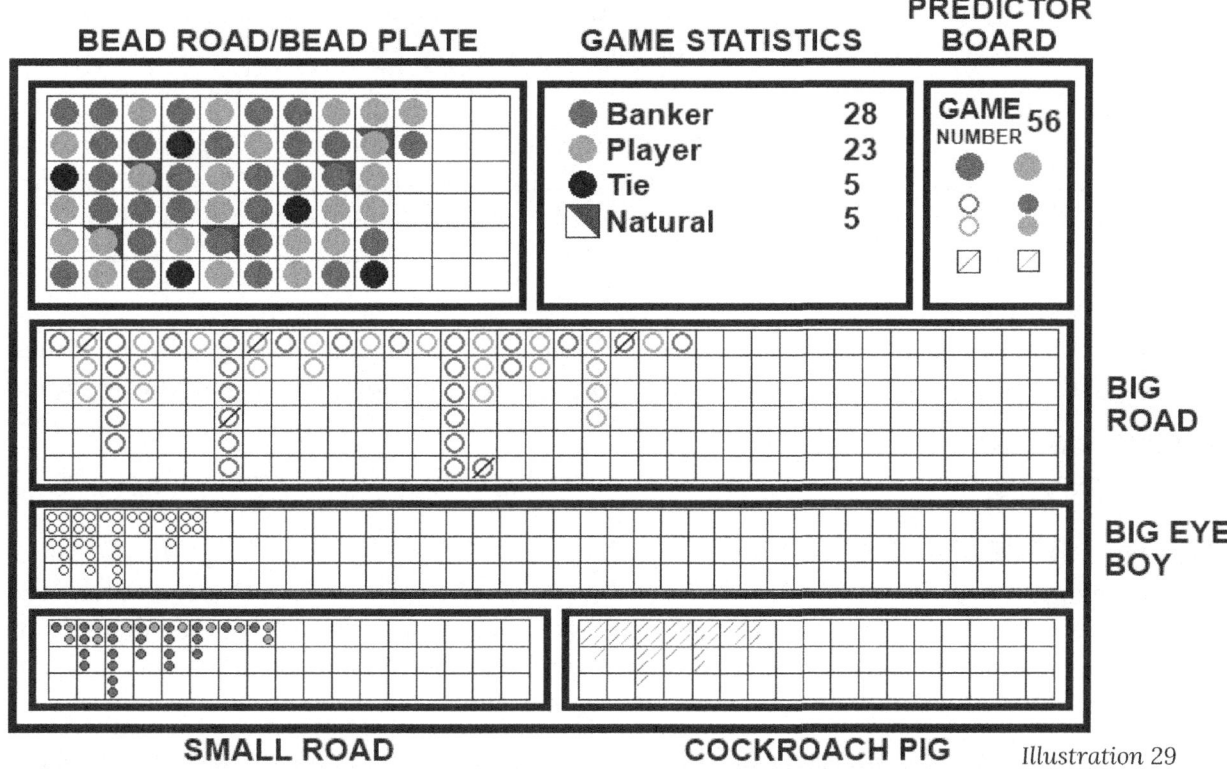

Illustration 29

The display boards are automatically updated as each hand ends. Blue dots represent a Player win, Red dots for a Banker win, and Green dots (or a slash "/") for a Tie. Naturals, Player and Banker Pairs, and even algorithm-based predictions can all be found on this type of display. Side bets, such as Dragon 7 or Panda 8, may also be displayed. Advanced grids will even flash winning side bets that pay significant odds. Each board continues to track until there are no more cards to deal from that shoe, then it is cleared completely for the next shoe. Digital display boards may show none, some, all, or more than what's presented here. A common display board is examined:

BEAD ROAD/BEAD PLATE

This is the most prominent display on the board; it records the history of the current shoe. Sometimes, it will also reveal the winning hand combination as numbers. The tracking order starts from the upper left-hand corner and works downward, completing the first column before starting atop a new column to the right of it.

BIG ROAD

This section is the easiest and most frequently referenced by players. The Big Road is an inverted bar chart that tracks strings of wins for the Banker or Player. It presents the same information as the Bead Road (or Bead Plate) but in a different format. Alternating columns of blue and red dots are used, with a new column starting whenever the leading position changes, such as from Banker to Player.

Tracking begins at the top-left corner and proceeds six rows downward. If the opposite hand wins, a new column starts to the right of the previous one. When a position achieves more than six consecutive wins, the streak pivots to the right upon reaching the bottom of the grid and continues along the last row. This pivoting is often referred to as a "dragon tail," and players consider it lucky to "follow the dragon." Ties are marked with a slash "/" through the previous result instead of taking up a new space.

BIG EYE BOY

This shows patterns, streaks, and trends by comparing one previous column from the Big Road. It aims to but cannot accurately predict the next set of cards for the Player or Banker hands.

SMALL ROAD

This scorecard derives two previous columns of results from the Big Road. It, too, does not predict the next set of cards or results for the Player or Banker hands.

COCKROACH PIG

Information for this scorecard is sourced from the previous 3 columns. Unlike all the other scorecards marked with a filled-in dot or an outline of a circle, slash marks show these results. Again, it is only information about the past cards. Properly and randomly shuffled cards will not show a bias in any accuracy of predictions of future hands.

GAME STATISTICS

This box shows a running tally of all the individual results, by identifying which hand won, if there was a tie, if either hand contained a Pair, or had a Natural 8 or 9, and how many of each has occurred.

PREDICTOR BOARD

This box uses an algorithm to predict what the next winning hand will be. It is frequently wrong.

STADIUM BACCARAT

Recent developments have found the inclusion of this game dealt "stadium-style." Players pick a seat from multiple rows of seats as if in a sport/concert stadium. Money is inserted into a digital game console where the player can wager "touchscreen" style. Each game is on a timer, and once the game closes, a live dealer, often on an elevated stage, deals the game.

Once the dealer reaches the cut card, one or two more hands/coup are drawn. Results are displayed on large digital screens and on the players' screen.

Players' bets are credited or debited accordingly. Players can add money or cash out any time. A cashout ticket, also known as T.I.T.O., is used.

BACCARAT ETIQUETTE

Baccarat is renowned for its elegant ambiance, particularly at high-limit tables. To maintain decorum, players are expected to observe these unwritten rules:

- Determine whether the table follows *punto banco*, *chemin de fer*, or *Baccarat banque* rules.
- Avoid touching the chips after placing bets.
- Dress suitably for high-stakes games.
- Settle any owed commissions before leaving the game.
- Show respect to the dealer and fellow players.
- Tip the dealers as appropriate.
- Understand the rules thoroughly.
- Be mindful of and respect other players' superstitions.
- Wait for the current hand to conclude before joining a table.

BACCARAT COMPARISON CHART

GAME FEATURE	MINI BACCARAT	MIDI BACCARAT	PUNTO BANCO	CHEMIN de FER	BACCARAT BANQUE
Number of Decks	6	8	8	6	3
Table Size	Up to 7 players	Up to 12 players	Up to 14 players	Up to 12 players	Up to 12 players
Betting Limits	Low minimums and maximums	Mid-range	High minimums and maximums	High	High
Game Pace	Fast	Moderate	Slow	Moderate	Moderate
Player Interaction	Minimal, dealer handles most actions	Some player interaction	High interaction, players handle cards	Players take turns being the Banker	One player is the permanent Banker
Atmosphere	Casual, social	Casual, social	Exclusive, high-stakes	Traditional and Formal	Exclusive and Formal
Side Bets	Few	More	Many	Few or none	Few or none

Different casinos may offer unique variations or house rules. Always check for specifics.

BIG WHEEL

The Big Wheel is one of the simplest casino games to deal and play. Players bet on which slot the wheel's pointer, arrow, or heavy leather indicator will land on. If it does, they win; if not, they lose. The Big Six wheel has late 19th and early 20th century roots.[4],[5]

Game:	Minimum 1 player/no maximum, as many players who can bet on the table.
Also Known As:	Big Six Wheel, Lucky Wheel, Money Wheel, Wheel of Fortune.
Object:	The player's objective is to bet on the layout's numbers/symbol hoping the wheel lands on the same corresponding number. Payouts vary.

EQUIPMENT

Wheel, table, layout, chairs, mirror, and cheques. (See illustration 30.)

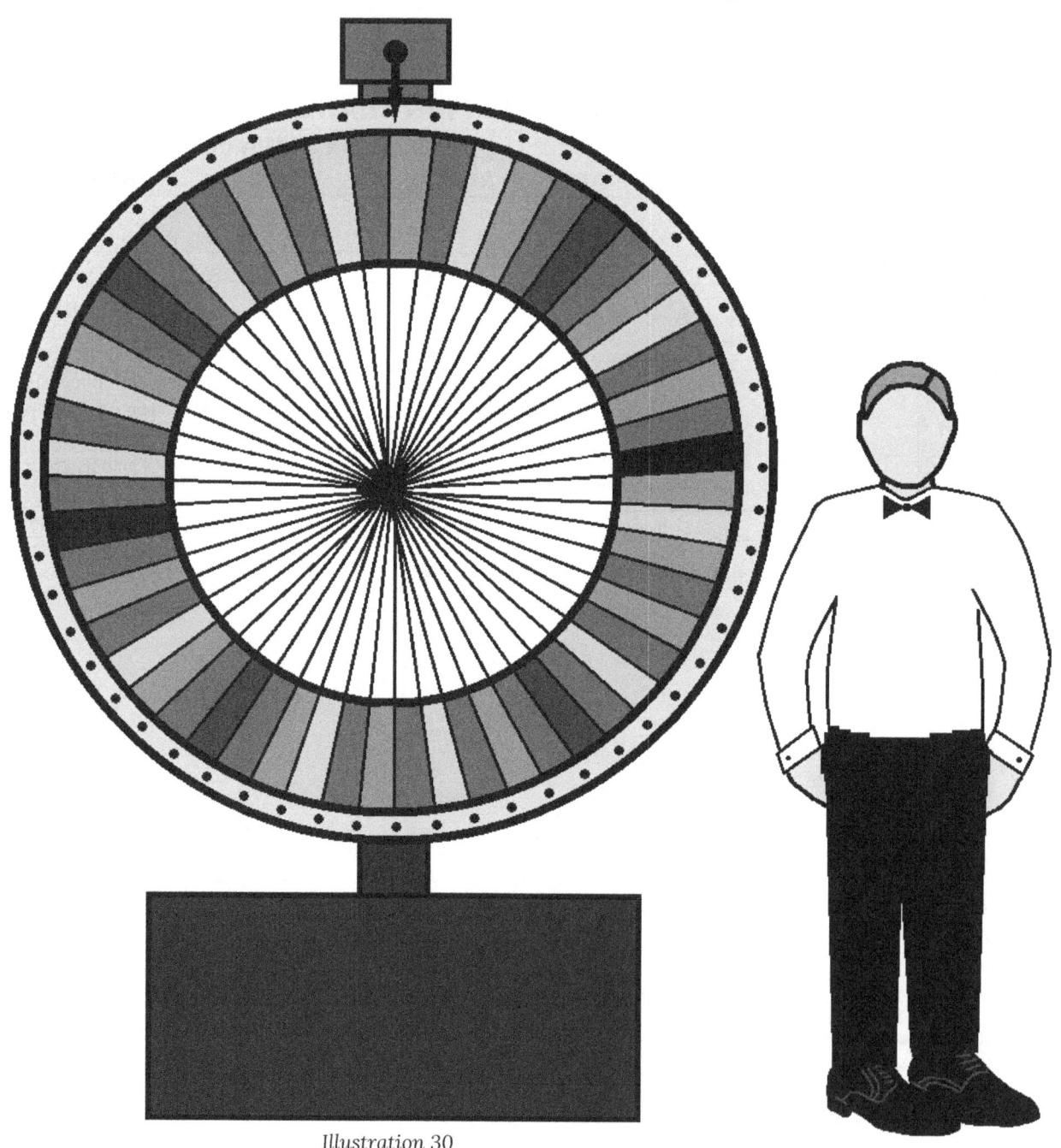

Illustration 30

46 CARNIVAL GAMES

Standing over 7 feet tall, the Big Wheel is a prominently adorned vertical rotating wheel, divided into equal segments with distinct symbols or numbers. The enticingly large design draws the attention of gamblers and onlookers. Players place bets on where they predict the wheel will stop, and as it spins, the anticipation builds until the final, heart-racing moment. This game of chance offers payouts ranging from modest to substantial, blending luck, excitement, and the appeal of significant winnings.

Sample Big Six wheel layout, complete with dealer mirror and cheque rack. (See illustration 31.)

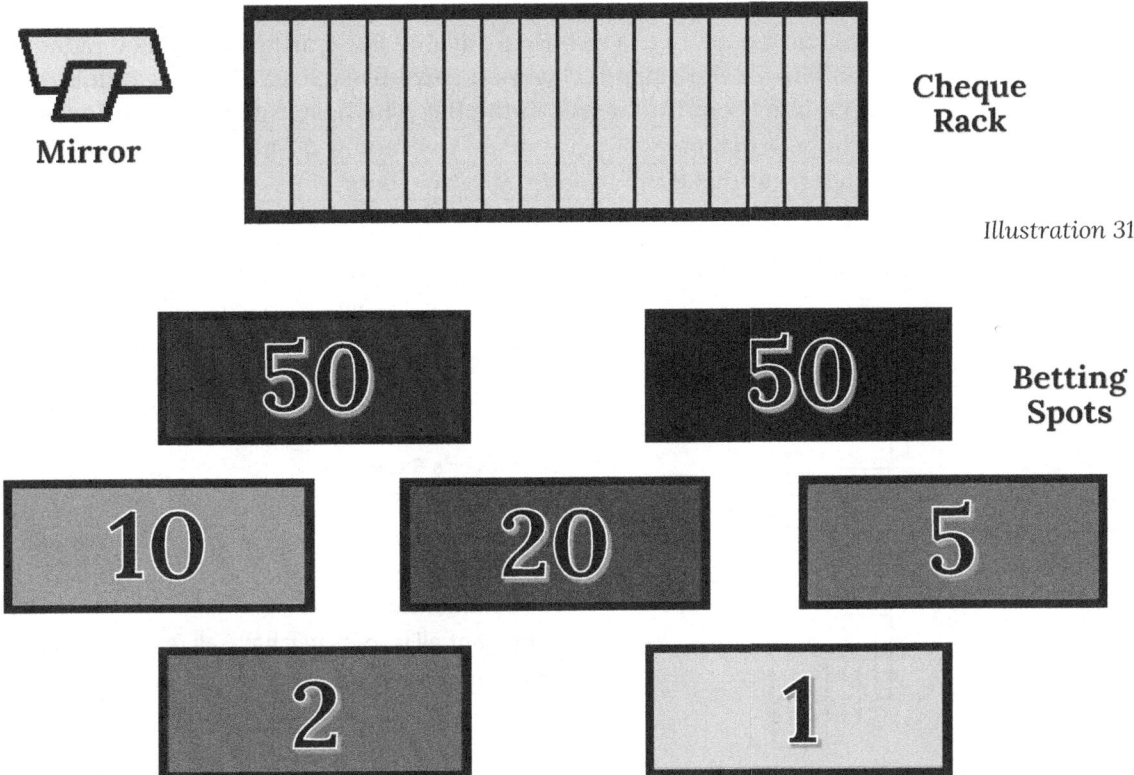

Illustration 31

Versions commonly found in the casino:

WHEEL TYPE	FEATURE
Classic Big Six Wheel	The traditional large wheel divided into segments and labeled with different payouts.
Dice Wheel	Players bet on numbers one to six using a wheel with three six-sided dice combinations.
52-Slot Wheel	The UK version with 52 slots and six different payouts.
High-Stakes Big Six	Higher betting limits and larger payouts.
Mini Big Six	A smaller wheel version with fewer segments and lower betting limits.
Money Wheel	Similar to the Big Six Wheel, it uses dollar bills in each slot to represent payout amounts.
Stadium Wheel	A dealer-less, machine-operated wheel where players bet via a touch screen.

DEALING AND PAY PROCEDURES

1. Players may wager as many bets as they wish.
2. Dealer spins the wheel. Make no change once the wheel spins.
3. Once the wheel slows down, extend arm over the layout and wave off any more bets, stating "No More Bets."
4. Dealer always looks forward. Look at the mirror that reflects where the wheel's arrow or pointer is. Announce the winning number(s) out loud. Use a marker if required by the casino.
5. Remove all the losing bets first. Place them into the cheque rack.
6. Pay the winning bets according to the correct payout that bet receives. Bets are self-service, and players need to remember which bet is theirs.
7. Remove marker if used, otherwise, announce that bets are open.

CARIBBEAN STUD POKER

The origin of Caribbean Stud Poker is unclear—unusual for a modern game. Conflicting authorship credits go to David Sklansky and James Suttle.[6,7] As poker's popularity grew, casinos introduced this five-card, no-draw, house-banked game to attract enthusiasts.

Game:	7-player maximum.
Also Known As:	Casino Poker, Casino Stud Poker, Super Stud, Multi-Hand Caribbean Stud, Caribbean Poker, Caribbean Draw Poker.
Object:	The player's objective is to have a payable five-card hand ranked higher than a qualifying dealer's hand. Players receive five cards. Players can fold, or play by doubling their Ante wager in the Bet. The best high hand is a Royal Flush.
Dealing:	Deal only to players who have made the required Ante bet.
Betting Structure:	Ante, Bet, various Bonus and Progressive bets.

EQUIPMENT

Table, layout, chairs, two decks of cards used alternatively, shuffle machine, discard tray, and cheques. (See illustration 32.)

Illustration Key

A – Progressive
B – Ante
C – Bet
D – Player's 5 Cards
E – Dealer's 5 Cards
F – Community Card #1
G – Community Card #2
H – Community Card #3

(Note: not all layouts will have all features shown.)

Illustration 32

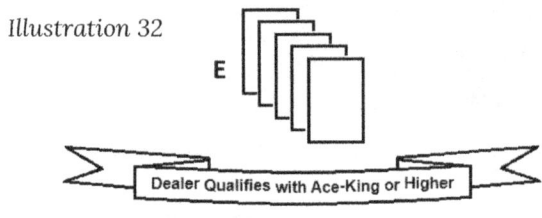
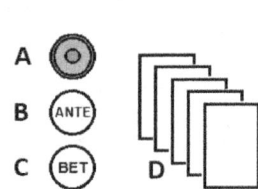

DEALER QUALIFYING HAND

The Dealer's five cards must be an Ace-King-high or higher to qualify/play against the Player's hand.

TYPES of BETS and PAYOUTS

- **Ante** – Pays even money if dealer qualifies and player beats the dealer, OR if the dealer doesn't qualify.

- **Progressive** – An optional side bet based on player's 5-card hand.
  - Royal Flush 100% of Jackpot
  - Straight Flush 10% of Jackpot
  - Four of a Kind $500
  - Full House $100
  - Flush $50

- **Bet** – Pushes if the dealer doesn't qualify, otherwise pays if the player beats the dealer:
  - Royal Flush 100:1
  - Straight Flush 50:1
  - Four of a Kind 20:1
  - Full House 7:1
  - Flush 5:1
  - Straight 4:1
  - Three of a Kind 3:1
  - Two Pair 2:1
  - All other hands 1:1

DEALING AND PAY PROCEDURES

1. Player must minimally wager an Ante bet and have the option to wager the Progressive bet.
2. Dealing order: Each player receives five cards face down, all at once. The dealer also receives five cards face down, but turns up the top card. The remaining cards are discarded.
3. Each player examines his own cards. He can bet or fold. Players may choose to play blind.
4. If the player folds, he forfeits his Ante bet and loses the hand. Discard the player's hand.
5. If the player plays, the player must double their Ante wager on the Bet spot.
6. After all players act, the dealer reveals his four remaining cards. Determine if the dealer hand qualifies. Compare each player's hand to the dealer's hand. Perform take/pay procedures counterclockwise starting with the dealer's right. Discard hands, shuffle, and deal next game.

CASINO WAR

Casino War embodies the simplest sense of player versus casino action. Bet Technology (now owned by Light & Wonder) developed and patented this game in 1993 based on the childhood game of War.[8] Players look to beat the dealer's total. If they do, they win. If they don't, they lose. Ties (or going to "WAR") make the game gut-wrenchingly exciting.

Game:	7-player maximum.
Also Known As:	Multi-Hand War, Progressive War, Speed War, Super War, War, One-Card Blackjack.
Object:	The player's objective is to obtain a higher card that the dealer's card. In case of a tie, the player may surrender or risk additional wager(s) for subsequent cards to determine who (player or dealer) has the higher hand. Suits don't matter. Rank of cards: Deuce is the lowest card. Ace is always high.
Dealing:	Deal only to players who have made a wager.
Betting Structure:	Main wager bet, additional "WAR" wagers, various Bonus bets.

EQUIPMENT

Table, layout, chairs, up to six decks of cards, shuffle machine, shoe, discard tray, and cheques. Players make a wager in the betting circle. One card is dealt face up to each player, and one card face up to the dealer. A player with a higher-ranked card(s) than what the dealer has will win for the player. A player's lower ranked card(s) than the dealer has will lose for the player. Ties are treated separately.

DEALING AND PAY PROCEDURES

1. A player must make a minimum wager in the betting circle.
2. The dealer usually deals from a shoe but may deal from a single or double deck if used.
3. Deal one card face up to each player, then one card face up in front of the dealer. Deuce is low, Ace is always high. Determine who has the higher card, the dealer or the player. Repeat for all hands that are not tied. Remove the bets from hands whose card rank is lower than the dealer, and pay even money to those hands that are higher than the dealer. Collect those cards.
4. For hands that tie the dealer, there are two scenarios.
    a. The player can inform the dealer he does not wish to go to "WAR" with the dealer, in which case, he will surrender (lose) half of his wager, and his hand is forfeited. If this is the case, bring the entire wager to the left side (money coming in), count it, then bring out half that amount on the right side and give this smaller amount to the player, bank the original wager. Collect his cards, and move onto the next player or hand.
    b. The player can go to "WAR" (compete for a higher hand by obtaining additional cards) with the dealer. If the player has not already informed the dealer, the dealer should ask the player if he wishes to go to "WAR." If yes, then the player will need to add an, equal wager to the original wager. Remember, the casino is always willing to go to "WAR" with the player. Ensure at this point that all remaining players have added the additional wager. Some casinos will have the dealer automatically put a special lammer next to the original wager to indicate the "WAR." Subsequently, the dealer will burn the next three cards, then issue one card to each player who tied the dealer with their first card. If the second cards are not the same, the higher-ranked card wins. Otherwise if the second card also results in a tie, this whole process repeats itself and will continue until there is a clear winner. Pay or take bets/cards as appropriate.
5. There is an optional Tie Bet wager that can be placed before any cards are dealt. If the dealer's and player's first cards result in a tie, this independent wager wins 10:1; else it loses.
6. Once all bets have been settled, clear the table of cards and begin dealing the next round to wagers that have been made.

CRAZY 4 POKER

Crazy 4 Poker is a poker-based, casino table game invented by Roger Snow and introduced in 2004 by Shuffle Master, now owned by Light & Wonder (formerly Scientific Games).[9] Each player's hand competes against the dealer's hand. Higher hand values result in bigger payouts. Players make an Ante bet equal to the Super Bonus bet to receive cards. Players either fold or elect to play by placing a Play bet. Additional Bonus or side bets are also available.

Game:	7-player maximum.
Also Known As:	Crazy Four Poker, Crazy 4 Poker Deluxe, Four Card Poker, Primero/Primera.
Object:	The player's objective is to have a payable best four of five-card hand ranked higher than the dealer's hand. The player starts with an Ante bet and receives two cards. Players can fold or play to compete in a showdown versus the dealer. The best high hand is a Royal Flush.
Dealing:	Deal only to players who have made the required Ante and Super Bonus bet.
Betting Structure:	Ante, Super Bonus, Play, various Bonus and Progressive bets.

EQUIPMENT

Table, layout, chairs, two decks of cards used alternatively, shuffle machine, discard tray, and cheques. (See illustration 33.)

Illustration 33

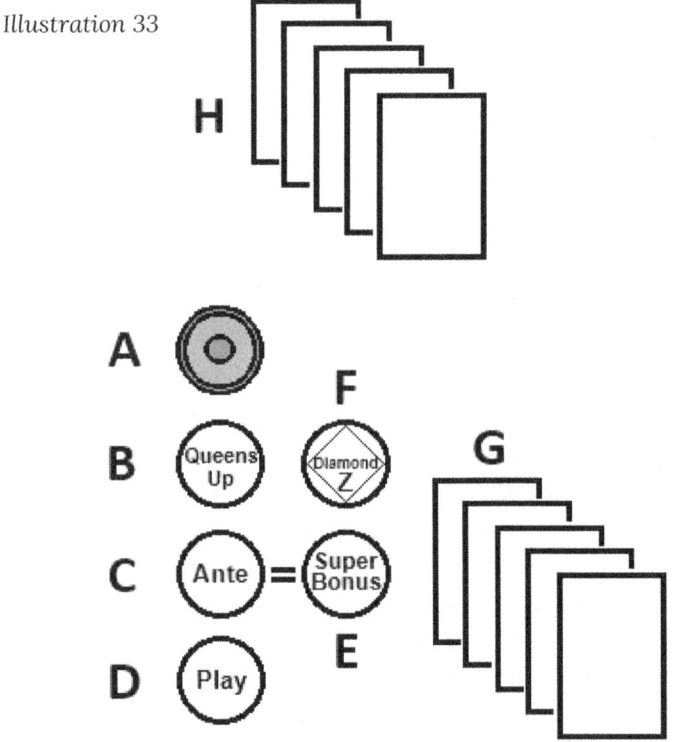

Illustration Key

A – Progressive Light
B – Queens Up
C – Ante
D – Play
E – Super Bonus
F – Diamond Z
G – Player's 5 Cards
H – Dealer's 5 Cards

(Note: not all layouts will have all features shown.)

DEALER QUALIFYING HAND

Dealer qualifies with a King High or better.

Play Bet: Players may triple the Ante bet holding a Pair of Aces or better.

TYPES of BETS and PAYOUTS

Crazy 4 Poker is a poker-based casino table game in which each player's aim is to have his best 4 of 5-card hand beat the dealer's best 4 of 5-card hand. Poker hand rankings vary from the standard order and are listed from highest to lowest. Verify specific payouts, as they can differ from each casino. Payouts are typically printed on the table felt. To receive cards, players must place two equal bets (Ante and Super Bonus) but can also wager optional side bets. Using a 52-card deck, players receive five cards each and can either fold or continue by making a Play bet. Since only the best 4 of the 5 cards are used, hands are ranked from highest (Four of a Kind) to lowest (high card).

50 CARNIVAL GAMES

If the player's hand beats the dealer's, the Ante and Play bets pay even money, If the first four cards tie, then the bets push. Other payouts are determined by the strength of the player's hand:

- **Queens Up**
  - Four of a Kind 50:1
  - Straight Flush 40:1
  - Three of a Kind 7:1
  - Flush 4:1
  - Straight 3:1
  - Two Pair 2:1
  - Queens or Better 1:1

- **Super Bonus**
  - Four Aces 200:1
  - Four of a Kind 30:1
  - Straight Flush 15:1
  - Flush 3:2
  - Straight 1:1

- **Diamond Z**
  - 10 Diamonds 1000:1
  - 9 Diamonds 400:1
  - 8 Diamonds 200:1
  - 7 Diamonds 100:1
  - 6 Diamonds 15:1
  - 5 Diamonds 4:1
  - 4 Diamonds 2:1

VARIATION

Four Card Poker – Primarily found in the Eastern U.S., this simpler game is the precursor to the more popular Crazy 4 Poker found in Las Vegas. The dealer receives six cards, while players only receive five cards to make their 4-card hands. The mandatory Super Bonus side bet does not exist.

DEALING AND PAY PROCEDURES

1. Players minimally make Ante and Super Bonus bets. Players can wager optional bonus bets. Players may or may not bet more than one player betting spot.
2. House dealing order: Verify and collect any Progressive wagers. The dealer gives each player, then himself, five cards face down. (Check with house policy on specific dealing procedures.)
3. Dealer discards any remaining, undealt cards into the discard tray.
4. Players look at their cards and decide if they wish to play. If the player folds, they are usually no longer eligible for any of the other payouts. Lock up their wagers and discard their cards.
5. If the player continues with the hand, he must equal his Ante wager in the Play betting circle. Players holding a Pair of Aces or better may raise their Play bet up to 3x their Ante.
6. If all players fold their hands, play has ended. Gather all cards, riffle the deck if the house requires it, and replace all cards into the shuffle machine.
7. The dealer reveals and arranges, in order, his best 4-card hand. Turn the 5th card sideways.
8. Working counterclockwise, start from the dealer's right side, turn one player's hand up and visually determine the best hand. Then, determine which 4-card hand is higher: the player or the dealer.
9. Collect the bets that lose. Follow the printed payout tables for payout amounts. Offset cheque stacks needing a colored-up payout. All winning Ante and Play wagers are paid even money (1:1). In the case of a tie, push these bets. If the dealer does not qualify with at least a King high, the Ante bet pushes and the Play bet wins automatically.
10. Pay winning bonus/side bet wagers according to the printed payout charts. Queens Up bet requires a player's hand to have a Pair of Queens or higher, otherwise it loses. The Super Bonus wins if a player's hand has a 4-card Straight or higher. All other hands push if the player's cards beat or tie the dealer. Generally, if the dealer does not qualify and the player has less than a Straight, the Super Bonus is automatically pushed. Discard player's hand.
11. Pay accordingly if the player wins their Progressive bet. (The light will be on if he wagered it.)
12. Repeat hand examination and payouts, if any, for each remaining player.
13. Any significant payout (including Progressive bets) will require an approval callout to the floorman. Play is often halted to have surveillance review the hand before any payouts. Know the house requirements.
14. Check to see if any remaining cards are on the table, collect them, then start a new game.

REMINDERS: House procedure may require a burn card and have the dealer stack or spread apart his cards, face down after all players have received their five cards. A cut card may or may not be used. A 6-Card Bonus bet may be offered.

DJ WILD

DJ Wild, first introduced in 2014 at the Las Vegas Global Gaming Expo, is currently owned and distributed by Light & Wonder.[10] It is a poker-based game using a 53-card deck including one joker. The joker and the four deuces are all considered wild and can be used to substitute for another card to complete a hand. Players play against the dealer's and optional bonus wagers are offered.

Game:	7-player maximum.
Also Known As:	DJ Wild Stud Poker.
Object:	DJ Wild is a poker-based casino table game where all four deuces and a joker are wild. A player's aim is to have his 5-card hand beat the dealer's 5-card hand and/or obtain hands that win certain Bonus bets. Best hand is 5 Wilds, (Four Deuces and the Joker.)
Dealing:	Deal only to players who have wagered an Ante and a Blind bet.
Betting Structure:	Ante and Blind bets, Play Bet, various Bonus bets.

EQUIPMENT

Table, layout, chairs, two decks of cards used alternatively, one joker per deck, shuffle machine, discard tray, and cheques. (See illustration 34.)

Illustration 34

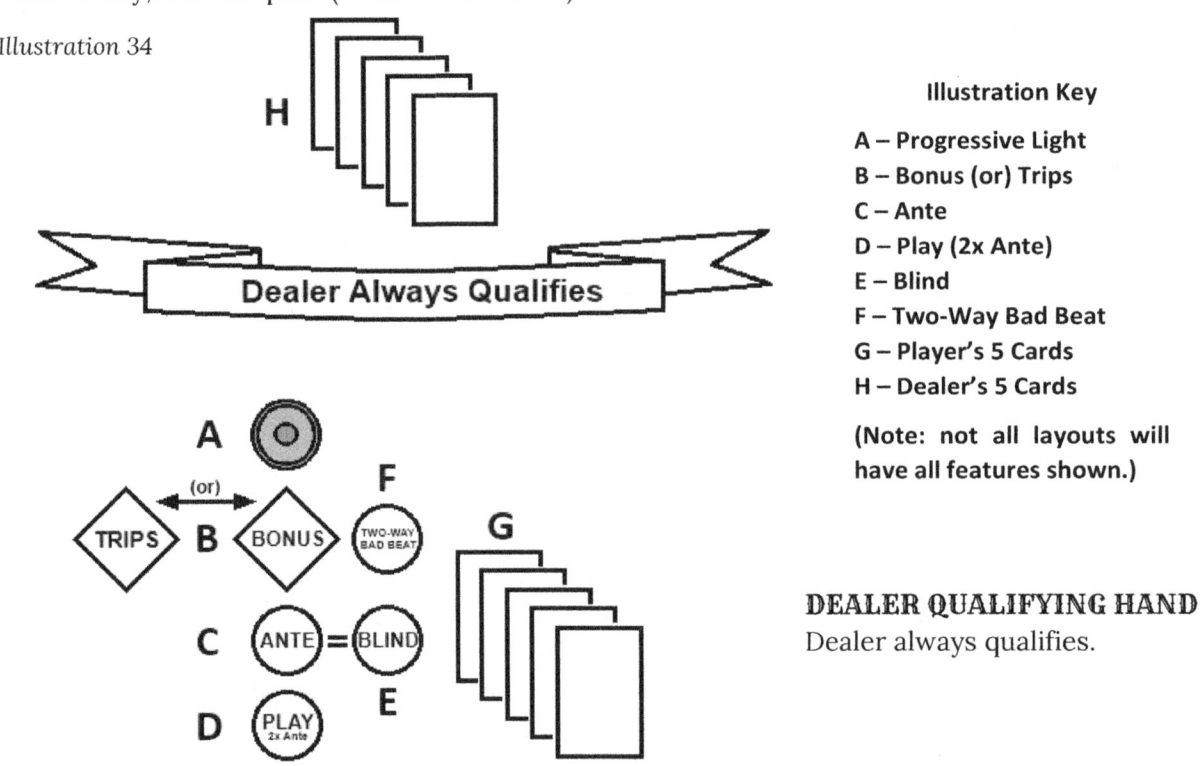

Illustration Key

A – Progressive Light
B – Bonus (or) Trips
C – Ante
D – Play (2x Ante)
E – Blind
F – Two-Way Bad Beat
G – Player's 5 Cards
H – Dealer's 5 Cards

(Note: not all layouts will have all features shown.)

DEALER QUALIFYING HAND
Dealer always qualifies.

TYPES of BETS and PAYOUTS

Players aim to beat the dealer's hand, with unique poker hand rankings listed from highest to lowest. Payouts vary by casino and are typically printed on the table felt. Players must place two equal bets (Ante and Blind) and can add side bets.

Using a 52-card deck plus a joker, there are 53 cards in total, with the four deuces and joker designated as wild. Players receive five cards each and can either fold or make a Play bet, equal to twice the Ante. Hands are ranked from highest (five wilds) to lowest (high card).

If the player's hand beats the dealer's, the Ante and Play bets pay even money. The Blind bet payout is determined by the player's hand as shown on the pay table.

Poker hand rankings vary from the standard order and are listed from highest to lowest. Verify specific payouts, as they can differ from each casino.

- ◊ **Blind Payout**
  - ➢ Five Wilds: 1000:1
  - ➢ Royal Flush: 50:1
  - ➢ Five of a Kind: 10:1
  - ➢ Straight Flush: 9:1
  - ➢ Four of a Kind: 4:1
  - ➢ Full House: 3:1
  - ➢ Flush: 2:1
  - ➢ Straight: 1:1
  - ➢ Three of a Kind: Push

- ◊ **Bonus (or) Trips Payout (Natural)**
  - ➢ Royal Flush: 1000:1
  - ➢ Straight Flush: 200:1
  - ➢ Four of a Kind: 90:1
  - ➢ Full House: 40:1
  - ➢ Flush: 30:1
  - ➢ Straight: 20:1
  - ➢ Three of a Kind: 6:1

- ◊ **Bonus (or) Trips Payout (Wild)**
  - ➢ Five Wilds: 2000:1
  - ➢ Royal Flush: 100:1
  - ➢ Five of a Kind: 100:1
  - ➢ Straight Flush: 30:1
  - ➢ Four of a Kind: 6:1
  - ➢ Full House: 5:1
  - ➢ Flush: 4:1
  - ➢ Straight: 3:1
  - ➢ Three of a Kind: 1:1

- ◊ **Two-Way Bad Beat**
  - ➢ Royal Flush: 10000:1
  - ➢ Five of a Kind 10000:1
  - ➢ Straight Flush 5000:1
  - ➢ Four of a Kind 500:1
  - ➢ Full House 400:1
  - ➢ Flush 300:1
  - ➢ Straight 100:1
  - ➢ Three of a Kind 9:1

As players receive their cards, they look at them and decide if their hand is strong enough to play and hopefully beat the dealer. A player either folds and will lose all of his current bets, or he will decide to play the hand in which case he must wager a Play bet at 2x his Ante bet.

Exception: Check house rules to determine if the player can still get paid on a valid Bonus/Trips bet even if he folds his Ante and Blind wagers.

DEALING AND PAY PROCEDURES

1. Players minimally make an Ante wager equal amount to the Blind wager. Optional Two-Way Bad Beat, Bonus/Trips, or Progressive wagers are also available before the hand starts.
2. Generally, the shuffle machine will dispense 5 cards. Deal each stack of cards to each player, then to the dealer (in one neat pile.) Some casinos will have the dealer hold off dealing his own stack of cards or will do so with a cut card or button to protect/cover the dealer hand.
3. Players will look at their hands, decide to play the Play bet or fold.
4. Collect any bets that are forfeited by the player, then collect their cards. Look around to see that every player has made their decision. Players continuing the hand must make a Player wager equal to the Ante bet and will also turn their hand up.
5. The dealer turns over his hand and arranges them from highest to lowest. The dealer will always qualify (have a hand that is playable).
6. Working counterclockwise from right to left, the dealer compares each player's hand, one at a time to see which hand is better, the player's or the dealer's. If the player's hand is better, their Ante and Play are both paid at 1:1. If not, they both lose.
7. Next, examine if that player has a hand containing Three of a Kind or better. If so, push or pay the Blind, Bonus/Trips, and/or Progressive bets according to the payout chart.
8. The dealer will also look to see if the Two-Way Bad Beat wager warrants a payout or not. To win, either the player must beat the dealer with a qualifying hand or the dealer beats the player with a qualifying hand. In case of a tie, the lower-ranked hand wins. Otherwise it loses.
9. Complete all action with one player before moving onto the next. Scoop up cards, begin again.

HIGH CARD FLUSH – I LOVE SUITS

A former dealer, Mike Pertgen of Las Vegas invented this game in 2010.[11] High Card Flush is a poker-flush-only based, casino table game now owned by Galaxy Gaming. Players compete against the dealer for the best flush hand. Players hope to be dealt as many same-suited cards as possible. Straight Flush hands result in bonus payouts when wagered.

Game:	6-player maximum.
Also Known As:	I ♥ Suits Poker, I Luv Suits.
Object:	The player's objective is to have a payable higher flush-only hand than the dealer's hand in each round of play. Players and the dealer each receive seven cards. Players sort their cards according to suits. Each player decides if he has a strong enough hand to play (generally, a 3-card jack-high, or higher.) More cards of the same suit help the player. Straights found within the same suit qualify for bonus payouts when wagered. The best high hand is a 7-card Straight Flush.
Dealing:	Deal only to players who have made an Ante bet.
Betting Structure:	Ante and Raise bets, various Bonus bets.

EQUIPMENT

Table, layout, chairs, two decks of cards used alternatively, shuffle machine, discard tray, and cheques. (See illustration 35.)

Illustration 35

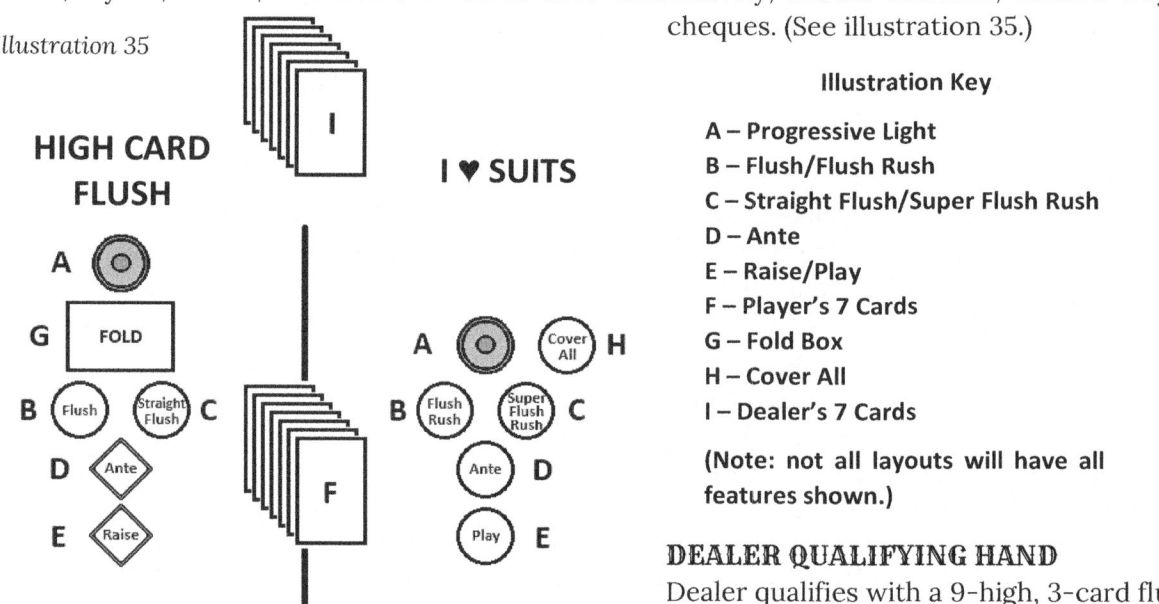

Illustration Key

A – Progressive Light
B – Flush/Flush Rush
C – Straight Flush/Super Flush Rush
D – Ante
E – Raise/Play
F – Player's 7 Cards
G – Fold Box
H – Cover All
I – Dealer's 7 Cards

(Note: not all layouts will have all features shown.)

DEALER QUALIFYING HAND

Dealer qualifies with a 9-high, 3-card flush.

TYPES of BETS and PAYOUTS (noted as "High Card Flush/I ♥ Suits" on winning hands)

- **Ante** – Minimum bet to receive two cards to play. Pays 1:1.
- **Raise/Play** – Player wager to compete against the dealer. Pays 1:1 if the dealer qualifies. Players may raise their bet to 2x the Ante with 5 flush cards, and to 3x for 6 or 7 flush cards.
- **Flush/Flush Rush** – Player wager that pays on a hand containing at least 4 of the same suit. Pays according to the payouts listed:
  - 7-Card Flush 300:1
  - 6-Card Flush 100:1
  - 5-Card Flush 10:1
  - 4-Card Flush 1:1
- **Straight Flush/Super Flush Rush** – Player wager that pays on a hand containing at least 3 straight, numerically successive cards of the same suit. Pays according to the payouts listed:
  - 7-Card Straight Flush 8000:1
  - 6-Card Straight Flush 1000:1
  - 5-Card Straight Flush 100:1
  - 4-Card Straight Flush 60:1
  - 3-Card Straight Flush 7:1

- **Progressive** – Optional bonus bet to reward players for a Three-Card Straight Flush or higher. Pays according to the jackpot payouts listed:
  - 7-Card Straight Flush (or 6 with Ace High)   100% of Main
  - 6-Card Straight Flush (King High or Lower)   10% of Main
  - 5-Card Straight Flush   300 for 1
  - 4-Card Straight Flush   50 for 1
  - 3-Card Straight Flush   3 for 1

  (Note: Original Bet is not returned.)
- **Cover All** – This bonus pays if player or the dealer receives one of the qualifying hands. Payouts are based on the highest hand only. Payouts adjust depending on the number of players in that hand and will pay only the highest hand of that game.

  Cover All payouts are listed:

COVER ALL						
	2 Players	3 Players	4 Players	5 Players	6 Players	7 Players
Royal Flush	400	250	200	150	125	100
Straight Flush	150	100	80	60	50	40
Four of a Kind	60	50	40	35	35	25
Full House	10	6	4	3	2	2

As players receive their cards, they will sort their hand by suits. Hands with the highest number of suited cards should receive preference. If a player's hand is three-suited—for example, one club, three hearts and three spades—the player will normally opt to play the higher ranked hand from the hearts or spade combination. Depending on house rule, a player either keeps all seven cards together and wagers a Play or Raise bet or will discard towards the dealer, the unwanted cards not associated with the suit they are playing. Should a player decide not to make a Play/Raise wager to continue the hand, they will lose all bets. Collect the bets first, then discard their cards.

Exception: if a player has a low-ranked three card Straight Flush (such as a 3-4-5 of a suit), they can opt not to Play/Raise the hand but will still get paid on the Straight Flush/Super Flush Rush payout and any Progressive light wager. Have the player tuck these three cards under this bet.

DEALING AND PAY PROCEDURES

1. Players minimally make an Ante wager.
2. Generally, the shuffle machine will dispense 7 cards. Deal each stack of 7 cards to each player, then to the dealer (in one neat pile.) Some casinos will have the dealer hold off dealing his own stack of cards or will do so with a cut card or button to protect/cover the dealer hand.
3. Players will look at their hands, decide to play the Play/Raise bet or fold. Collect any bets that are forfeited by the player, then collect his cards. Look around to see that every player has made their decision. A player may keep his cards for the Straight Flush/Super Flush Rush.
4. The dealer turns over his hand and sets his cards. The best dealer hand will prominently be pushed up towards the players. If the dealer has at least a three-card Flush hand containing a nine or higher, he qualifies. If he does not, every remaining player's Ante automatically gets paid, and their Play/Raise bet is a push.
5. Working counterclockwise from right to left, the dealer will reveal each player's hand, one at a time. He will compare the hands to see which hand is better, the player or the dealer's. The hand with the greater number of Flush cards wins. (For example 5 Flush cards beats 4 Flush cards.) If the player's hand is better, their Ante and Play/Raise are both paid at 1:1. If not, they both lose. Next, examine if that player has 4 or more Flush cards of the same suit. If so, pay according to the payout chart. Otherwise, it loses. Check if the player has a Straight Flush of 3 or more cards. If so, pay out the proper amount. Else, it loses. Same for the Progressive bet.
6. Complete all action with one player before moving onto the next. Scoop up cards; begin again.

LET IT RIDE

Let It Ride is a poker-based, casino table game introduced in 2005 by Shuffle Master, now owned by Light & Wonder (formerly Scientific Games).[12] Unlike many other table games, players do not compete against the dealer but combine their three cards with two community cards to achieve a hand. Higher hand values result in bigger payouts.

Game:	7-player maximum.
Also Known As:	Let 'Em Ride, Free Ride, Keep 'Em Going, Ride 'Em Poker.
Object:	The player's objective is to have a payable five-card hand in each round of play. Players do not compete against the dealer or other players. Instead, they combine their three cards with the two community cards to make a five-card poker hand. A player bets all three betting spots and receives three cards. Players decide to withdraw one or both of the first two bets or "let it ride." The 3rd bet, the ⓢ, may not be withdrawn. From all five cards, a Pair of 10s or higher wins. The best high hand is a Royal Flush.
Dealing:	Deal only to players who have made all three Player bets.
Betting Structure:	Three Player bets (of which two can be withdrawn), various Bonus bets.

EQUIPMENT

Table, layout, chairs, two decks of cards used alternatively, shuffle machine, discard tray, and cheques. (See illustration 36.)

Illustration 36

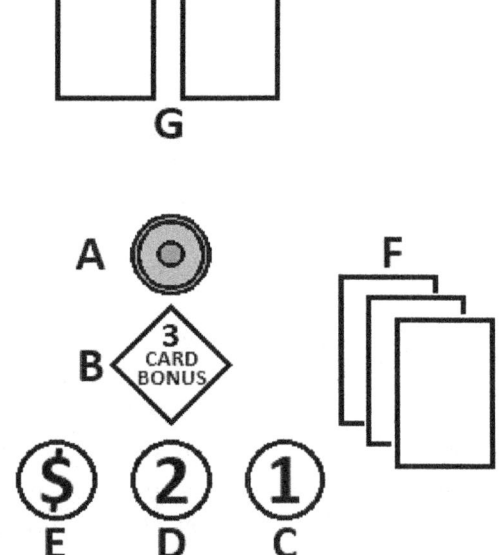

Illustration Key

A – Progressive Light
B – 3 Card Bonus
C – Bet #1
D – Bet #2
E – Bet #3
F – Player's 3 Cards
G – Community Cards

(Note: not all layouts will have all features shown.)

DEALER QUALIFYING HAND
None.

TYPES of BETS and PAYOUTS

Poker hand rankings can vary from the standard order and are listed from highest to lowest. Verify specific payouts, as they can differ from each casino. Payouts are typically printed on the table felt. Players make three equal bets and have the option to withdraw the first two of them ① and/or ②. The 3rd bet, ⓢ, cannot be withdrawn during play.

- **Payouts**
  - Royal Flush 1000:1
  - Straight Flush 200:1
  - Four of a Kind 50:1
  - Full House 11:1
  - Flush 8:1
  - Straight 5:1
  - Three of a Kind 3:1
  - Two Pair 2:1
  - Pair of 10s or Better 1:1

- ✧ **3 Card Bonus** – Optional Bonus bet based solely on the three community cards. Payouts are:
    - ➢ Straight Flush – one-suited, three-card Straight. Pays 40:1
    - ➢ Three of a Kind – three same-ranked cards. Pays 30:1
    - ➢ Straight – three consecutively ranked unsuited cards. Pays 6:1
    - ➢ Flush – three cards of the same suit. Pays 3:1
    - ➢ Pair – two cards of the same rank. Pays 1:1
- ✧ **Progressive** – Optional Bonus bet to reward players for achieving Three of a Kind or higher.

DEALING AND PAY PROCEDURES

1. Players wagers all three bets: ①, ②, and Ⓢ. Players can make optional Bonus bet wagers but may or may not bet more than one player betting spot.
2. House dealing order: Verify and collect any Progressive wagers. The dealer gives each player three cards face down. The dealer gives himself three cards, from which he needs to discard one, either the top or bottom. Check with house policy on specific dealing procedures.
3. Determine if the 3 Card Bonus bet is to be settled, win or lose, immediately, or during the hand evaluation/payout phase. Determine if the player's three cards contain a Pair or higher. If so, pay the 3 Card Bonus bet the correct amount. If not, take the player's wager. Check with house procedure.
4. Players look at their cards and decide if they wish to withdraw the ① bet by stating this and/or showing a hand motion of "no" or "bring the bet back." Otherwise, they're letting the bet ride. Ask each player in clockwise order from the dealer's left side to his right.
5. The dealer then reveals one community card, the left one, face up for all players.
6. Players look at their cards and decide if they wish to withdraw the ② bet by stating this and/or showing a hand motion of "no" or "bring the bet back." Otherwise, they're letting the bet ride (remain). Ask each player in clockwise order from the dealer's left side, to his right.
7. The dealer then reveals the second community card, the right one, face up for all players.
8. Play is complete. Start with the player on the dealer's right and work counterclockwise to the far left player. Evaluate each player's hand, one player at a time. Collect bets that lose. Follow the payout table for payout amounts. House procedure may have the dealer stack all winning Street bets and size-in payouts; or require the bets to be kept separate.
9. Offset cheque stacks that require a multi-color payout. If the player hasn't done so, turn up his cards. All wagers are paid at the same multiplying ratio for each payout. For example, a player wins with a Three of a Kind hand, payouts for all bets receive 3x the amount the player had placed in those three spots. Pay, push, or take wagers according to the printed payout chart. Discard player's hand.
10. Determine if the player has a Progressive bet, (the light will be on if it is.) If the win amount is significant, contact the floorman before paying out the bet.
11. Repeat hand examination and payouts, if any, for each remaining player.
12. Any significant payout (including Progressive bets) will require an approval callout to the floorman. Play is often halted to have surveillance review the hand before any payouts. Know the house's requirements.
13. Check to see if any remaining cards are on the table, collect them, then start a new game.

REMINDERS: Always check with specific house dealing and payout procedures.
- ➢ Payouts to players on the dealer's right side and across from him are paid with the right hand. First two players on the dealer's left side are paid with the left hand.
- ➢ The first two betting spots on the left side of the table are paid with the left hand.
- ➢ House procedures may eliminate the use of burn cards. Instead, the dealer spreads all three community cards face down after players have received their two cards. A cut card may or may not be used.

MISSISSIPPI STUD

Mississippi Stud is a poker-based, casino table game introduced in 2005 by Shuffle Master, now owned by Light & Wonder (formerly Scientific Games).[13] Unlike many other table games, players do not compete against the dealer but combine their two cards with three community cards to achieve a hand. Higher hand values result in bigger payouts. Players make an Ante bet and can fold or place additional bets required to see the next card until all three community cards are revealed.

Game:	7-player maximum.
Also Known As:	Mississippi Stud Poker, Mystic Stud, Southern Stud, Let It Ride on speed.
Object:	The player's objective is to have a payable five-card hand. Players do not compete against the dealer or other players. Instead, they combine their two cards with the three community cards to make a five-card poker hand. The player starts with an Ante bet and receives two cards. Players can fold or pay to see up to three streets of community cards (3rd, 4th, and 5th Streets). From all five cards, a Pair of 6s through 10s will push, and a Pair of Jacks or better wins. The best high hand is a Royal Flush.
Dealing:	Deal only to players who have made an Ante bet.
Betting Structure:	Ante wager, three streets of wagers, various Bonus bets.

EQUIPMENT

Table, layout, chairs, two decks of cards used alternatively, shuffle machine, discard tray, and cheques. (See illustration 37.)

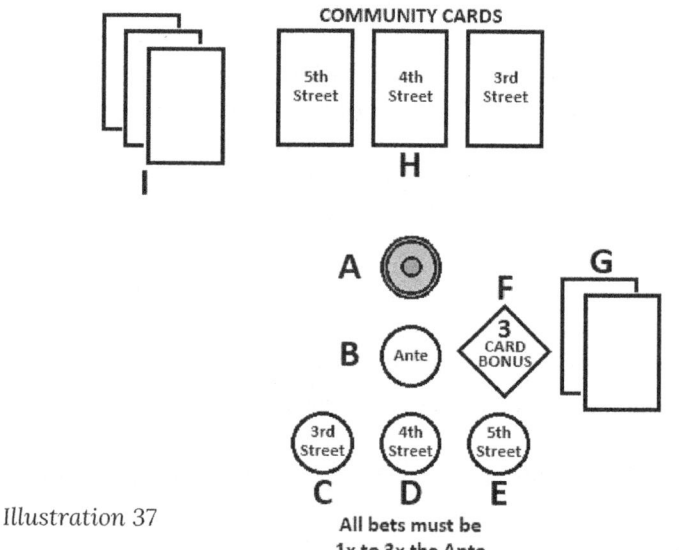

Illustration Key

A – Progressive Light
B – Ante
C – Player's 3rd Street
D – Player's 4th Street
E – Player's 5th Street
F – 3 Card Bonus
G – Player's 2 Cards
H – Community Cards
I – 3 Burn Cards

(Note: not all layouts will have all features shown.)

Illustration 37

All bets must be 1x to 3x the Ante

DEALER QUALIFYING HAND
None. Dealer does not receive a hand.

TYPES of BETS and PAYOUTS

Poker hand rankings can vary from the standard order and are listed from highest to lowest. Verify specific payouts, as they can differ from each casino. Payouts are typically printed on the table felt.

- **Ante** – Minimum bet to receive two cards to play.
- **3rd Street** – First of three community cards a player must pay before seeing.
- **4th Street** – Second of three community cards a player must pay before seeing.
- **5th Street** – Third and last of three community cards a player must pay before seeing.

Ante and Street Payouts

- Royal Flush 500:1
- Straight Flush 100:1
- Four of a Kind 40:1
- Full House 10:1
- Flush 6:1
- Straight 4:1
- Three of a Kind 3:1
- Two Pair 2:1
- Pair of Jacks or Better 1:1
- Pair of 6s through 10s Push

- **3 Card Bonus** – Optional Bonus bet based solely on the three community cards. Payouts are:
  - Straight Flush – one-suited, three-card straight. Pays 40:1
  - Three of a Kind – three same-ranked cards. Pays 30:1
  - Straight – three consecutively ranked unsuited cards. Pays 6:1
  - Flush – three cards of the same suit. Pays 3:1
  - Pair – two cards of the same rank. Pays 1:1
- **Progressive** – Optional Bonus bet to reward players for achieving Three of a Kind or higher.

DEALING AND PAY PROCEDURES

1. Player minimally makes an Ante bet. Players can make optional Bonus bet wagers. Players may or may not bet more than one player betting spot.
2. House dealing order: Verify and collect any Progressive wagers. The dealer gives each player two cards face down. Check with house policy on specific dealing procedures.
3. Players look at their cards and decide if they wish to play. If the player folds, they are still eligible for the 3-Card bonus. Take their Ante wager but leave their cards.
4. If the player continues the hand, they must equal their Ante wager 1x to 3x on 3rd Street. The dealer burns a card and deals one community card face up for all players.
5. If the player continues the hand, they must equal their Ante wager 1x to 3x on 4th Street. The dealer burns a card and deals one community card face up for all players.
6. If the player continues the hand, they must equal their Ante wager 1x to 3x on 5th Street. The dealer burns a card and deals one community card face up for all players.
7. Dealer discards any remaining stub into a discard rack.
8. Any time a player wishes to fold, collect their Ante and Street wagers, then collect their cards. Leave their cards if the player wagered the 3 Card Bonus bet.
9. If all players fold their hands, play has ended, gather all cards, riffle the deck if the house requires it, and replace all cards into the shuffle machine, or follow house shuffle. **EXCEPTION:** if any player has an outstanding 3 Card Bonus bet, appropriately burn and deal the remaining cards to complete the community cards.
10. Working counterclockwise, start from the dealer's right side, turn one player's hand up and visually combine those two cards to the three community cards. Collect bets that lose. Follow the payout table for payout amounts. House procedure may have the dealer stack all winning Street bets and size-in payouts; or require the bets to be kept separate.
11. Offset cheque stacks needing a colored-up payout. All Ante and Street wagers are paid at the same multiplying ratio for each payout. For example, a player wins with a Three of a Kind hand, payouts for each Street wager and the Ante bet all receive 3x the amount the player placed in those four spots. Pay, push, or take wagers according to the printed payout chart. Discard player's hand.
12. Determine if the three community cards contains a Pair or higher. If so, pay the 3 Card Bonus bet the correct amount. If not, take the player's wager.
13. Pay if the player wins their Progressive bet. (The light indicates whether the bet was placed.)
14. Repeat hand examination and payouts, if any, for each remaining player.
15. Any significant payout (including Progressive bets) will require an approval callout to the floorman. Play is often halted to have surveillance review the hand before any payouts.
16. Check to see if any remaining cards are on the table, collect them, then start a new game.

REMINDERS: Always check with specific house dealing and payout procedures.
- Payouts to all players on the dealer's right side and across from him are paid with the right hand. The first two betting spots on the left side of the table are paid with the left hand.
- House procedure may eliminate burn cards and have the dealer spread apart all three community cards, face down after all players have received their two cards. A cut card may or may not be used.

PAI GOW POKER

Pai Gow Poker, invented around 1985, is credited to Sam Torosian, who sought a way to save his failing casino in California. [14] A friend introduced him to "*Puy Soy*," a predecessor in which both player and dealer receive 13 cards, divided into three hands. Torosian simplified the game to two hands per player and dealer, reducing the cards from 13 to 7. Both player and dealer set their hands into a 5-card high hand that must beat a 2-card low hand. The game also introduced a Joker, a wild card used to complete a Flush, a Straight, or, as a last resort, to represent an Ace. Despite Pai Gow Poker's unique popularity, Torosian's attempt to patent it was thwarted by incorrect legal advice, claiming it wasn't patentable. By the time he discovered the error, the game had entered the public domain.

Pai Gow Poker uses a standard 52-card deck with one Joker, unlike the original Pai Gow game, which is played with dominoes. In this context, "Pai Gow" refers to a hand without a Pair, Straight, or Flush—hence the term "Ace-High Pai Gow." Pai Gow ranks among the oldest of table games used in the casino. Pai Gow, in its original and true sense, refers to the game using dominoes. The more popular Pai Gow Poker, is often misidentified and shortened to Pai Gow, which is incorrect. **Pai Gow uses dominoes; Pai Gow Poker uses cards.**

Game:	6-player maximum.
Also Known As:	Pai Gow (incorrect), Fortune Pai Gow Poker, Two Hands, Face Up Pai Gow Poker.
Object:	Each player splits their seven cards into a five-card high hand and a two-card low hand, aiming for the best combination. Players compete against the dealer, and to win, both the player's high and low hands must beat the dealer's respective hands. If a player wins one hand but loses the other, the bet pushes. A tie in either hand results in a loss for the player in that hand. The dealer wins by securing both high and low hands. The strongest high hand is five Aces (four Aces plus the Joker), while the best low hand is two Aces.
Dealing:	Deal to every betting spot on the table, whether or not it is wagered.
Betting Structure:	Main bet, various Progressive and bonus bets.

EQUIPMENT

Pai Gow Poker uses some of the standard equipment found in other Carnival Games. Refer to the **Equipment** section of this book: Table, layout, chairs, two decks of cards used alternatively (each with a Joker), shuffle machine, discard tray, and cheques. In addition, these tools of the trade are used: Ace-High Lammer, Dice Cup and Dice, Envy Lammer, and House Way Lammer.

ACE-HIGH LAMMER

When the dealer has an Ace-High hand, he'll display this circular 3-inch Ace-High disc to designate that all hands push on the main bet. (See photo 68.)

Photo 68

DICE CUP and DICE

When the dealer must manually originate a random number, a dice cup and 3 dice are used. (See illustration 38.) The three dice are noticeably smaller and the edges are more rounded than professional craps dice. To determine which player/dealer is dealt the first set of cards, the dealer covers the dice with the dice cup, shake and uncover. (Some casinos will let a player shake the covered dice.) Add up the total number of Pips (the dots located on the top of each die), and arrive at one number. The dealer is always #1, 8, and 15. The counting of numbers is always counterclockwise.

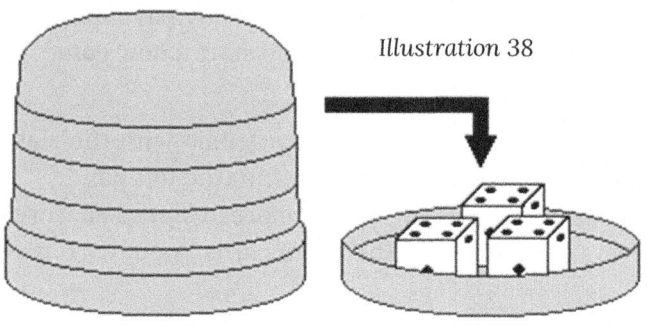

Illustration 38

PLAYER SPOT NUMBERS

The initial card distribution follows either the digital random number generator (RNG) or the result of shaking three dice. The dealer is always position #1. If dice are used, the dealer also occupies positions #8 and #15. Counting is always counterclockwise. The player to the dealer's right is #2 (also #9 and #16), while the player to the dealer's left is #7 (or a dice total of #7 or #14). (See illustration 39.) Once the number is determined, deal to that spot first, then deal every betting spot counterclockwise, including the dealer, until four stub cards remain. Collect and discard all unused hands. For Face Up Pai Gow Poker, reveal and spread the dealer's hand immediately after dealing

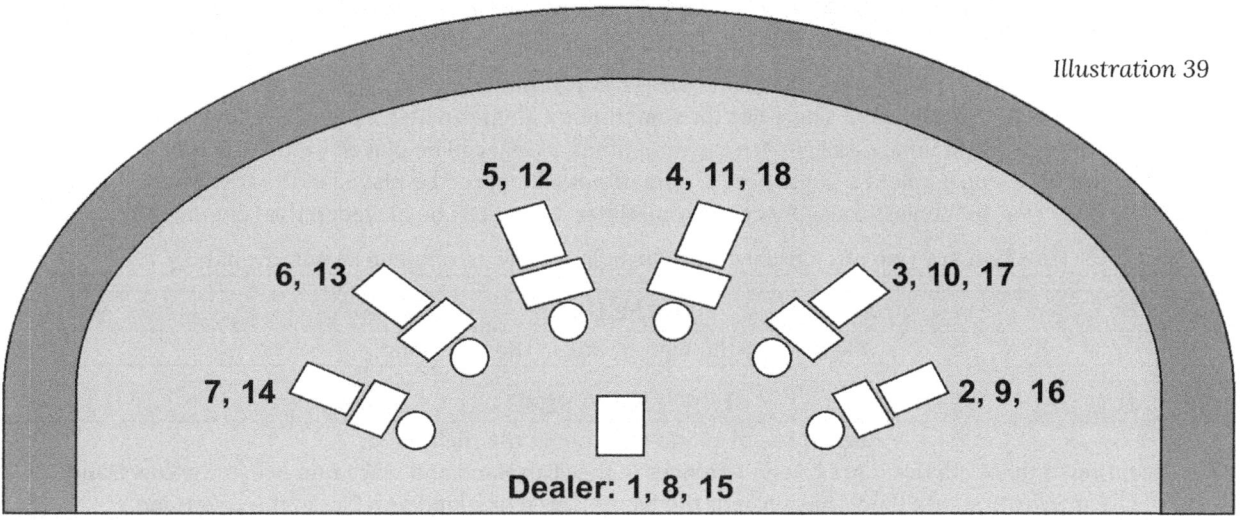

Illustration 39

ENVY LAMMER

This lammer shows a player has made a bonus or side bet, paying out if another player at the table achieves a specific winning hand during the same hand. It allows players to benefit (piggyback) from others' successes. Normally, a minimum bet amount (often $5 or higher) is required.

HOUSE WAY LAMMER

This lammer is used when the dealer sets a player's hand according to the casino's rules, known as the "House Way." This lammer may or may not be available if this option is not offered to players.

TABLE

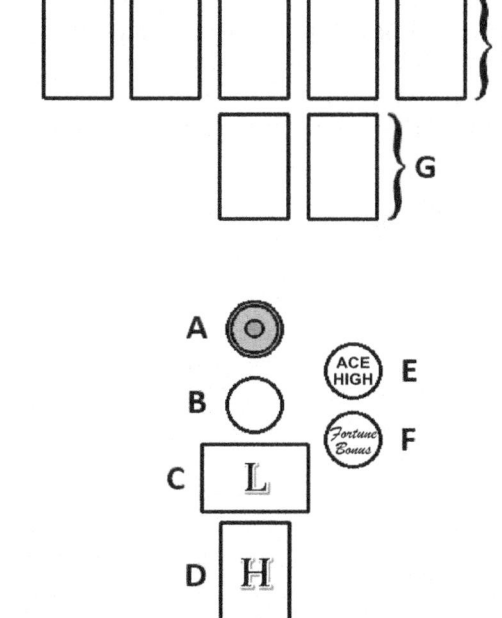

Illustration Key

A – Progressive Light
B – Main Bet
C – Player's 2-Card Low Hand
D – Player's 5-Card High Hand
E – Ace High Bet
F – Fortune Bonus Bet
G – Dealer's 2-Card Low Hand
H – Dealer's 5-Card High Hand

(Note: not all layouts will have all features shown.)

DEALER QUALIFYING HAND

None. However, when employed, a dealer's "Ace-High Pai Gow" hand will cause all Main bets to push.

Illustration 40

COMMON HOUSE WAY GUIDE to SETTING HANDS

HIGH CARD (No Pair, Straight, or Flush)

H: Place the highest and 4th through 7th ranked cards in the High Hand.	L: Place the 2nd and 3rd highest ranking cards in the Low Hand.

ONE PAIR

H: Place the Pair and 5th through 7th ranked cards in the High Hand.	L: Place the top two non-paired cards in the Low Hand.

TWO PAIR

HP + HP – Always Split.
HP + MP – Always Split.
MP + MP – Split unless a single Ace (or sometimes a King) can be played in the Low Hand.
HP + LP – Split unless a single Ace (or sometimes a King) can be played in the Low Hand.
MP + LP – Split unless a single Ace (or sometimes a King) can be played in the Low Hand.
LP + LP – Split unless a single Ace (or sometimes a King) can be played in the Low Hand.

(The Two Pair rule often breaks up a Flush or Straight to obtain a better low hand.)

THREE PAIR

Always play the highest Pair in the Low Hand.

THREE OF A KIND

Keep Three of a Kind together in the High Hand.
Exception: If there are three Aces, keep two Aces in the High Hand and place one Ace in the Low Hand.
(For two Three of a Kinds: always split the higher Three of a Kind as a Pair in the Low Hand.)

FULL HOUSE

Most always, split a Full House, placing the Three of a Kind in the High Hand and the Pair in the Low Hand.
If the Pair is 2s and an Ace-Jack or higher can be played in the Low Hand, then keep Full House together.
Set as a Full House when a Joker can be used to make either a Straight, Flush, or Straight Flush.

(For a Full House with a Pair, always play the higher Pair in the Low Hand. Exception: Some rules allow to break up three Aces into a Pair and placed in the Low Hand with the other Two Pair in the High Hand.)

STRAIGHTS, FLUSHES, AND STRAIGHT FLUSHES

When a Full House can also be made using a Joker, Use Full House Rule.
With Three of a Kind Aces, make a Straight, Flush, or Straight Flush, allowing for the highest possible Low Hand.
All other Three of a Kinds, split into a Pair for the Low Hand to preserve the Straight, Flush, or Straight Flush.
For Three Pair (Joker used as an Ace), use Three Pair Rule instead of making a Straight, Flush, or Straight Flush.
With Two Pair, always use the Two Pair Rule, unless the Straight, Flush, or Straight Flush can be preserved in the High Hand with a Pair in the Low Hand.
With One Pair, place the Pair in the Low Hand if the 5-Card Straight, Flush, or Straight Flush can be preserved.

If the 7-Cards contain a Straight, Flush, or a Straight Flush with a Pair of 10s or better along with any Ace, place the High Pair in the High Hand, and the Ace with the next highest card in the Low Hand.

FOUR OF A KIND

Four Aces with a Pair: split Aces unless the hand contains 7s or higher to be placed in the Low Hand.
Four Aces: always split two Aces into the Low Hand.
Four of a Kind with Three of a Kind: split to place the highest Pair in the Low Hand.
Four of a Kind with a Pair: place the Pair in the Low Hand.
Four of a Kind with a Full House: use Full House rule. (Also see Full House exception.)
Four of a Kind Jacks or higher: always split.
Four of a Kind 7s – 10s: split unless an Ace can be placed in the Low Hand.
Four of a Kind 2s – 6s: never split, keep together in the High Hand.

FIVE ACES

Five Aces (Four Aces plus the Joker): split two Aces into the Low Hand, unless the hand is Five Aces and a Pair of Kings, then put the two Kings in the Low Hand.

TERMS
Common (and abbreviated) words:
- **H** – High, High Hand, Big Hand, Back Hand, Major Hand, Highest, Bottom. (5 cards placed on the card-outlined "H" spot in the back of, or horizontally behind the Low Hand).
- **L** – Low, Low Hand, Small Hand, Front Hand, Minor Hand, 2nd Highest, Top. (2 cards placed on the card-outlined "L" spot in front of, or horizontally on top of the High Hand).
- **HP** – High Pair (any Pair from Jacks through Aces).
- **MP** – Medium Pair (any Pair from 7s through 10s).
- **LP** – Low Pair (any Pair from 2s through 6s).
- **HC** – High Card (any hand that does not contain a Pair, a 5-card Straight, or 5-card Flush.)
- **Joker** – A versatile card that substitutes for any card needed to complete a Straight Flush, Flush, or Straight. Otherwise, it will always represent an Ace.
- **Pai Gow** – A 7-Card hand that fails to make a Pair or better. (Hence, Ace-High Pai Gow).

PAI GOW POKER HAND RANKINGS
Five-Card High Hand:
- Five Aces – Four Aces plus the Joker
- Royal Flush – Any one-suited Ace-High Straight
- Straight Flush – Any one-suited Straight
- Four of a Kind – Four same-ranked cards
- Full House – Three same-ranked cards plus two same-ranked cards
- Flush – Any five one-suited cards
- Straight – Five consecutively ranked cards
- Three of a Kind – Three same-ranked cards
- Two Pair – Two same-ranked cards plus two same-ranked cards
- Pair – Two same-ranked cards
- High Card (HC) – Five unmatched cards (also known as Pai Gow)

Two-Card Low Hand:
- Pair – Two same-ranked cards
- High Card (HC) – Two unpaired cards

HOUSE WAY ON SETTING HANDS
Since Pai Gow Poker is in the public domain, casinos can implement their own "House Way" of setting hands, as long as it meets state or national gaming requirements. The House Way provides standard rules for dealers to follow for every possible seven-card hand. Dealers cannot choose how to arrange hands; they must follow their casino's House Way. Astute players can often visually determine how the dealer will set their hand the moment the dealer's cards are revealed. A written copy of the casino's House Way and rules for every table game is available for inspection by asking the floorman.

Every Pai Gow Poker dealer must memorize their casino's House Way for setting hands. This ensures they never second-guess how to set any hand and allows them to identify and adapt to subtle variations when working across different casinos. Evaluating hand strength is key for House Way.

BANKING
As in Baccarat, the regular version of Pai Gow Poker may allow some casinos to offer players, in rotation, the chance to be the Banker. This lets a player take on the risk of covering all the main bets from other players that would typically belong to the house. One player is selected and must cover all main wagers for that hand. If no player volunteers to be the Banker, the role defaults to the house. A special Banker lammer is used to indicate who the Banker is.

REMINDERS:
- The dealer can never foul a 7-Card hand. The High Hand must always beat the Low Hand.
- Preference is almost always given to make the Low Hand the strongest it can be.
- Set cards neatly in descending order by rank and/or suit.
- The A-2-3-4-5 is the second highest Straight, and the second highest Straight Flush.

PAYOUTS
- **Main Bet** – When the player's high and low hands beat the dealer's, the main bet pays 1:1. (A 5% commission may be applied to all winning payouts. See the **Baccarat: Commission** section on how to calculate this.) When one of the player's hands beats the dealer's but the other loses, the bet pushes. When both player's hands lose, the bet loses. Any tie between the player's and dealer's hands results in a loss for the player, as the dealer wins all ties.
- **Fortune Pai Gow Bonus** – $5 bet or larger qualifies for Envy Payout:

HAND	PAYS	ENVY
7-Card Straight Flush – No Joker	8000:1	$5000
Royal Flush Plus Royal Match	2000:1	$1000
7-Card Straight Flush – with Joker	1000:1	$500
Five Aces	400:1	$250
Royal Flush	150:1	$50
Straight Flush	50:1	$20
Four of a Kind	25:1	$5
Full House	5:1	
Flush	4:1	
Three of a Kind*	3:1	
Straight	2:1	

*Note: Three of a Kind pays higher than a Straight but ranks lower when comparing hands.

- **Ace-High Pai Gow** – Pays if the dealer has an Ace-High Pai Gow hand
    - Dealer and Player Ace-High 40:1
    - Dealer Ace-High with Joker 15:1
    - Dealer Ace-High No Joker – 5:1
- **Progressive** – Payouts shown on each casino's Digital Display Board (where offered).
- **Pai Gow Insurance** – Pays if the player receives any of the following:
    - 9-High 100:1
    - 10-High 25:1
    - Jack-High 15:1
    - Queen-High 6:1
    - King-High 5:1
    - Ace-High 3:1

DEALING AND PAY PROCEDURES
1. Players minimally make a Main bet. If allowed, Players can play two hands (two betting spots) so long as they complete action on one hand before moving onto the 2nd hand. The Progressive and Bonus bets are available at this time.
2. Cards must be shuffled and the first player to receive cards must be determined. Two ways:
    a. Shuffle Machine and RNG Digital Display: Most Pai Gow Poker tables use a shuffle machine to dispense 7 cards at a time, plus 4 extra cards to discard at the end. The built-in RNG displays a number from 1 through 7 which player (or dealer) receives cards first. Deal the first set of cards to the position corresponding with that number.
    b. Hand shuffle and deal the cards into seven piles of seven cards each. Discard the remaining four cards. Vigorously shake the dice cup, lift the lid, and if one or more dice land on top of another, state "No roll" or "No result" and roll again. A valid roll shows three dice flat on the cup's bottom. Add and deal to that corresponding spot.
3. **Deal to every player betting spot, regardless of wagers.** Unlike other casino games, deal the entire deck: seven cards to each betting spot and the dealer. After dealing to each of the six player spots and the dealer, there will be four extra cards. Slide these four cards face down to show they are accounted for and place them in the discard tray.
4. Verify if a player is folding due to not setting their hand(s), then collect their wagers and cards.
5. On Face-Up Pai Gow Poker, the dealer hand is turned face up and players see this hand before setting their own. In regular Pai Gow Poker, the dealer's hand is revealed after all players have acted. Once the dealer has set his hand, and after players have acted, work counterclockwise starting from the dealer's right. Turn up each player's hand. Use take/pay procedures (or push hands with a visual table tap.) Pay any Envy bets. Collect cards. Shuffle. Deal again.

TEXAS HOLD'EM BONUS POKER

Texas Hold'em Bonus Poker is owned and licensed by Mikohn Gaming/Progressive Gaming International Corporation and has been available in Las Vegas, NV at least since 2005.[15] The similar, but more popular and better-paying Ultimate Texas Hold'em overshadows this game. Players and the dealer receive two hole cards, and five community cards to make the best 5 of 7 card hand.

EQUIPMENT
Table, layout, chairs, one deck of cards, discard tray, and cheques. (See illustration 41.)

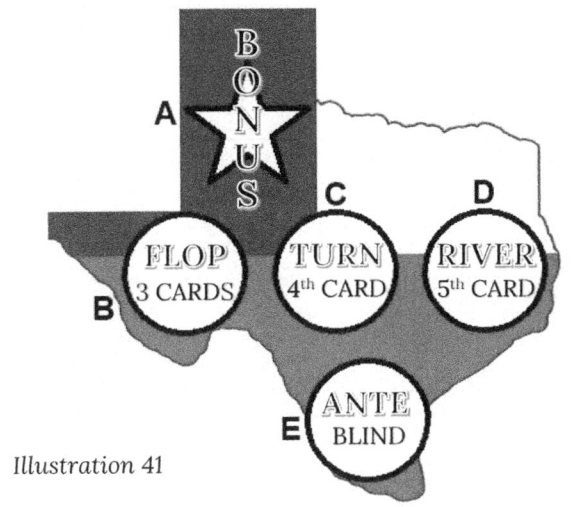

Illustration 41

Illustration Key

A – Bonus
B – Flop (3 Cards)
C – Turn (1 Card)
D – River (1 Card)
E – Ante
(Note: not all layouts will have all features shown.)

DEALER QUALIFYING HAND
None. Dealer plays every hand.

SHUFFLE
See the section on **Skillful Card Shuffling**.

TYPES of BETS and PAYOUTS

- **Ante** – Required bet for player to receive two cards. Player Straight or better pays 1:1.
- **Flop** – Wager 2x the Ante bet or Fold. 1:1.
- **Turn** – Wager 1x Ante bet or Check. 1:1.
- **River** – Wager 1x Ante bet or Check. 1:1.
- **Bonus** – Optional bonus bet combines the player's two cards with three community cards. A pair of 2s or higher wins.

➤ A-A (Player and Dealer) 1000:1
➤ A-A (Player Only) 30:1
➤ A-K (Suited) 25:1
➤ A-Q or A-J (Suited) 20:1
➤ A-K (Unsuited) 15:1
➤ K-K or Q-Q or J-J 10:1
➤ A-Q or A-J (Unsuited) 5:1
➤ 10-10 through 2-2 (Pairs) 3:1

DEALING AND PAY PROCEDURES

1. Player must minimally wager an Ante bet. The optional Bonus wager is available at this time.
2. Dealing order: The dealer deals five community cards face down. Next, the dealer deals each player two cards face down, and deals himself two cards face down. Discard remaining cards.
3. There are three betting rounds, each made available to players before the dealer reveals the card(s). Each player examines his own cards. For the Flop, the player must either wager 2x his Ante bet or Fold. Players may choose to play blind.
4. If the player folds, he forfeits his Ante wager. The dealer reveals the first three cards, (Flop).
5. Each player can either bet 1x the Ante wager or Check and not bet anything for the Turn bet. The dealer reveals the Turn card. Identical process for the River (Check or Bet, reveal River).
6. After all player action is complete, the dealer reveals his two hole cards. Two of the seven cards that do not play should be turned diagonally. (See illustration 42.)
7. Work counterclockwise from the dealer's right. Reveal a player's 2-card hand. (Complete take/pay procedures for each player.) Compare player's best 5 of 7 cards to the dealer's best 5 of 7 hand. If the dealer's hand beats the player's hand, the Ante, Flop, Turn, and River bets lose. Bets win if the player has the better hand. Collect cards, deal the next game.

Illustration 42

THREE CARD POKER

Three Card Poker is a Carnival Game staple in many casinos. Popular citations give full credit for the patented 1994 "invention" of Three-Card Poker to Derek Webb. However, his is a large borrowing from the 16th century British game Three-Card *Brag*.[15],[16] Hoyle's *Rules of Games* in 1983 also mentions a form of three-card poker. Today, players bet on one or more spots and receive three cards to form a hand to play against or combine with the dealer's three cards. Dealer qualifies with a Queen-high. 6 Card and Progressive bets combine the player's and dealer's cards for bonus payouts. House rules dictate required bets and prerequisites for bonus bets.

Game:	7-player maximum.
Also Known As:	Three Card Hold'em, Prime Three Card Poker, Three Card Shine, Teen Patti, Bragg, Brag, Three Card Brag, Primero, Primera.
Object:	The objective is to have a higher 3-card hand than the dealer. Players play against the dealer. Players make an Ante bet and receive three cards. Players can fold or play against the dealer. Best 3-card hand is a same-suited A-K-Q.
Dealing:	Deal only to players who have wagered.
Betting Structure:	Ante and Play wagers, various Bonus bets.

EQUIPMENT

Table, layout, chairs, two decks of cards used alternatively, shuffle machine, discard tray, and cheques. (See illustration 43.)

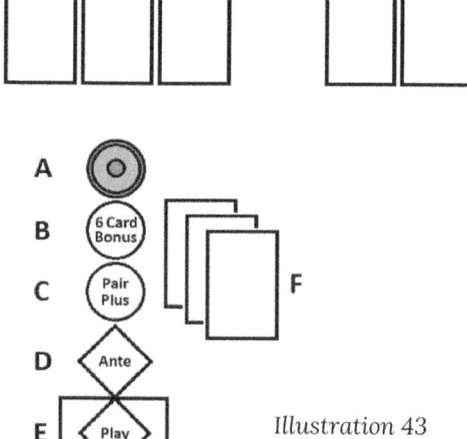

Illustration 43

Illustration Key

A – Progressive Light
B – 6 Card Bonus
C – Pair Plus
D – Ante
E – Play
F – Player's 3 Cards
G – Dealer's 3 Cards
H – Progressive 2 Cards

(Note: not all layouts will have all features shown.)

DEALER QUALIFYING HAND

The Dealer's three cards must be a Queen-high or better to qualify/play against the Player's hand.

OUTCOME	Ante Bet*	Play Bet
Dealer does not qualify	Pays 1:1	Push
Dealer qualifies; Player wins	Pays 1:1	Pays 1:1
Dealer qualifies; Player loses	Lose	Lose
Dealer qualifies; Tie	Push	Push

*Ante Bonus always pays a player's Straight, Three of a Kind, or Straight Flush regardless of outcome.

TYPES of BETS and PAYOUTS

Poker hand rankings can vary from the standard order and are listed from highest to lowest. Verify specific payouts, as they can differ from each casino. Payouts are typically printed on the table felt.

- **Ante** – Table minimum bet to play against the dealer. Pays 1:1 if the player's three cards beat the dealer's. An Ante Bonus payout is awarded should a player receive the following:
  - Straight Flush 5:1
  - Three of a Kind 4:1
  - Straight 1:1

  Note: Ante Bonus is paid regardless of the dealer's hand. Ante can lose, but pay the Bonus.

- **Play** – If the player bets the Ante and wants to play his three-card hand against the dealer's three-card hand, a bet equal to the Ante wager is placed here. The bet pays 1:1 when it wins. See **Pair Plus** on the next page for hand rankings. **Note:** a 3-card Straight beats a 3-card Flush.

- **Pair Plus** – Optional bonus bet based solely on the strength of the player's own hand. Any pair or higher wins. Depending on house rule, a player may/may not be required to place an Ante bet hoping to achieve a qualifying hand of a pair or better. Payouts are:
    - Straight Flush – one-suited, three-card straight. Pays 40:1
    - Three of a Kind – three same-ranked cards. Pays 30:1
    - Straight – three consecutively ranked unsuited cards. Pays 6:1
    - Flush – three cards of the same suit. Pays 3:1
    - Pair – two cards of the same rank. Pays 1:1
    - High card – three unmatched cards. Bet loses
- **6 Card Bonus** – Optional bonus bet that combines the player's three-cards and the dealer's three-cards. If the result is a Three of a Kind or higher, it wins. Must have an Ante wager. If the player does not wish to play the hand, he is still eligible to win this bet.
    - 6-Card Royal Flush – $100,000
    - 5-Card Royal Flush – 1000:1
    - 5-Card Straight Flush – 200:1
    - Four of a Kind – 50:1
    - Full House – 20:1
    - 5-Card Flush – 15:1
    - 5-Card Straight – 10:1
    - Three of a Kind – 5:1 (or 7:1)
- **Progressive** – Some casinos have a five-card progressive bonus bet. It combines the player's three-card hand with the dealer's two-card hand. To join, players place a $1-$5 wager on the "light," which flashes until acknowledged by the dealer and stays lit until the hand ends, indicating eligibility for progressive jackpots. High jackpots can trigger "Envy" bonuses for other players.

VARIATION

Prime – In the United Kingdom, an optional wager pays 3:1 if all three player's cards are of the same color. By combining a player's and dealer's cards, for a six card, same color combination pays 4:1.

DEALING AND PAY PROCEDURES

1. Player minimally makes an Ante and/or Pair Plus bet.
2. House dealing order: The dealer gives each player three cards face down, deals himself three cards face down in the center, and if there's a Progressive, deals himself three more cards off to the side, discarding the bottom card of the Progressive hand, leaving two cards.
3. Each player examines his own cards. Players may choose to play blind.
4. If the player wagered the Ante bet, he must either fold or place an equal amount on the Play.
5. If the player folds, he forfeits his Ante bet, the Pairs Plus and Progressive bets.
6. If the player decides to play, he places a bet equal to his Ante bet on the Play bet.
7. The dealer reveals his main three cards. The dealer needs a Queen-high or better to qualify.
8. If the dealer does not qualify, the player's Ante bet automatically pays 1:1. The Play bet pushes. Some casinos require the dealer to push back Play bets to all players and pay all Ante bets.
9. If the dealer qualifies, the dealer's hand is compared to each player's hand, one at a time, starting from the dealer's right to the next player counterclockwise. The higher hand wins.
10. If the dealer has the higher 3-card poker hand versus the player, both Ante and Play loses.
11. If the player has the higher three-card poker hand versus the dealer, Ante and Play wins 1:1.
12. If the dealer and player tie (have the same ranked cards), the Ante and Play bets will push.
13. A 3-card straight or better on the Ante bet earns an Ante Bonus, despite the dealer's hand.
14. The Pair Plus bet pays based on the strength of the player's hand. Any pair or better wins.
15. Visually combine the player's 3 cards with the dealer's 3 cards for the 6-card Bonus wager; it wins with Three of a Kind or higher, else it loses. Do the same for the player's 3 cards with the two Progressive cards separately.
16. Collect the cards, deal the next game.

ULTIMATE TEXAS HOLD'EM

Originally invented in the late 1990's by Stephen Au-Yeung, the originator of Casino Hold'em, this game takes root from the popular Poker variant, Texas Hold'Em.[18],[19] Further developed and reinvented by Roger Snow of Shuffle Master (now Light & Wonder) and introduced in the 2000s is the game known as Ultimate Texas Hold'em. This game is often abbreviated as UTH.

Game:	7-player maximum.
Also Known As:	Casino Hold'em, Casino Hold'em Open, Texas Hold'em Bonus Poker, Heads-Up Hold'em Poker, Extreme Texas Hold'em, Caribbean Hold 'Em.
Object:	Each player and the dealer combine their two hole cards dealt face down with five community cards to form their best five-card hand. The goal is to achieve a higher hand than the dealer. Players can: ➢ Check or Raise 3x/4x the Ante before any community cards are revealed. ➢ Check or Raise 2x the Ante after the first three cards (Flop) are revealed. ➢ Fold or Call the Ante after the last two cards (Turn and River) are revealed. The dealer qualifies with a Pair or higher from their five-card combination. The best possible five-card hand is a Royal Flush.
Dealing:	Deal only to players who have wagered at least the Ante bet.
Betting Structure:	Ante, Blind, and Play wagers, various Bonus bets.

EQUIPMENT

Table, layout, chairs, two decks of cards used alternatively, shuffle machine, discard tray, cut card, and cheques. (See illustration 44.)

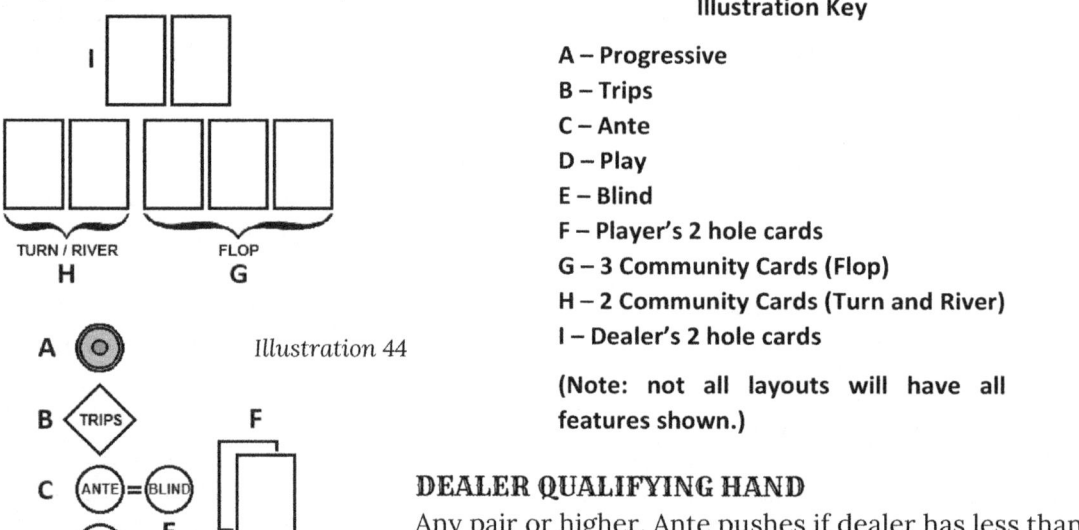

Illustration 44

Illustration Key

A – Progressive
B – Trips
C – Ante
D – Play
E – Blind
F – Player's 2 hole cards
G – 3 Community Cards (Flop)
H – 2 Community Cards (Turn and River)
I – Dealer's 2 hole cards

(Note: not all layouts will have all features shown.)

DEALER QUALIFYING HAND
Any pair or higher. Ante pushes if dealer has less than a pair.

TYPES of BETS and PAYOUTS

Standard Poker hand rankings are listed from highest to lowest. Each player and the dealer visually combine their two hole cards with the five community cards to make the best 5 out of 7 card hand. Verify specific payouts as they can differ from each casino. Payouts are printed on the table felt.

- ✦ **Ante** – Required bet to receive cards. Winning hand pays 1:1. Pushes if dealer does not qualify.
- ✦ **Blind** – Required bet equal to the Ante bet. Payouts are:
    - ➢ Royal Flush – 500:1*
    - ➢ Straight Flush – 50:1*
    - ➢ Four of a Kind – 10:1*
    - ➢ Full House – 3:1*
    - ➢ Flush – 3:2*
    - ➢ Straight – 1:1*
    - ➢ Other Hands – Push*
      * Must Beat the Dealer
      Tie Dealer – Push
      Lose to Dealer – Loss

68 CARNIVAL GAMES

- ◌ **Trips**– Optional bonus bet that combines the player's cards with the community cards. If the result is a Three of a Kind or higher, it wins. Otherwise, it loses. Must have an Ante wager to start the hand. If the player does not wish to play the hand and loses the Ante wager, he is still eligible to win this bet, (leave the Trips bet until the hand is revealed), when community cards show Three of a Kind, but the player's hand is not strong enough to wager the Play.
  - ➢ Royal Flush – 50:1
  - ➢ Straight Flush – 40:1
  - ➢ Four of a Kind – 30:1
  - ➢ Full House – 8:1
  - ➢ Flush – 7:1
  - ➢ Straight – 4:1
  - ➢ Three of a Kind – 3:1
- ◌ **Play** – If the player wants to play his hand against the dealer's hand, a wager is placed here. Pays 1:1. **Note:** Some casinos may require the player's hand to beat the dealer's non-qualifying hand to receive the payout. Otherwise, this bet may lose.
  - ➢ Before the Flop – 3x or 4x
  - ➢ After the Flop – 2x
  - ➢ After the Turn/River – 1x
- ◌ **Progressive** – Some casinos have a five-card progressive bonus bet. To win, the player must FLOP the winning payout to be eligible for one. Thus, achieving a winning hand type on the Turn/River will not count. It uses the player's 2 hole cards and <u>only</u> the community Flop cards. To join, players place a $1-$5 wager on the "light," which flashes until acknowledged by the dealer and stays lit until the hand ends, indicating eligibility for progressive jackpots. High jackpots can trigger "Envy" bonuses for other players. Types of hands and payouts vary.

DEALING AND PAY PROCEDURES

1. Player must minimally wager the Ante bet and an equal Blind bet. The optional Trips and Progressive wagers are only available at this time.
2. Dealing order: With the use of the shuffle machine, deal the five community cards face down first in front of the dealer. These cards may use a cut card, be kept stacked, or spread apart. Next, each player from the dealer's left to right is dealt their two cards together face down before dealing the next player his two cards. Depending on house rule, the dealer may immediately deal his two hole cards face down, or leave them in the shuffle machine to retrieve after all players have acted on their hands completely. Discard remaining cards.
3. Each player examines his own cards. Players may play blind.
4. Players can Check or Raise 3x or 4x their Ante before any community cards are revealed, Check or Raise 2x their Ante after the first three community cards (Flop) are revealed, or Fold or Call the Ante bet after the last two community cards (Turn/River) are revealed. Once a Play bet is made, it can't be changed.
5. If, after seeing all the community cards, the player wishes to fold, he forfeits all of his bets. (See exception in Trips above). Remove his bets and discard the player's hand.
6. After all player action is complete, the dealer reveals his two hole cards. Two of the seven cards that do not play should be turned diagonally. (See illustration 45.) If the dealer does not qualify, some casinos will require the dealer to pick up and return all Ante bets to the players; otherwise, it can be left and ignored for this hand.

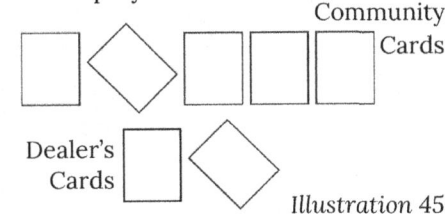

Illustration 45

7. Starting from the dealer's right, working counterclockwise, the dealer will reveal each player's 2-card hand. (Complete the take/pay procedure before moving on to the next player.) Compare the player's best 5 of 7 cards to the dealer's best 5 card hand. If the dealer doesn't qualify, both Play and Blind bets must beat the dealer to win. Collect cards, deal the next game.

REMINDERS: Be aware of the house rules on player collusion. Some casinos allow players to share information about their cards, while others strictly prohibit it. In such cases, signs like 'No Sharing of Player's Cards Allowed' may be posted, and players caught sharing information risk having their hands voided or being removed from the table.

PROPER CARNIVAL GAMES ETIQUETTE

Carnival Games etiquette is defined as the common protocols, courtesies, formalities, and codes of polite and accepted behavior expected from all players at the gaming tables (or even casino) toward other players, dealers, and staff members. So much of the dealer's attention involves making change, assisting players, watching for cheating, and controlling the game, to ensure that the game's rules are followed, and a fair game is played. Unfortunately, he must also be aware to correct players on their mannerisms, lack of courtesy, unfair play, or informalities. Sometimes these unwritten rules are broken unintentionally by a novice player who might need a quick reminder/education on what is considered proper. Occasionally, veteran players willfully cross the lines of gambling etiquette.

Etiquette can be required or optional. Sometimes, there's a gray area between the two. A floorman may be required to settle disputes or issue a corrective action/rule. Poor etiquette may or may not have consequences.

PROPER ETIQUETTE FOR PLAYERS	
Be respectful to everyone (players, staff)	Avoid asking the same questions repeatedly
Don't use electronic or magnetic devices at the table	Always use proper terminology
Observe the "One betting spot per player" rule	Speak clearly and loud enough
Don't disturb or crowd the ongoing action	Collect payouts once dealer is completely finished paying
Buy sufficient cheques for playing	Never hand dealers money or chips; place on table
Pay attention and keep the game moving along	Stop betting when "No more bets" has been announced
Keep anger in check	Avoid discussing sensitive or controversial topics
Avoid name-calling, putdowns, and arguments	Win and lose like a gentleman
Avoid fighting or any unwanted touching	Never abuse/assault anyone (verbally or physically)
Keep all cards on the table in full view of the dealer	Buy large amounts of cheques from the cashier
NEVER cheat, lie, or steal EVER	Don't blame the dealer for bad cards/repeated losses
Don't linger if finished playing, leave the table	Never pretend an action (betting)
Know the game being played before sitting down	Don't over-celebrate a win to put down others
Apologize if a mistake is made	Don't slam the table or damage any equipment
Avoid making illegal/unclear bets	Never touch another player's money or cheques
Never touch any casino equipment used by dealer	Be careful when betting near others' bets
Don't offer advice or give it at the table	Don't talk on the phone or play loud music
Don't criticize another's play, including strategies	Don't wear headphones and ask someone to repeat
Don't use foul language	Respect and tip the dealer and staff
Never grab payouts, let dealer push the cheques	Observe table minimum/maximum bets
Do not eat on or spill drinks onto the table	Avoid constantly asking where the cocktail server is
Remain at the table with placed bets	Never collude with another player
Maintain a healthy hygiene	Wash/sanitize hands after coughing/sneezing
Report mistakes to the dealer promptly	Be orderly and welcoming to other players
Know and comply with the game rules	Go with the flow of the game; don't be the odd man
Report offensive remarks and rule breakings	Be of legal age before sitting down to play
Accept dealers are human and make mistakes	Never compare home rules to casino rules
Use common sense when playing	Don't drink excessively at or arrive drunk to the table
Color up all cheques to that table before leaving	Avoid shouting or constant loud talking
Avoid discussing or showing hands to other players	Abide by all rules in that casino, even if it differs elsewhere
A player absent more than one hour should end his session before leaving to go on an extended break	Do not dominate the conversation at the table, allow others a chance to talk or enjoy their quiet moments

CALLOUTS: ALERT versus APPROVAL

Casinos have callouts defining an alert versus an approval. When a dealer communicates a callout to the floorman, it helps with the flow of the game and makes the floorman aware of the game. Something out of the ordinary progress of the game has happened or is about to happen.

Below is a standard list of what a dealer should do during regular or irregular situations while dealing:

CALLOUT	SITUATION	ALERT	APPROVAL	DEALER ACTION
Change Only	Exchanging cash for cheques, more than $100	X	X	Varies each casino
Cheque Change	Exchanging a player's higher (more than $100) denomination cheque(s) for a lower one	X	X	Varies each casino
Cheque Down Inside	A cheque has dropped inside the pit area	X		Continue play
Cheques Play	A bet of cheque(s) more than $100		X	Wait for approval
Cheques Play to the Limit	A player betting table maximum		X	Wait for approval
Color Coming In	Announce before bringing in chips/cheques; player exchanging lower denomination cheques for higher ones		X	Wait for approval
Color Up $____	After approval for Color Coming In, a player trading lower denomination cheques for higher ones		X	Wait for approval
Drink Down	A drink has spilled onto the table		X	Call for towels
Floor	Any other time a dealer needs the floorman for any reason		X	Wait for floorman
Foreign Cheque	A cheque from another casino		X	Wait for approval
Marker Request	Player requested to use casino credit or to take out a marker		X	Follow supervisor direction
Money/Cash Plays to the Limit	(Where allowed) A player betting cash, instead of chip/cheques for playing, to table limit		X	Wait for approval
Outside	Dealer wishes to leave his position at an empty table to straighten the chairs		X	Wait for approval
No More Bets	Betting action is closed and no more bets are allowed	X		Start dealing the game
Place Your Bets	Dealer declaration to start new betting	X		Start new game

Casinos often have a special callout or action a dealer takes when dealing with cheating, theft, or vandalism. It may be verbal or non-verbal. It may require a hand over the head, or the paddle removed from the slit. Whatever the policy or methods used, know exactly how the casino management wants this reported. Use professional discretion.

CARNIVAL GAMES EMPLOYMENT

At some point, students and readers of this book will have already decided to work in a professional casino. Steps vary widely from each state in the United States and countries abroad. The general outline is:

EDUCATION / TRAINING

Nothing substitutes or beats a solid, formal education and hands-on training that one receives from a gaming school to build a career in casino dealing. Gaming schools are a type of trade school, much like plumbing, cosmetology, electric, or carpentry are in their respective fields. The more in-depth, knowledgeable, patient, and congenial the instructors at a gaming school are, the better off the student will be. The course should include at a minimum: A course syllabus, daily lesson plans, classroom lecture, an instruction manual, hands-on instruction from an experienced dealer, hands-on practice with professional-like equipment used in casinos, and a course evaluation/exam. Graduates of the course should receive a certificate of completion/graduation. Informal home training from a friend and the annual home "casino night" are no match to the detailed foundation a professional receives from a certified gaming school. Prospective students should invest time and money to equip themselves in their craft, their skill, their trade. Some casinos require job applicants to complete a professional dealer/gaming course in order to audition or be hired. If a casino is nearby, most likely a gaming school, or two, can be found. A casino will provide additional training on specific house rules. Financing, grants, and student loans may also be available.

JOB SEARCHING

After receiving solid training from a certified school, a student may look to see which casinos have job openings. Students can work locally or find a relocation if warranted. Gaming schools are a great source for finding job openings. Often, they have developed a working, business relationship with casino managers locally to funnel their students, giving them priority over non-trained applicants. Searching online for dealing positions and visiting websites, as well as meeting with the shift manager during slow times, can often answer many questions of job openings, pay, benefits, shift availability, and more. Word of mouth, internet searches, and in-person visits to casinos can all aid the student in choosing where he would like to work.

APPLICATION

Most companies require an online application. It can help to know another dealer, as a reference, who already works in that casino, and who can vouch for the applicant. If a paper application is used, write legibly! Sloppy and/or incomplete applications often result in a quick rejection.

AUDITION

After submitting a job application and the hiring manager's interest has been piqued, the next stage of the hiring process is going in for an audition. Rather than a traditional interview where the applicant and hiring manager sit down to discuss the job, the applicant is placed onto a mock (or sometimes live) table with real players/real money to demonstrate his hands-on skill and knowledge of dealing several types of casino table games. Usually, knowledge of three or more games is required of the applicant during the audition. The role of management is to see what the applicant knows, the dexterity of the hands, and the overall running of the game as a dealer. Nervousness is natural and to be expected. Applicants are usually told to wear industry standard "black and whites" to the audition, meaning, a white button-down long-sleeve dress shirt, black pants, black belt, black socks, and black shoes.

GAMING LICENSURE ♥ FINGERPRINTING ♦ CRIMINAL BACKGROUND CHECK ♣ DRUG TESTING

Once the applicant has passed the audition and is offered employment, the casino will send the newly hired dealer to get licensed by the state, county, or country. Fingerprinting, a criminal background check, and drug testing may be required. The casino may cover some of these costs, while others will be the responsibility of the applicant. National, state, and local laws vary too much to be covered in this section but understand that a dealer must pass all legal requirements for employment to commence. If unsure of the laws or the process, ask the casino questions.

ACCEPTING EMPLOYMENT and STARTING

Once the gaming license is issued to the dealer and all other requirements have been met, the student is now a hired professional casino dealer. Congratulations! It is time to start work. Always arrive at the designated area 10 to 15 minutes prior to the start of the shift. Casinos may offer/discuss some, all, or even more than this list of "first day of employment" topics:

- Location of designated employee parking area
- Parking lot shuttle service
- Employee entrance and exit doors
- Employee badge/ID
- Employee name tags
- Employer-provided uniform/in-house laundry
- Employee-provided clothing
- Employee changing areas/locker room/lockers
- Break area/EDR/smoking area
- Time clock location
- Learning the table rotations/breaks and brushes
- Weekly schedule location/time-off requests
- Early out (EO) list
- Manager's office
- Employee cashier/cage location
- Callout procedures/direct phone numbers
- Paycheck schedule/direct deposit information

PERMANENT 💰 FULL-TIME WORK

Permanent, full-time work may happen immediately, after a waiting period, or when there's availability. Benefits can be quite good at some casinos, mediocre at others, or non-existent. It is important to compare the entire benefits package offered among casinos and not just the pay/toke rates. An employee can expect and be expected to work full-time hours each week.

PART-TIME WORK

Part-time work can include some benefits, but the hours scheduled/worked each week are less on a part-time basis. This may suit employees not wanting to work full-time for various reasons.

ON CALL ▦ EXTRA BOARD

On-call or extra board employees are scheduled irregularly and infrequently on the casino's whim and need for extra dealers due to sick/vacationed employees, the casino is short staffed, or a big event is planned. This type of employment may suit some people, but not others. A dealer should ask his manager periodically if more or fewer hours are desired—or if a consistent schedule is wanted.

TEMPORARY WORK

Temporary work (often through a temporary casino dealer staffing agency) can offer a dealer the chance to work at a different casino or for a group of local casinos. This type of work is need-based and often an inconsistent schedule on a first-come, first-served priority to pick up shifts. It can be a good way to scope out a new place of employment without fully committing to working there as a full-time, permanent employee. Usually, a small fee can be paid as part of an employee's gaming licensure that will allow the dealer to work multiple locations.

BREAKS versus BRUSHES

Breaks and brushes refer to the paid time covering a dealer when he is away from his table dealing. Casinos want their dealers alert to avoid costly errors. It is customary for dealers to get a break every hour or two (depending on the push rotation) to relax or eat. A break is time away entirely from the casino floor or poker room. A brush is usually a poker room's need for a dealer to step away from dealing to help the poker room with various short and simple duties such as putting players' names on waiting lists, seating new players at tables, getting cheques for those new players, completing a fill order for a seated dealer, among other things. Brushes and breaks are, at most, 30 minutes, but usually less. No matter when the dealer is sent to break or brush, it is his responsibility to make sure he is not late for the next push to start dealing again, even if this means his break is only 10 minutes.

RELIEF DEALING

Typically, a dealer is assigned to a specific table for the entire shift. However, when it is time for him to take a short break, an assigned relief dealer will step in and cover until the main dealer returns. This relief (dealer) will repeat this for the next few tables until finally getting a break himself. This type of dealing requires the dealer to be knowledgeable in several possible different games and may migrate from one pit to another.

SHILLS versus PROPOSITION PLAYERS

Shills and proposition players are players hired by the house (or in-house dealers) to play any casino game with the sole purpose of keeping tables looking full and to keep the action at the tables going. In the much older sense, these were "skilled" or "lucky" players (depending on point of view) who played at one table and can be asked to move to another short-handed or new table being set up. Today, these players are often poker dealers who want to play poker while on the clock instead of dealing.

Instead of sending a dealer home during a slowdown, a floorman may opt to let the dealer play with the understanding he may be pulled off the table and told to deal at another table at a moment's notice. These dealers often must wear a jacket over the uniform that can be instantly removed at and thrown in the back room. A dealer may play to avoid being sent home and thus remain on the clock in order to get the required weekly hours to maintain health insurance benefits.

Shills use the house's money to play and have an agreement to split any profits with the house but are usually not responsible for any losses incurred. Shills are rarely found anymore. Proposition players, however, are much more common as they use their own money and keep 100 percent of all their profits but must absorb their own losses. Most gaming laws require the casino or poker room to identify to any player who inquires, any and all shill and proposition players currently playing and which player(s) they are.

DUAL RATE

An employee who is a dealer part-time and, at other times, a supervisor has a dual-rate status. This gives the employee an opportunity for job advancement by accepting more responsibilities.

GAMBLING ADDICTION

With the rise in popularity and availability of all forms of gambling, it would be ignorant and remiss not to address gambling's downside: Addiction.

Gambling addiction is also known by many other names: Problem gambling, ludomania, degenerate gambling, compulsive gambling, gambling disorder, and pathological gambling. The National Council on Problem Gambling states:

> *Problem gambling—or gambling addiction—includes all gambling behavior patterns that compromise, disrupt or damage personal, family or vocational pursuits. The symptoms include increasing preoccupation with gambling, a need to bet more money more frequently, restlessness or irritability when attempting to stop, "chasing" losses, and loss of control manifested by continuation of the gambling behavior in spite of mounting, serious, negative consequences. In extreme cases, problem gambling can result in financial ruin, legal problems, loss of career and family, or even suicide.*

Make no mistake about it, casinos are in the business to make money, and, to put it bluntly, casinos need losing players to support their business model. Casinos regularly need high rollers to lose large amounts of money, along with many small- and medium-average bankrolled players to lose. Every person who gambles or is in the business of gambling has a desire to get someone else's money into his own pocket. There are recreational gamblers to professional gamblers, and everything in between. Yet, anyone can become addicted to gambling. Play long enough, everyone will lose at some point. Some more than others. Some more painful than others. One person's win is someone else's loss. Luck, and odds, favor the house, not the players.

However, there is good news! Casinos have adopted policies required by state and federal mandates to prevent, help, curb, and direct players to information regarding problem gambling. Casino employees (dealers and management staff) receive training to pass information along to players who ask for help. Brochures on getting help from Gambling Addiction are always found near the casino player rewards desk and cashier cage among other places.

There is a national organization gambling helpline that provides 24/7 confidential assistance to anyone needing help with gambling issues. This organization's website is a valuable resource full of definitions, symptoms, screening tools, programs, services, help, treatment, toolkits, and so much more. Every person who ever sets foot in a casino would be well advised to read up on this information. In addition, Gambler's Anonymous provides a wealth of resources and support.

These U.S. organizations also provide state-specific contact lists for regions where gambling is permitted.

National Council on Problem Gambling*

>Website: https://www.ncpgambling.org
>Phone: 1-800-GAMBLER
>Chat: 1800gamblerchat.org
>Text: 800GAM

Gambler's Anonymous

>Website: https://gamblersanonymous.org/
>Phone: (909) 931-9056 (Main)
>Every state's local chapter has its own telephone number.

*The author used this source for this summary: https://www.ncpgambling.org/help-treatment/faqs-what-is-problem-gambling/, accessed January 4, 2024.

CLOSING

Whatever your reason(s) for reading this book, I hope you have found its contents enjoyable to read, educational to learn, easy to implement, noteworthy to remember, and hopefully valued to share with others. Carnival games can be easy to learn to deal or play, but as the saying goes, "For every obstacle, there is a solution. Persistence is key. The greatest mistake is giving up!" (Eisenhower)

The best advice I have to all my readers and students alike: Practice, practice, practice.

Practice to get better; to improve dexterity, technique, and speed; to memorize rules; to calculate quicker and more accurate payouts; to be open to learning something new; or to teach someone else who asks for your help or demonstration.

As a dealer, you will come across players in life who are polite, nice, and generous in their tokes you receive. Kind people are memorable. Some players are quiet, yet knowledgeable and efficient. Busy looking, but prompt, efficient, and attentive when it is time to bet or collect their winnings. Some days, some tables—or even a single player or two—can make your entire day. Some will offer words of praise or encouragement. Some players will tip you for just showing up at the table, or as they leave the table. Hopefully, you'll work with fabulously smart, professional, and amazing managers and floormen as I have. Sometimes a simple "Thank you" is all a dealer needs to hear. Dealers wish for these days often.

However, this is the one paragraph of the entire book I wish I could leave out. Life gives us the good, but also the bad, and the ugly. And regrettably, I must tell you some of the common bad and uglies. I'm purposely cramming those two things into this one paragraph. Sorry, there's no sugar coating this. Dealers deal with mean, cheap stiffers. Old people who fall asleep at the tables. Drunk and belligerent people. People with bad manners. People who sneeze or cough in their hands and don't wash or sanitize them. Inattentive phone and tablet gawkers. Players who need constant reminders to place their bets or collect their winnings. Stinky, smelly, unclean, bad-breathed, and unbathed people. People who reek of too much cologne, or cigarette/cigar/weed smokers who return to your table stinking to high heaven feeling as lofty as the clouds they just blew. Even when it is not allowed, players will try to sneak vaping blows when you're not looking and will continue to do so after being warned. Lazy players who walk through the pit area instead of around it. Players will constantly ask where the cocktail server is so they can order more drinks only to later drunkenly, carelessly, or sloppily spill those drinks onto your tables. They'll eat food, leaving a trail of popcorn behind, potato chips, rice, crackers, and handle BBQ chicken wings bare-handed that ants could just move in and build monumental colonies at, atop, or under the table. Rule breakers. People who put down others. People who put you down as a dealer. People who tell you how to deal or run your game. Players who don't listen to dealers. Players will demand a color up in the middle of another player's payout or leave with numerous cheques leaving a hole in your bank. Worse, some will reach into your bank. Players will try to cheat and past post bets. Players will disagree with the official outcome. Players who complain about your "poor/inept" dealing to management when you did nothing wrong, especially after they lost a big bet. Players who complain about 'rigged' shuffle machines. You'll encounter super novice players who never played a casino game in their life and now you must teach them a few things every hand, that they won't remember a minute later, while they're drunk. You'll also come across underage players, or those who get mad at you because you decided to ID them. Some of those players won't even carry their ID with them and are upset at you and must be kicked off the gaming floor. Players will try to remove their own losing bets before you can. Players will shout out loud for themselves, toward other players, their dealer, management, and even while security is escorting or carrying them out of the casino. Players will slap and punch people and get into fights. They'll be angry at other players. Losing players will blame you, for "cheating" or call you a mechanic. These idiot donkeys blame you for losing over and over instead of quitting the game for the night, or forever! It's funny to see them whine like toddlers. And boy will they whine when you overhear one losing story after another that no one ever really cares to listen to. You might work with bad management along with incompetent dealers. You'll call for the supervisor, but they won't show up promptly even after you've already called, and now started YELLING for three, four, five, even six times! You'll see wrong floor rulings and players who benefit from them. Security who can't get to your table to fill your near-empty tray or bank fast enough or the lazy/inattentive floorman who doesn't request a proper or timely fill. You'll also push dealers while noticing their bad and incorrect dealing forms due to not learning proper techniques from professional dealer training. Some people will purposely go out of their way to make your time at that table hell. There are a million and one more examples, but you get the idea. You'll need to grow a thick skin and learn to deal with all this.

Dealers should never take their frustrations out on the players. Politely tell them what they can or cannot do. Explain the rules. If they don't like it, refer them to the floorman. Let him handle the problem or dispute. Never let these people or situations bring you down. Always go to the next table, next day, month, etc. (and beyond) with a fresh, open mind and a great spirit. If you're a good or even a great dealer, you'll know it. If you're not, but you have the desire to improve, ask for help. Leave your work, at work. When it's time to come home to your loved ones or go out with friends, turn off those depressing parts of your day like a light switch and leave them in the dark forever. Don't burden others with your daily miserable sob stories. Apologize, forgive, forget, learn, and move on. Have hope. Your next push to the next table is coming soon!

Like many things in life, Carnival Games evolve. Always have an open mind to learn new games, tips, tricks, and yes, good shortcuts to improve your total understanding and proficiency.

I never started writing this book with any intention (whole or in part) of telling, teaching, advising, or showing people how to play the games strategically or how to win money. There are plenty of those books already in stores, websites, podcasts, and numerous vlogs floating online. And, for as long as carnival games remain as vibrant as they are, there will be plenty more written, discussed, demonstrated, and videos to watch. Finding just one of those books that fits your playing style, level of risk, and bankroll level is like finding a needle in a haystack. Those authors have a lot of good things to say, and players can learn from them. But remember, those authors explain how THEY would have played. Their techniques, advice, and betting systems most often may not match yours. Should you become a player on any serious level, learn what is useful but develop your own playing style.

I also did not write this book specifying how errors and mistakes made by either players or the dealer might be ruled by the floorman or the house. Rules vary so much and often change within a casino, city, province, territory, state, country, or even internationally. It is up to the casino to stay current on its own rules, the players to know and act within those rules and to ask the supervisor for clarification. And then for dealers to deal accordingly within those rules/norms/customs. When in doubt, a dealer should never be afraid to seek help, guidance, or a correct ruling from a supervisor. Standardized house rules will always favor the house. However, honest mistakes will be made, and it is not up to the dealer to make the ruling or correction himself; inform a supervisor and let the supervisor make the ruling. Once they make a ruling, don't argue with them. Follow their ruling.

Always do the right thing. The number one expectation and responsibility of every dealer is to always maintain full integrity. This is noted very early and throughout this book and is worth repeating. INTEGRITY reflects HONOR, CHARACTER, and TRUSTWORTHINESS. Protect it.

In parting, ALWAYS DO YOUR BEST. Be nice, be professional, and grow to help others. None of us started out as experts.

Thank you for reading this book.

See you at the tables...

– Edward

ACKNOWLEDGMENTS

Writing a book is never easy. It takes ideas, research, planning, energy, working space, and all the time an author must find to get the project off the ground from a single blank page to a finished product. And while much of the writing takes time, lots of time, all the time, it does take time away from others one would normally spend sharing fun activities.

Writing also involves pestering and inundating people with questions for bits and pieces of information. Thank you for putting up with all that. Here is a short list of people who left an imprint on me writing this book:

THANK YOU, Almighty God, for everything.

THANK YOU to my professional gaming instructors: Rick DeBonis and Raymond Nichols. Solid teachers.

THANK YOU to Ricky P. Richard, gaming school owner, who allowed me to teach many students in his school. This gave me the inspiration to write a complete set of gaming dealing books and start my own gaming school.

THANK YOU to all my students, many of whom I have kept in contact with, and who come to me with more questions long after finishing their classes, always eager to learn. Encountering former students always brings a smile to my face.

THANK YOU to all the casinos who hired me to put into practice what I've learned, and for hiring my students to work, often right alongside me, giving me credence that my teachings are correct and accepted in the professional gaming industry.

THANK YOU to those who invented, developed, progressed, promoted, offered, or dealt the games presented in this book, no matter how long ago. Refreshingly, casinos, players, and dealers alike always look forward to embracing new games or side bets to add to the current repertoire. Keep 'em coming!

THANK YOU to Ellie Race for her invaluable assistance in refining this manuscript.

THANK YOU to my patient yet skillful graphic designer, Syeda Ayesha Shah, who accommodated numerous change requests to give this book cover a great professional look.

THANK YOU to my proofreaders, Anthony Desmoni, Candy Baron, Jinky Buenaseca, and Robert Giordano. All willingly reviewed different sections of this book (prepublication) and lent their supervisory and/or dealing experience to ensure a correct and complete handbook.

And finally, THANK YOU to my deaf parents, my mother Irene Cervinski and my father Edward J. Cervinski, for having me, raising me, loving me, and who taught me to always put God first.

CARNIVAL GAMES QUOTES

"A pack of cards is the devil's prayer-book." – German Proverb

"At gambling, the deadly sin is to mistake bad play for bad luck." – Ian Fleming

"Baccarat is a game whereby the croupier gathers in money with a flexible sculling oar, then takes it home. If I could have borrowed his oar I would have stayed." – Mark Twain

"By gaming, we lose both our time and treasure – two things most precious to the life of man." – Owen Feltham

"Don't be suckered into making sucker bets, unless, of course, you don't know the difference, in which case you're a sucker anyhow." – John Gollehon

"Everyone you will ever meet knows something you don't." – Bill Nye

"Gambling is a loser's chance to be a winner." – Anonymous

"Good luck has its storms." – George Lucas

"I feel like I am involved in an obscure and complex version of poker in a pitch-dark room, with blank cards, for infinite stakes, with a dealer who won't tell me the rules, and who smiles all the time." – Neil Gaiman

"If you ain't just a little scared when you enter a casino, you are either very rich or you haven't studied the games enough." – VP Pappy

"If you can learn to quit when you are ahead, then you have an excellent chance of being a successful gambler." – Baltasar Gracián y Morales

"It is better to trust in knowledge than in luck." – American Proverb

"Luck never gives; it only lends." – Swedish proverb

"The gambler who does not practice self-restraint will soon be led to ruin." – Chinese Proverb

"The majority of casino players leave too much to chance when playing in a casino. To put it bluntly, they don't have a clue as to how to play." – Henry Tamburin

"The only impossible journey is the one you never begin." – Tony Robbins

"The only way to do great work is to love what you do." – Steve Jobs

"When you gamble, you get thrills and chills; When you keep it, you stay rich and well." – Chinese Proverb

A few of my own quotes:

"Believe in yourself, just as God believes in you."

"Dream big, plan, execute, but don't fail."

"I'm regularly asked when dealing, 'drop the toke or gamble it?' I drop the first toke and gamble the rest. That way, I'm never broke."

"While playing cards with the elderly, I noticed they moistened their fingers with saliva to deal or fan the sticky cards."

GLOSSARY

A, Ace – (symbol) 1. The highest ranked card in the deck above a King, and at times, the lowest ranked card below a Deuce. 2. In Baccarat, the ace always has a value of one point.

A-Game – 1. Optimal playing. Playing at the highest level. 2. The highest stakes game offered.

According to Hoyle – Named after 18th-century author Edmond Hoyle for authoring books on card game rules. Generally used as an authoritative way to play card/casino games.

Ace in the Hole – Used metaphorically to describe a hidden advantage.

Ace Out – Winning a hand with just a high card Ace.

Ace Up the Sleeve – 1. An act of cheating by hiding an Ace from any player and restoring it back into play, often to the cheater's advantage. See also *Jacob's Ladder* and *Vest Holdout*. 2. Any form of hidden but legitimate advantage. 3. Any form of cheating.

Ace-High – 1. The highest-ranking card of an unpaired hand, with or without making a Straight or Flush. 2. A hand at showdown that did not make a Pair, Straight, or Flush and has a single Ace as the high card. 3. The best type of Straight, Flush, or Straight Flush.

Ace-High Pai Gow – 1. Any player or dealer in Pai Gow Poker who receives a hand that does not contain a Pair, Straight, or Flush while having the Ace as the high card. 2. The optional wager on a Pai Gow Poker layout.

Aces Full – A Full House with three Aces and any other Pair.

Aces Over – A Two Pair hand containing one pair of Aces. Same as *Aces Up*.

Aces Up – A Two Pair hand containing One Pair of Aces. Same as *Aces Over*.

Ace-to-Five – 1. The low Straight, A-2-3-4-5. In Pai Gow Poker, the 2nd highest Straight. 2. See *Wheel* and *Bicycle/Bike*.

Act – 1. Any executed action by a player to either bet, check, call, fold, raise, or go all-in. 2. A staging of a deliberate "tell" intended to mislead other players about the strength or weakness of his hand.

Action – 1. Any bet or wagering of chips, cheques, or money with the hopes of winning. 2. Any game in which there is a lot of betting to fuel interest of other players. 3. Sometimes an alert or approval callout to the floorman for a $100 bet or more. 4 The busyness or lack of it at a table.

Active Hand/Player – Any player who has current bets, is making bets, or is buying into the game.

Advantage – 1. A player who is seen as more skilled at the table. 2. Holding a strong hand. 3. Having a favorable position.

Advantage Player – A player who seeks to exploit weaknesses or detect flaws or imperfections in the rules or equipment of any casino game. By using this knowledge, they aim to play better, gain an edge, and/or make money. This may not always be illegal.

Advantage Tool – An illegal method or device used to cheat or to hide casino equipment. See *Cheat*, definition 1.

After-Hours Game – A private game, oftentimes for high-rollers, played in a card room or casino after it has closed for the night.

Agent – 1. Someone who colludes with one or more cheaters to gain money unethically, favors, an advantage, or position. 2. A person who lures another into a crooked game with the hopes of defrauding him. 3. Any player who works with the dealer on an inside job to cheat the casino.

Air – 1. A hand that has little value at showdown. 2. Nothing. 3. A deceptive tactic used as "giving air" during table talk to lure another player that he should stay in the hand convincing him he could win.

Alert Call – A dealer callout/verbal notification to the floor supervisor or pit boss about the action the dealer or player is taking. No reply is necessary. See also *Callout*, definition 1.

All Black – 1. A Flush consisting of all black cards, either spades or clubs. See also *All Blue* or *All Purple*. 2. A request by the player to receive all black, $100 denomination cheques.

All Blue – 1. (ambiguous) A Flush consisting of all black cards, either spades or clubs, and sometimes diamonds. Also called All Black or All Purple. In some online poker games, a player has the option to change from the two black and red suit colors to four different colors. Diamonds change to a blue color and clubs change to a green color.

All Green – 1. (ambiguous) A Flush consisting of clubs. In some online poker games, a player has the option to change from the two black and red suit colors to four different colors. Diamonds change to a blue color and clubs change to a green color. 2. A request by the player to receive all green, $25 denomination cheques.

All Pink – A Flush consisting of all red cards, either hearts or diamonds. Also known as *All Red*.

All Purple – A Flush consisting of all black cards, either spades or clubs. Also known as *All Black* or *All Blue*.

All Red – 1. A Flush consisting of all red cards, either hearts or diamonds. Also known as *All Pink*. 2. A request by the player to receive all red, $5 denomination cheques.

Alligator Blood – A short-stacked player, or his playing style, who plays fearlessly and wins, usually just enough of the time to remain in the game.

All-In – A bet in which a player wagers his entire stack of chips/cheques. Also known as *Shove*.

Alone Player – A cheat who works without an accomplice or partner in crime.

Ammo/Ammunition – Also known as *Chip* or *Cheque*.

An Ace Working – A player holding an Ace in his hand.

Announce – A player's verbal intention. This can be a bet size, amount, or action.

Announced Bet – A player's verbalized wager that is immediately booked by the player placing the cheque(s) on the table to cover that bet.

Ante – 1. In Poker, money collected by the dealer from a) each player or b) the big blind (see *Big Blind Ante*) before any cards are dealt. This money is not part of the blinds or normal betting and is brought to the pot. It is often regarded as required for the privilege of being dealt cards. 2. In Carnival Games, usually the minimum required bet to be dealt cards. Normally, it will pay even money when it wins.

Apologizer/Apology Card – In most poker games, the appearance of a card that would have been most useful the previous hand. Oftentimes this card is shown to other players.

Apple – Refers to a big or the biggest (highest stakes) game in the casino or poker room.

Approval Call – A dealer callout/verbal notification to the floor supervisor or pit boss about the action the dealer or player is taking. The dealer must wait for a response from the floorman or pit boss, whether the action is accepted or rejected, and must follow accordingly. Usually, rejections are followed by a corrective or substitutive action. Also known as *Response Call*. See also *Callout*, definition 1.

Apron – A piece of uniform clothing issued by the casino worn around the waist designed to protect the dealer and the casino from any chip/cheque to fall into the dealer's front pant pocket.

Armrest Rail – The foamy outer edge of the table where players often rest their elbows while playing.

Artist – An agent, grifter, or mechanic. See also *Agent*, definition 1, *Cheater*, *Grifter*, and *Mechanic*.

B&M – Short for "brick and mortar." See *Brick-and-Mortar*.

Baby – A low ranking card (two, three, four, or five) used to complete a low Straight.

Baby Pair – Any of the low-ranked Pairs that a player is dealt. A Pair of twos through sixes are examples.

Baccarat – A type of Carnival Game where players bet on Player or Banker to win.

Back of the House (BOH) – Any place an employee is not in view of the guest. Opposite of *Front of the House*.

Back Off – The act of a casino's management informing a player that he is no longer allowed to play. The message can come politely, discreetly, professionally, but almost always abruptly and usually as a surprise to the player. Since casinos are private entities, they may allow or deny any player to play in their casino they deem. This player's ban from playing can be temporary or permanent and may be specific to one or more games in that casino. A player may be backed off from Blackjack, for example, but may or may not be totally banned from the casino; thus, he may still be allowed to play a different type of table game or slots. Also known as ban, *Blacklisted*, and *Heat*.

Backer – Someone who backs, stakes, or finances another to gamble. See also *Stake*, definition 2.

Back-to-Back – Anything done in successive order.

Ball(er) – (slang) The tables (in a string of tables) a current dealer sits at (including dead spreads) before a break or brush table. Usually prefaced with a number and discussed among dealers, one might say, "I had a 5-ball (or 5 ball-er)" meaning "I dealt a string of five tables before going on break."

Bank – House cheques in front of the dealer. See also *Bankroll*, definition 1, *Banque*, and *House*, definition 2.

Bank Cover – The lockable cover that protects and safeguards the house's bank cheques when the table is not in use/closed. Also known as a lid.

Banker – 1. In Baccarat, the second hand to receive and reveal the cards. This is often referred to as the "house." A player will wager this bet if he thinks the Banker's card total will be higher than the Player's card total. Any tie with the Player hand results in a push. This bet pays 1:1. A 5% commission may or may not be applied to all winning Banker bets. 2. In Pai Gow Poker, a player electing take the risk of personally covering the main bets should it win, but also collecting bets should they lose. See also *Banque*.

Bankroll – 1. The house's bank/cheques used to color up a player's chips. 2. A specific amount of money set aside specifically for gambling. 3. To back, stake, or finance another to play or gamble.

Banque – In Baccarat, any player who is selected to financially assume the role of the house bank.

Bar – To exclude or prevent a player from playing in the casino or is off-limits to certain games. Similar to a ban. See also *Blacklisted*.

Barn – (slang) A Full House. Also called full barn. See *Full House*.

Barrel – 1. A bet. See *Bet*. 2. A player's successive bets each betting round.

Base Deal(ing) – Any deck manipulation to allow the dealer to deal from the bottom of the deck. Very good or very bad cards can be dealt and is a serious form of cheating. Also known as *Bottom Dealing*, *Greek Bottom*, and *Hanger*. See also *Cheat*, definition 1, and *Mechanic*.

Basic Strategy Card – A wallet-sized card filled with simple helpful hints and optimal strategies that a player can oftentimes use while gambling. Some casinos allow the use of this card, some forbid it. Players should always check with a supervisor regarding the house's policy.

Bay and a Gray – A $6 bet made with a red $5 cheque and a white/gray $1 cheque. In horse racing, a bay is a reddish-brown horse with black markings. A red $5 cheque often comes with black streaks.

Beat the Board – To have a hand in any flop game that is better than using the five community cards as the player's best five-card poker hand. See also *Play(ing) the Board*.

Behind – 1. A player who is losing and needs to win to "catch up." 2. The amount of money remaining in front of a player at any time.

Behind a Log – After a player increased his chip stack, he plays conservatively to protect his gains.

Belly Buster – Any of the missing three middle cards to complete a Straight. See *Inside Straight (Draw)*.

Benjamin (Franklin) – (slang) A U.S. $100 bill of a U.S. founding father pictured on its front. Also known as Benji or Franklin. See *C-Note* and *Yard*.

Best of It – To be in the most advantageous position. Opposite of *Worst of It*.

Bet – The money a player risks overall or for a specific hand, roll of the dice, or spin of the wheel before the outcome. Winning bets can pay less than, equal to, or greater than what is wagered based on casino odds. Dealers are expected to not only know winning and losing bets but also all the proper payouts of every bet and which hand is used to collect and pay the bets. Also known as *Wager*.

Bet Blind – Any bet made by a player before either a) looking at his cards or, b) before the next card is dealt. Also known as a bet in the dark.

Bet Into – To take a stance against an aggressive opponent by making a bet or even raising the bet.

Bet on the Layout – Any bet (chip/cheque/money) placed on the layout.

Bet the Limit – The maximum allowable bet.

Betting Area – Specific spots on the layout where players can make wagers. See *Layout*.

Betting Spot (Circle) – The circle or square on the layout where players place their wagers.

Betting Stakes – 1. (slang) Layout. See *Layout*. 2. The chip or dollar betting limits.

Bicycle/Bike – 1. (slang) Refers to a poker hand of A-2-3-4-5, also known as *Wheel*. 2. The U.S. playing card manufacturer, or its logo. 3. Name of the casino and/or poker room in Bell Gardens, California.

Big Baccarat – The largest Baccarat table that seats up to fourteen players (seven on each side) and normally has two dealers. Also known as *Maxi Baccarat*.

Big Cat – A hand without a Pair, Straight, or Flush and all cards rank from eight to King.

Big Dog – An underdog. A player who has a low chance of winning.

Big Full – The higher and best Full House in poker. Opposite of *Underfull*. See *Full House*.

Big Pair – Any of the high-ranked Pairs that a player is dealt, for example a Pair of Queens.

Big Wheel – A type of Carnival Game where players bet the outcome of a large spinning wheel.

Bird Dog – A recruiter who oversees new player development. Also known as a casino host.

Biscuit – A $1000 or £1000 cheque. See also *Yellow*.

Black Action – A bet of one or more black chips/cheques generally worth $100 each.

Black and Whites – Industry standard, casino audition attire. Applicants are usually told to wear a white, button-down, long-sleeved dress shirt, black pants, black belt, black socks, and black shoes when auditioning for a dealing job. Dealers wear this outfit if the casino does not provide uniforms for temporary workers.

Black Book – A casino's private list of names and detailed profiles of players who are unwelcome to play or even be on a casino's property without risking a trespassing charge or greater. In the past, a physical black book was kept by the casino, but now player information is stored digitally and accessible anytime, anywhere, a known or suspected blacklisted person enters the casino property. A player, such as an addicted gambler, can choose to ask the casino to place his name voluntarily in the Black Book. Also known as *Griffin Book*. See also *Blacklisted*.

Blacklisted – A player whose name appears in a casino's *Black Book*. Some of the many reasons a player can be blacklisted are: cheating, violence, bad-mouthing, stealing, being an advantage player, being a card counter (in Blackjack), or tampering with any casino equipment. Casinos are in business to make money, provide great entertainment, and make guests feel safe. It takes a lot to get blacklisted, and this is the casino's way of saying management doesn't want a person on the property. Drinking excessively and falling down drunk will either get the person escorted back to his hotel room onsite or kicked off the property for the rest of the day. Being blacklisted can be a temporary ban, such as one month or one year, or a permanent ban. Also known as *86'd*.

Blacks – Any black-colored chip/cheque.

Blank – A card that a player gets that does not help with completing any hopeful draws, such as Straights or Flushes. This "blank" card can appear on the community board in flop games, when drawing cards in a draw game, or in stud games.

Blaze – (slang) A hand containing five face cards.

Bleed – To consistently lose money over a playing session. Also known as bleeding.

Blind – 1. In Poker, the forced bet required of the player. 2. Players who decide to play (wager) any bet after receiving cards but without looking at them. Also known as *Playing Blind*.

Blind Raise – To increase a current bet without looking at one's cards.

Blistering – See *Pegging*.

Blocker – Any card a player has that prevents or reduces the possibility of another player making or improving his hand.

Bloodbath – A situation in which two or more players have large amounts of chips/cheques going into the pot and a losing player will either be eliminated or lose most of his stack.

Blow Back – A situation in which a player loses much or all of his previous winnings.

Blue – The color associated with the Player in Baccarat.

Blue Chip – (uncommon/obsolete) A high-value chip. Used more to describe investment and finance of high and stable value. Black Chip is more commonly used. See also *High-Limit/High-Stakes Games*.

Board – Same as community board or community cards. See *Community Cards*.

Board Cards – Cards that are dealt face-up for all players to see. In Holdem or Omaha, these are the community cards. In stud games, these are each player's face-up cards.

Boat – (slang) A Full House. See *Full House*.

Bonus – Anything that is considered extra, or in addition to a regular bet or payout.

Bottom Card – See *Cut Card*.

Bottom Dealing – See *Base Deal(ing)*.

Bottom Pair – The smallest Pair using a player's hole card and the lowest-ranked card on the board.

Box – The dealer taking one-third of the top of the deck and putting it on the bottom of the deck. Or the dealer taking the bottom third of the deck and placing it on the top of the deck. See also *Strip*.

Boxed Card – A face-up, exposed card in the deck discovered during any part of dealing. In poker, it is a dead card not legally playable. This may or may not result in a misdeal. In Carnival Games, it most likely is a misdeal. House rules vary on treatment of the exposed card.

Break – The rest time a dealer is not dealing and is away from the table.

Breakage – The result of payouts being rounded down to the nearest dollar because a table game cannot issue denominations less than their minimum cheque standard (usually $1). Unusual or sub-optimal bet amounts, while legal, won't reflect a full payout.

Break-In Dealer – A dealer with very little or no dealing experience in a live casino often showing a "deer in the headlights" fear with complex bets. See also *Lump/Lumpy*, definition 2.

Breaking Streaks – A betting strategy to "go against the grain" and bet the opposite number(s), because the thought is that if it won before, it is due to change soon. "Yin and Yang" applies here.

Brick – A card that stops short of improving a hand, usually with some disappointment. For example, a player failing to complete his Flush or Straight is said to have "bricked out." Also known as idle card.

Brick-and-Mortar – A physical casino location as opposed to online gambling. Also known as *B&M*.

Bring It In – An acknowledgment by the supervisor to a dealer's "Color Coming In" alert or approval call allowing the dealer to bring in a player's chips and/or cheques to Color Up. See also *Color Coming In* and *Color/Color Up*.

Broadway – An Ace-High Straight with cards of at least two different suits that contain T-J-Q-K-A. The term derives from the oldest north-south thoroughfare in Manhattan (New York City) and the spectacle of bright lights, abundance of money, high class, and the allure of world-famous musicals and theatre shows. A one-suited Broadway is a *Royal Flush*.

Broadway Cards – Any T-J-Q-K-A needed to complete the Broadway Straight.

Broadway Straight – See *Broadway*.

Broke – Anyone (or an entity) without money.

Broke Money – (rare) Transportation money that a casino will give to a broke player.

Broken – A player who consistently loses.

Broken Game – Any game at a table that has emptied itself of all players.

Brush – 1. Any cleaning object with a handle and bristles used to consolidate dust or dirt from a table. 2. An employee of a brick-and-mortar poker room not dealing at a table but who helps with putting players' names on a waiting list, seating players, making change, getting chips/cheques, or processing fill orders for dealers, among other duties.

Buck – 1. The original version of the dealer button being a clasp knife with a buckhorn handle. A player holding the dealer button acts last and is regarded as the most advantageous position. At each hand's conclusion, the buck/button is rotated clockwise to the next player. 2. One dollar. See *Dollar*, definition 1.

Bug – (slang) In some variations of poker, such as Pai Gow Poker, a joker that is used to represent an Ace, or to substitute another card to complete a Straight, a Flush, or a Straight Flush. See *Joker*.

Build(ing) a Stack – A player gradually increasing the amount of his chips/cheques. See *Chip Up*, definition 2, and *Robusto*.

Bump – An extra dealer break when the table is overstaffed or has no activity.

Bump/Bump It Up – To raise or increase the betting amount. See *Raise*.

Burn/Burn Card – The removal of the top card from the deck before dealing, to prevent players from gaining an advantage by identifying imperfections or marks. Burn cards are never shown to players and serve to protect the stub, not to preserve card order. Typically, one card is burned for each street or draw dealt.

Bury Card – (obsolete) The top card taken from the deck and placed into the middle of the deck.

Bust Out – The result of a player losing all his chips during a tournament.

Bust/Busted – 1. A player who lost all of his money in any casino game. Opposite of *Robusto*. Also known as busto. 2. A player who is responsible for another player's exit. 3. A hand that failed to improve as the player had hoped.

Busted Hand – 1. A hand that lost. 2. A hand that failed to complete a desired Straight or Flush.

Butterfly(ing) – Interlacing cards after a riffle and setting them aside without squaring up the deck. This shows how evenly the cards have been riffled before being squaring up the deck(s) for cutting.

Button – See *Lammer*, definition 2.

Buy-In – 1. The exact amount of money a player puts down to purchase chips from the dealer in order to play. Some casinos allow for all kinds of payment methods (cash, casino cheques, cashier's check, credit or debit card transactions, wire transfer, account withdrawal, etc.). 2. The minimum/maximum amount of money for a player to pay to enter a game.

Cage – See *Cashier*, definition 1.

Call Bet – A player's verbalized wager without placing the chip(s) on the table to cover that bet. Casinos may allow or forbid this type of bet, as it is a form of credit. See also *Announced Bet*.

Call – To match the highest current bet by putting in an equal amount of chips/cheques. Also known as *Meet*, and *See*.

Callout – 1. Any dealer's verbal announcement during different stages of gameplay. Directed to the players or to the supervisor, it safeguards transparency and alerts (or requires approval) from the supervisor for any specific action. 2. An employee who calls the employer to state he will miss work.

Canary – (slang) A yellow $1000 cheque. See *Yellow*.

Capping – An illegal adding of more chips to a winning bet before the dealer issues the payout. Also known as capping a bet. See also *Past Posting*.

Card – 1. One of the 52 cards found in a standard deck. See *Cards*. 2. To ask a person for their identification to verify their age.

Card Sharp (Shark) – 1. (uncommon) A cheating player. 2. In non-poker contexts, someone who can perform card tricks.

Cardrack – (slang) A player who is dealt many very good and winning hands. See *Heater* and *Run*.

Cards – A complete deck of 52 unique pieces of stiff paper/plastic, each with one of the four suits and one of the 13 unique ranked cards. No two cards are ever identical from the same deck. Cards always come with one or two Jokers, and sometimes with one or two cards verifying authenticity. Oftentimes they are sealed and shrink-wrapped to ensure a verified, secure, clean deck. Cards used in Blackjack and Carnival Games are usually made of paper, while poker cards are usually plastic.

Cards Speak – 1. A hand's most favorable value is determined by the cards revealed face-up, regardless of the player's declaration. The dealer reads the hands. See *Reading*. 2. Verbal declarations of a hand's value are not binding in most poker rooms. Deliberate miscalls may result in penalties.

Caribbean Stud – A Carnival Game variant focused on a player using his five cards against the dealer's hand.

Carnival Games – Any of the other casino table games that do not include Blackjack, Craps, Poker, or Roulette.

Case Card – The fourth and last card of a rank that appears, oftentimes to help a player immensely.

Case Chips – A player's remaining chips.

Case the Layout – A player's examination or inspection of the arrangement of the table, bets offered, payouts, equipment used, players involved, and which dealer is at the table. Some, all, or even more of these factor into whether a player sits down to play, or not, and his wagering.

Cash – Money in coins or U.S. Federal Reserve Notes, or any other country's current valid currency used to exchange for cheques for a cash game.

Cash In – Same as Cash Out. See *Cash Out*.

Cash Out – To exchange cheques for cash at the cashier. Also known as *Cash In*.

Cash Plays/Cash Does Not Play – House rules that dictate whether actual cash can be used instead of exchanging it for chips/cheques. Generally, most house rules in the U.S. and state gaming laws forbid cash from being used to wager bets in poker or casino table games. When cash was allowed, a table games dealer would shout, "Money plays" to the pit boss, alerting them of cash being used. Cash was counted for wins, and all wins were paid in casino cheques.

Cashier – 1. The caged area in a casino responsible for all currency transactions, debit/credit card advances, markers and their paybacks, to exchange player's cheques for cash, issue receipts, and complete a chip runner's fill order for tables running low on cheques, among other duties. 2. The person who works in a casino cashier/cage is also known as a cashier.

Casino – [It. *casa* house] A building where gambling games are played. Though privately and/or publicly traded, casinos are considered private properties. Each casino is unique, due to location, size, zoning, amenities, theme, and available assets, among other considerations. Casinos can be found on land (indoors, outdoors, pool area), a train, a ship, or a riverboat, or in an airplane. Casinos are highly regulated by some government agency. In the U.S., each state's gaming commission/bureau/board oversees casinos, gambling establishments, lotteries, and more. There are many requirements to obtain and keep an ongoing casino license. Of all the assets, glitter, money, prime location, or trademarked fame, nothing is more important to a casino than its gaming license to operate in that location. See also *Gaming Commission* and *Underground Casino*.

Casino Credit – A line of credit (money) made available interest-free by the casino to creditworthy players. Players pay this money back either upon cashing out or within a short time period, usually 30 days. It eliminates ATM fees and the need for players to bring in large amounts of cash to where they gamble. Players get approved a limit upon which they can draw from and sign an agreement to pay back the money. Also known as a *Credit* and *Marker*.

Casino War – A single card "player versus dealer" type of Carnival Game.

Catch – 1. Any card(s) that appears and improves a player's hand, often turning a losing hand into a winning hand. 2. See also *Nice Catch*, both definitions.

Central Processing Unit (CPU) – A "thinking/calculating" component found in any electronic game that requires a computerized "brain" to function. This unit utilizes a random number generator (RNG) for random yet fair calculations to operate. See also *Random Number Generator (RNG)*.

Chameleon Strategy – The copying/mimicking system used by players who observe other players winning and bet as they do in the hopes, they too get lucky.

Change Gears – The act of a player altering the manner or technique of his playing.

Change Only – A dealer's announcement when exchanging a player's cash buy-in for chips/cheques without a bet being placed. This also protects the house that no Call Bet was placed during the transaction, either verbally or intentionally.

Charting (a Table) – A player who keeps track of outcomes at the table, either using pen and paper or sliding cheques in the player's cheque rack, ala abacus style.

Chase – 1. The act of a player who continues to play, hoping to improve his hand by catching a certain card or cards. 2. A losing player who keeps playing, hoping to win back his losses.

Chasing Losses – A losing player who keeps playing, hoping to win back his losses. Sometimes this player bets a larger and larger amount after a series/sequence of consecutive losses. The belief is that since he has lost so many times in a row, he is "due" for a win, and the latest big bet will cover all his previous losses. See also *Gambler's Fallacy* and *Martingale System*.

Cheat – 1. An intentional violation of ANY rule in any way to gain money or an advantage over other players or the casino. A person who cheats may act alone, with others, or with the dealer. Any foreign device, mechanical or not, is often used when cheating. See also *Alone Player*, *Agent*, all definitions, and *Mechanic*. 2. To avoid something undesirable by luck or skill. 3. Short for "cheater." See *Cheater*.

Cheater – A person who cheats. See *Cheat*, definition 1. The penalties are not kind to someone who is caught cheating. Aside from being banned from the poker room and/or casino, a cheat is embarrassingly escorted off the property if he is not already detained, arrested, and then charged with a felony. The cheater can also face court penalties, restitution, and even a prison sentence. And since many casinos share information about players, the cheater can also be blacklisted from other casino properties. See also *Black Book* and *Blacklisted*.

Check – 1. One of the six actions a player can take during a betting round. A player's action to decline to bet with no previous bets ahead of him. This player still retains the right to call or raise if faced with future action in the same round. A player in the big blind with no raise ahead of him in the initial betting round may check his option without adding more money to his forced bet. Also known as *Knock*, *Pat*, *Stand Pat*, 2. Any motion made by the player to indicate the action of a check by verbally saying the word "check"; by a finger, hand, or entire fist tapping the table; by tapping one chip to the table or to another chip; or any other accepted sign of a player checking (e.g., head nod, shoulder tapping). A dealer should always ask if the player's action is too vague or might be misunderstood. 3. Alternate spelling for cheque.

Check Blind – A check made by the first-to-act player before seeing the next dealt card.

Cheese – A generally agreed upon weak starting hand.

Cheque – A round disc or token slightly larger than a U.S. half-dollar coin, weighing around 11.5 grams used in the casino for all table games played with real money. Cheques are sometimes used alongside real money but are mostly used in place of real money. As opposed to chips, cheques always have a cash value clearly printed on both sides. Each denomination has its own color and monetary value. The use of these tokens speeds up the game immensely as players and dealers can quickly count a player's entire stack of chips in a few moments without the burden or cumbersome process of counting paper bills. See also *Chip*, *Fiche*, *Gratuity*, *Jeton*, *Mil*, and *Toke/Token*.

Cheque Change – A dealer's alert that a player is bringing cheques to the table and needs a different denomination (usually this is from larger to smaller).

Cheques Play – A dealer's verbal alert/approval callout that a player is betting a big amount (usually any amount over $100). State once; repeated callouts for the same player are unnecessary.

Chip – A round disc or token slightly larger than a U.S. half dollar coin, weighing around 11.5 grams used in the casino in roulette games and poker tournaments, or as promotional chips. Technically speaking, chips have no cash value. Players often but incorrectly use this term when they really mean cheque, which has a cash value. The use of chips ("cheques") speeds up the game immensely, as players and dealers can quickly count an entire stack of chips with one hand in a few moments without the burden or cumbersome process of counting paper bills. Chips, like cheques, are made from clay, ceramic, plastic injection molding, compression molded clay, metal, highly durable plastic resin, or a combination thereof. Higher denominations may have extra security features like a computer chip (RFID – Radio Frequency Identification) embedded into the chip itself or a blue light marking/stamp on the outside. Early chips were made of bone material, rhino horns, and even elephant tusks. See also *Cheque, Fiche, Gratuity, Jeton, Mil,* and *Toke/Token*.

Chip Carrying Case – A protective case that security uses to transport up to ten chip trays full of cheques along with matching fill order paperwork for any number of tables.

Chip Rack – See *Rack*.

Chip Tray – See *Tray*.

Chip Up – 1. Exchanging chips/cheques of a lower denomination for a higher one. See *Color/Color Up*. 2. To increase a player's stack by winning little by little.

Chocolate – (slang) A brown $5000 cheque.

Choppy Game – A game during which there are no noticeable winning/losing streaks or repeated numbers.

Chunking – The dealer's act of clearing lost bets on the layout by stacking (picking up) these individual stacks by hand and placing them in the cheque bank.

Cinch Hand – An unbeatable hand. See also *Nuts*, definition 1.

Clean Money – Chips/cheques straight from the dealer's bank from which to pay out winning bets. These payouts have been verified as having the same color/denomination and would not result in an incorrect payout. This is the professional way to pay out bets. Opposite of *Dirty Money*.

Clear – The act of a dealer showing his hands are free of any object. By demonstrating to surveillance and anyone watching, the hands clap together once, and both sides of the hands are shown. This is done before a dealer arrives at a table, touches any part of his body, or for any other reason during his time at the table, and when he leaves the table. Also known as wash your hands.

Closed Game – A game currently not available to anyone who wants to play. Opposite of *Open Game*.

Clubs ♣ – One of the four common suits in a deck of cards. Also known as clovers, paw prints, and puppies.

Coat Card – Any King, Queen, or Jack. Also known as *Court Card*. See *Face Card*.

Clear Spacer – See *Lammer*, definition 1.

C-Note – (slang) A $100 dollar bill. The "C" comes from Roman Numerals meaning 100. Also known as *Benjamin (Franklin)* and *Yard*. See also *Dollar*, definition 2.

Coat Card – Any King, Queen, or Jack. Also known as *Court Card*. See *Face Card*.

Coin Flip – Situation in which the outcome of any bet is nearly a 50/50 chance of winning.

Cold Deck – 1. A deck of cards that has been stacked or organized in a certain order to produce monetary losses to the cheater's intended victim. Literally, this cold-to-the-touch deck has been prepared ahead of time and is swapped with the warmer deck that has been played with. Astute players notice the difference in temperature change. Also known as *Ice*. 2. An honest deck that players want to change due to consistently receiving bad cards/unplayable hands. in hopes of better luck.

Cold Table – Any table where multiple players are losing repeatedly in a short time frame. Usually their frustrations and loud groaning draw the attention of other players.

Collusion – The act(s) of two or more players cheating/working together in any manner to influence the outcome of any casino game.

Color Change – 1. A request by a player to change from one denomination to another without increasing or decreasing the amount of money the chips/cheques represent. 2. In Roulette, a request by a player to change and get a different color of chips.

Color Coming In – A callout to notify the supervisor that a player wishes to cash out/exchange his chips/cheques for easier to carry, larger denomination amounts. This may be an alert in some casinos, a request for approval at others. This precedes a color up. See also *Color/Color Up*.

Color for Color – Paying a winning bet by matching the same denomination cheques as the bet.

Color/Color Up – A dealer callout for exchanging multiple low-denomination cheques into fewer, higher-denomination ones. The supervisor verifies the correct amount side by side before handing them to the player. This minimizes the number of cheques a player needs to carry and helps keep the dealer's bank/rack fuller, reducing the need for frequent fills. For example, a player with 40 red $5 cheques may request a color up, and the dealer exchanges them for two black $100 cheques, making it easier to transport to another table or the cashier/cage.

Combo Draw – An opportunity, usually in Holdem, which occurs after a player sees the flop or the flop and turn cards, then hopes to catch the right card to make either a Straight or a Flush because he has four cards to making either hand.

Community Board – See also *Board* and *Community Cards*.

Community Cards – The five cards in the center of the table during hands of any flop game (Holdem and Omaha) that are to be used by each player (and the dealer on Carnival Games) with the cards in their hands to form the best five-card hand, either high or low. See also *Board*.

Comp – Rewards earned by using a player's card for a loyalty program, allowing a player to receive certain benefits for playing often and/or big amounts. Short for "complimentary."

Complete Hand – A player's hand that contains all the necessary cards to make a Straight, Flush, etc.

Concealed Pair – Hole cards that contain a Pair unseen by other players.

Connectors – Any starting poker hand that is consecutive in rank but of two different suits. For example, 7 of Hearts, 6 of Clubs. See also *Suited Connectors*.

Conservative – A player or his playing style that tends to play with very good/premium starting hands and continues post-flop with a better-than-average chance of winning the pot.

Converting – Changing one denomination of cheques into a larger denomination.

Cooler – 1. Bad Luck. 2. A dealer or player who is brought in superstitiously (and sometimes successfully) to halt and even reverse a single or a group of players' winnings or hot streak. This is done so the house can recoup some, if not all, or even more than it had already lost to the player(s).

Coordinated – See *Wet Board*.

Copy – A tie hand in Pai Gow Poker. Players tying the dealer lose. Also known as *Tie*, definition 1.

Cosmetics – Any foreign substance used for marking cards. Also known as daub.

Count Room – The secure room in the BOH where large volumes of currency and cheques are counted, re-counted, verified and stored properly. Bank notes and paper currency are soft counts while the coins and cheques are hard counts. Heavy surveillance oversees this room.

Counterfeit – 1. Fake/Fake Currency. 2. A hand that may start out strong (oftentimes Baby Pairs) but the continuation of more dealt cards, such as in Holdem, may improve the hand but in effect weakens it. For example, a hand of 3-3 starts as One Pair. The flop is 6-7-9 still giving this player One Pair (a Pair of threes). The turn card brings a 6, and while the player improves to Two Pair (sixes over threes), he must consider that someone might have achieved their Straight by holding 10-8 or 8-5 or, made any Full House or even Four of a Kind. A 9 on the river negates or "counterfeits" his Two Pair hand since the board is made up of Two Pair (nines over sixes). The player's Pair of threes is bested by "playing the board" as neither of the threes will play as a kicker. See also *Play(ing) the Board*.

Coup – A hand or round of play during Baccarat. It begins with dealing of cards and ends with either a Player win, Banker win, or a Tie.

Court Card – See *Face Card*.

Covered – The reassurance that a particular number or bet is indeed in place or positioned properly.

Cow – A player sharing a buy-in with another player with the intention of splitting the proceeds afterwards. To "go cow" is to make such an arrangement.

CPU – Acronym for "Central Processing Unit." See *Central Processing Unit*.

Cranberry – A $25,000 cheque used in high-stakes games. Named because of its color.

Crazy 4 Poker – A Carnival Game poker variant where players use the best four of five dealt cards to beat the dealer's four of five card hand.

Credit – A pre-approved line of funds issued by the casino with its own payback timeframe and terms. Players with good credit scores and verifiable assets/sufficient bank funds are approved for a certain amount from which a player can draw upon. This feature allows players to arrive at a casino without cash, draw upon their available credit, play, pay it back during their visit or within a short period (a month or so), and not have to worry about carrying large amounts of cash. Winnings and payment can also be electronically transferred. Also known as *Marker*. See also *Lammer*, definition 3.

Credit Order/Credit Slip – The exact opposite of a Fill Order or Fill Slip. It is used when a high denomination or an abundance of cheques need to be removed from the table's bank.

Cross-Fire(ing) – Conversation between dealers at different live tables, especially with live players.

Croupier – Proper term for a Roulette dealer, and in some parts of the world, a Baccarat dealer.

Cup Holder – A circular cutout portion of the table, whether in the rail or racetrack, which serves to secure drink glasses, so they are less likely to tip over and spill onto the felt. Some tables instead use a plastic or metal container with an extended lip to tuck under the table.

Cut – 1. The process of dividing a shuffled deck into two sections and swapping their positions for fairness. If a card gets exposed, a reshuffle is required. 2. In Blackjack, players in rotation often cut the deck. See *Cut Card*. 3. In home poker games, it's usually done by the player to the dealer's right.

Cut Card – A plastic, metal, or other thin material with the same dimensions as a card deck, used to hide the bottom card in a poker deck and protect the stub after dealing a hand. In casinos, cut cards are used in some Carnival Games, but mainly in Blackjack, where players may cut the deck when offered the cut card. In Blackjack, the cut card near the end of the shoe or handheld deck reminds the dealer to finish the current hand and then shuffle. Also known as *Bottom Card*.

Cut the Cards/Cut the Deck/Cut the Pack – See *Cut*, all definitions.

Day – The late morning/early afternoon shift for casino workers. See *Graveyard* and *Swing*.

DC – Short for "dealer coordinator." Also known as *Pencil/Pencil Person*. See *Dealer Coordinator*.

Dead Card – A card that is not legally playable and removed from play. Either it was a boxed card, a mucked card, or an exposed card. Visibly damaged cards are removed permanently and replaced by a floorman bringing a new setup or replacing the same single card by rank, suit, and color backing.

Dead Game/Dead Spread/Dead Table – An open table with no players. A dealer is present, either waiting for a new game to start or because the previous game ended, and players left. Since the secure lid is either removed or unlocked, the table cannot be left unattended.

Dead Hand – 1. A fouled, mucked, or folded hand (or one that is declared as such by a player, dealer, or floorman) that is unavailable for further play, gets placed into the muck pile, and the player is not entitled to any portion of the pot, or refunds. 2. A new player to the game who is ineligible to receive a hand. 3. A player in a cash game who has moved two or more seats away from the blinds is not entitled to a hand unless he posts the big blind or waits until he is again the same number of seats away from the blinds from which he moved.

Deal – 1. The act and responsibilities of a dealer. Dealing can refer to a) the pitching of the correct number of cards to each player, or b) the entire process that starts with the dealer's first riffle of the shuffle and ends after pushing the pot to the winning player(s) and combining mucked cards. See *Dealer*. 2. The agreement by the remaining players at the end of the tournament to divide the prize money differently from the announced payouts.

Dealer – The person at the table who oversees, deals, and runs the casino game. A dealer makes change, explains game rules, monitors the game's efficiency, and notifies a supervisor/pit boss/floorman of any issues. Dealers also handle player questions, suspected cheating, rule clarifications, and equipment issues. In private or home games, a dealer can be a player. In live casinos, dealers are hired staff in uniform and may receive tips from players.

Dealer Change – The end of the timed session, usually 20 minutes, when a dealer is finished dealing at that table and is pushed out by another dealer. Also known as *Tap Out*.

Dealer Coordinator (DC) – The supervisory staff responsible for assigning and rerouting dealers to tables, or sending dealers home. Also known as *Pencil/Pencil Person*.

Deck – See *Cards*.

Defective Deck – A deck of cards that has something wrong with it that may compromise the integrity of the game. A short list of issues includes: a damaged, bent, torn, ripped, defective, or compromised card; too many or missing cards; cards not used for the current game; duplicate cards; or cards with different color backings or any manufacturing defect. Should a dealer or player discover this, a floorman should be called upon to replace the deck(s) in question. Some poker rooms will replace only the defective cards in question.

Denomination – The value assigned to a bill, coin, chip, or cheque within a series.

Deuce Dealer – A cheating dealer who deals not the top card to each player, but somehow deals one or more players the second card off the top of the deck.

Diamonds ♦ – One of the four common suits in a deck of cards. Also known as decked out and well dressed.

Dig – The ability to add money or chips/cheques to the game during an ongoing hand.

Digital Display Board – A two feet by three feet animated, digital screen roughly seven feet tall placed at the table's edge, displaying the running tally of a progressively larger jackpot amount. Some amounts increase, some are standard payouts. Often, a small disclaimer indicates the display may not have accurate/up-to-date information. A dealer error/machine malfunction may void hands.

Dime – (slang) $1000. Also known as *Yellow*.

Dirty Money – Disguised as a shortcut or laziness, a dealer taking cheques from a losing bet and directly paying a winning bet without properly verifying all of them by going back to his bank first. Cheques not verified as the same color/denomination would often result in an incorrect payout. This is an unprofessional way to pay out bets. Opposite of *Clean Money*.

Dirty Stack – 1. Any stack of cheques containing two or more different denominations in a column as visibly noticeable by any player or dealer. Other players or the dealer, as a courtesy, will alert to properly sort this stack to like-colored/same denomination cheques. 2. A dealer using money from a losing bet to pay a winning bet. This is a big no-no. Always pay bets from the bank or working stacks.

Discard – Any card no longer in play, for that hand, game, or round.

Discard(s) – 1. In a draw type of game, the cards players remove from their hand to exchange with the dealer for different cards. 2. Mucked cards that are folded and no longer playable.

DJ Wild – A Carnival Game poker variant where the joker and four deuces are wild. Player receive five cards to beat the dealer's five card hand.

Dog – Short for "underdog." See *Underdog*.

Dollar – 1. One U.S. Dollar, $1. 2. (slang) $100. See also *C-Note*.

Dominated Hands – Any hand that is an underdog. See *Underdog*.

Dominating Hand – Any hand that is better than another and oftentimes has room to improve.

Donk – Short for "donkey." See *Pigeon*.

Donk Bet – A bet made by a player that other players ridicule due to an unorthodox/foolish wager.

Donkey – Also known as donk. See *Pigeon*.

Dots – See *Pips*, definition 2.

Double – A ball that has landed on the same number in two consecutive spins.

Double Belly Buster – A situation in Holdem or Omaha when a player has two inside Straight draws. For example, a player holding 7-5 with a community board of 6-3-9 can make a Straight with an 8 or a 4. Also known as *Double Gutshot Draw*. See *Inside Straight (Draw)*.

Double Deal – An instance when the dealer dealt two cards to a player instead of one. Oftentimes accidental and easily correctable, it can be viewed as cheating as it gives an extra card to a player as an advantage.

Double Discard – A cheating technique when a player secretly removes a card(s) from his hand to be reintroduced later. The cheat will need to discard the extra card(s) at some eventual point.

Double Gutshot Draw – See *Double Belly Buster*.

Double Suited – A hand containing two or more different suits.

Double Up – Any bet that gets paid an equal amount that is wagered. For example, a $10 bet pays $10, (now worth $20 total.) Also known as double through and *Even Money Bet*. See also *Triple Up*.

Double-Up System – See *Martingale System*.

Down Card – The dealer's hidden card, face down for the players not to see while acting on their hands. Players can only guess what this card is, but often inflate the value this card to be a 10-value card. Opposite of *Up Card*.

Downswing – A series of losses by a player either during a session or any time period. Opposite of upswing. See also *Draw Down*.

Dragging – A fraudulent act by a player (or even a dealer) who moves a losing or non-paying bet to a different nearby spot on the layout to make it a winning bet eligible for a payout. This method of cheating occurs before the dealer collected the losing bets or paid out the winners. See also *Pinching*.

Draw Down – An amount of money a player's bankroll loses or can withstand to lose, before quitting or a turnaround is needed to continue playing. See also *Downswing*.

Drawing Dead – A hand that has already lost, even if it improves. No drawn cards can help this doomed hand win. Also known as *Wooden Hand*.

Drawing Hand – Any player's hand that needs to improve to win. Also known as on the come.

Drop – 1. The amount deposited by the player. 2. The amount lost by a player. 3. The toke rate amount collected for each eight-hour shift of a dealer. 4. The casino's income tally from every *Drop Box*. 5. To fold a hand. See *Fold*.

Drop Box – The locked metal container that holds a shift or an entire day's worth of players' cash buy-ins, fill slips, and marker receipts. These boxes are located on the dealer's side of the table, each with a paddle plunger to push the contents securely into the box below the table. See also *Toke Box*.

Drop Cut(ting) – The professional sectioning off and table placement of any number of cheques from a handful containing more cheques. This often leads to sizing-in the remainder of the cheques to count or pay a bet properly. See *Sizing-In*.

Drop Out – 1. Fold. To resign from continuing a hand any further. See *Fold*. 2. A player who removed himself from any further contention, such as an emergency during a tournament, for example.

Drop Slot – The table's small slot/slit where dealers drop cash, fill slips, foreign cheques, and promotional bets into the drop box below. Normally used in conjunction with a *Paddle*.

Dry Board – See *Rainbow*, definition 2.

Dual Rate – An employee who is a dealer some shifts, and at other times, a supervisor. This gives the employee an opportunity for job advancement by accepting more responsibilities.

Dummy Up/Dummy Up And Deal – A phrase one utters to the dealer to resume dealing after an unnecessarily long chit-chat delay. It also alerts other players to get serious about playing/gambling.

8, Eight – Any eight. The ranking numbered card above a seven but below a nine.

86'd – See *Blacklisted*.

Early Out (EO) – A voluntary sign-up list where dealers can register their names to leave work before completing their full shift, provided management determines the pace of operations is slow enough to allow early departures.

Edge – An advantage. The larger the house's edge, the worse the odds or chance a player has to win.

EDR – Acronym for "Employee Dining Room." See *Employee Dining Room (EDR)*.

Employee Dining Room (EDR) – A break area where food is served buffet style, usually free for employees before, during, or after their shift. Usually, a badge is swiped to enter, and some casinos have limits on how many times per shift an employee may eat.

End Strippers – Cards tampered along the edges by a cheater. Such devices to shave off a thin part of the card lengthwise are known as card trimmers. See also *Pegging*.

Envy – 1. A player who has placed a bonus or side bet that pays out if another player at the table achieves a specific winning hand during the same round. This allows players to benefit from the successes of others. Normally, a minimum required wager is needed to qualify and is most often found at the Pai Gow Poker tables. 2. The "Envy" lammer used for bets that qualify for Envy payouts.

EO – Acronym for "Early Out." It is an open list on which dealers can add their names to leave work earlier than their full shift should management deem it slow enough to release them.

Ethics or Etiquette – The common protocol, courtesies, formalities, and codes of polite and accepted behavior expected from all players at the casino table (or even casino playing) toward other players, dealers, and staff members.

Even Money – A payout of the same amount as wagered; 1 to 1.

Even Money Bet – Any bet that pays 1 to 1 (1:1). The original bet is returned. Same as *Double-Up Bet*.

Exposed Cards – Any card turned face up. It can be intentional, such as in Face up Pai Gow Poker, or DJ Wild games; or unintentional, such as a dealer error, a bad shuffle, a player's hand knocked the card over during dealing, a player flashing his card, or a boxed card. See also *Show*.

Exposed Pair – Two cards of the same rank that all players can see.

Extra Board – See *On Call*.

Eye in the Sky – 1. Closed-circuit cameras installed in the casino ceiling. Although they can also be placed on walls, they are positioned anywhere to monitor casino tables, players' seats, restaurants, gift shops, hotel check-in, hallways, elevators, parking garages, and the casino cage. All camera recordings are stored as digital files in the Surveillance/Security office. The current standard is the PTZ (pan-tilt-zoom) function that allows a camera to be hidden inside a dark dome (so anyone looking at it from the floor cannot see the direction of the camera). These are mounted with a series of gears and levers with two axes of rotation and can see virtually anything that happens 24 hours a day. See also *Security* and *Surveillance*, both definitions. 2. Human Inspectors. See also *Human Inspectors*.

4, Four – Any four. The ranking numbered card above a three but below a five.

5, Five – Any five. The ranking numbered card above a four but below a six.

Face Cards – Any King, Queen, or Jack and are normally worth 10 points, as in Blackjack. In Baccarat however, these four ranks are worth 0 points. Also known as *Coat Card, Court Card, Liner, Monkey, Paint Cards/Paints, Picture Cards,* and *Rembrandts*.

False Cut – A cheating maneuver in which the deck of cards seemed to be cut, but the top cards remained unchanged.

Fast – Quick speed of playing.

Favorite – Any hand that has a statistical advantage over another player's hand to win that hand.

Fell – A card that appeared. For example, "A Queen fell on the turn means that a Queen appeared on the turn."

Felt – The general term for the cloth surface found on casino table games. Most casinos use the professional Suited Speed Cloth grade. See *Speed Cloth/Suited Speed Cloth*.

Fiche – See also *Cheque, Chip, Gratuity, Jeton, Mil,* and *Toke/Token*.

Fifth Street – 1. In Holdem and Omaha games, it is the river card, the fifth of five community cards. 2. In Seven-Card Stud games, it is the fifth card (third up card) dealt to a player. 3. In Mississippi Stud, it is the last community card to be dealt.

Fill – A chip rack or dealer's bank at the table in need of more cheques to look fuller and have more available to pay, make change, or to color up players. Management, security, or a chip runner brings these cheques out. See also, *Fill Order/Fill Slip*.

Fill Order/Fill Slip – A receipt for the transfer of cheques (a Fill) from the main cage to the table. Both the dealer and supervisor verify/sign off on this before dropping into the drop box. See also *Fill*.

Fill Up – Drawing cards to complete a Full House.

Fish – See *Pigeon*.

Fist Pump – A motion used to celebrate a bet that won.

Five Aces – A hand containing four natural Aces plus a fifth card (wild, or joker) that substitutes for a fifth Ace. Found mostly in DJ Wild and Pai Gow Poker. Often, this hand ranks higher than a *Royal Flush*.

Five of a Kind – Five cards of the same rank. Impossible in a standard 52-card deck unless another card substitutes, or a Joker is used as a wild card. Oftentimes, this hand ranks above a *Royal Flush*.

Flashed Card/Flashing – A card that is exposed, whether intentional or not.

Flea – (slang) A table-minimum bettor for an extended period of time.

Floor – Short for "floorman" or "floorperson." When a dealer or a player needs a floorman, "Floor on table ___" is shouted. See *Floorman*.

Floorman – An employee of the casino, usually in a supervisory or managerial role, who oversees the casino table games or a poker room. Responsibilities are numerous. A few of the most important to dealers are: dealer/table number assignment; dealer rotation/break schedule; opening and closing tables; listening to player disputes and issuing a ruling based on facts and the best interest of the game; and scheduling of dealers. In more serious situations, a floorman can call security when needed to de-escalate physical confrontation, or to have surveillance look at a video of a certain incidence of a hand or player's action, or when cheating is suspected. Also known as *Floor*, floorperson, floor manager, *Supervisor*, and *Table Inspector*.

Flop – The first set of community cards revealed by the dealer for everyone's use to make or complete a full poker hand. See *Turn/River*.

Flop a Set – When a community card on the flop matches a player's pocket Pair. See also *Set*, definition 1, and *Three of a Kind*.

Flush – Any five cards of the same suit.

Flush Draw – A four Flush needing one more of the same suit. See *Four Flush* and *Flush*.

Fold – The act of a player releasing/surrendering his hand to the dealer, no longer wishing to play that hand. Also known as *Drop*, *Drop Out*, definition 1, *Get Away*, *Lay Down*, muck, *Put Down*, pass (when facing a bet), surrender.

Fold Equity – The amount of money a player expects to gain as a result of another player folding.

Following Streaks – A betting strategy to "ride the wave" and keep betting the same number(s), because the thought is that if it won before, it would keep winning. Quotes of "An object in motion stays in motion" and "going with the flow" apply here.

For – A house designation that the original wager is included in the payout. For example, 15 for 1 means for every unit, the winning wager will receive fourteen more, for a total of 15. See also *To*.

Foreign Chip/Cheques – 1. Any cheque from another casino that does not belong to the current gaming establishment or casino. Foreign chips generally are not played in cash games due to gaming laws. Players can ask the cashier or floorman to properly exchange foreign chips for the current casino's equivalent cheques. 2. In tournaments, the introduction of foreign chips is the equivalent of cheating by a player trying to increase his stack of chips. Not only will the chips come out of play, but the player is also disqualified from the tournament, receives no refund of entry fees, can be banned from ever entering that casino or playing in another tournament, and may face criminal arrest, fines, and/or jail time.

Forward Motion – A rule or the act of a player pushing chips forward toward the center of the table is said to have bet those chips and is committed to that bet. Some card room rules require the actual release of the chips from the hand to be considered a bet/call/raise/all-in.

Foul – The setting of a Pai Gow Poker hand where the Low Hand outranks the High Hand and is not allowed.

Fouled Deck – Any discovery of two or more same-ranked cards and suits in a deck (i.e., two King of spades), or a deck with more than one different backing (i.e., red deck backing versus blue deck backing). This nullifies the current hand, and all bets must be returned to all players regardless of the progress of the hand. This deck must be corrected or switched to another deck before a new hand can be dealt.

Four Flush – An incomplete four card Flush. See *Flush*.

Four of a Kind – Four cards of the same rank. When announcing the A-A-A-A-3 hand, the correct way to say it is, "Four of a Kind Aces." Also known as *Quadruplets* and *Quads*.

Four to the Royal – A player who currently has any four of the five cards used to make a *Royal Flush*.

Four-Color Deck – Typically used in online poker, this deck features four distinct colors for the card suits: spades remain black, hearts remain red, diamonds are blue, and clubs are green. It aids online players and those with impaired vision in easily distinguishing between suits.

Fourth Street – 1. In Holdem and Omaha games, it is the turn card, the fourth of five community cards. 2. In Seven-Card Stud games, it is the fourth card (second up card) dealt to a player. 3. In Mississippi Stud, it is the second community card to be dealt.

Fox Hunting – The curious act of seeing just the next single card that would have been dealt (cards to come) if the hand had continued further. This is usually asked of the dealer when the hand is over. Similar to *Rabbit Hunting*.

Free Bet – A free wager given to players (in the form of a chip, voucher etc.) for players to bet without having to place any money (as in Match Play). Similar to *Match Play*. See also *Promotional Chips*.

Free Collection – A lammer placed on the rake drop handle to indicate to surveillance, the players at that table, and any other floorman that supervisory approval has directed the dealer that no rake is being collected for that hand or for the duration of that down.

Front of the House (FOH) – Any time an employee is in full or partial view of the guest. Opposite of *Back of the House*.

Full Barn – (slang) A Full House. See *Full House*.

Full Boat – (slang) A Full House. See *Full House*.

Full Buy – See *Maximum Buy-In*.

Full House – Three same-ranked cards plus two same-ranked cards (three of a kind plus a pair). When comparing two full-house hands, the player holding the higher three of a kind will win. If both three of a kinds are the same, then the player with the higher pair will win. Otherwise, this is a Tie. When announcing the 7-7-7-9-9 hand, the correct way to say it is, "Sevens full of nines."

Full Ring (Game) – A full cash game table. Opposite of *Short-Handed*.

Full Tub – (slang) A Full House. See *Full House*.

Gallery – Spectators who are not playing the game. Usually found on the rail.

Gamble – See *Gambling*.

Gambler – A person who participates in gambling. See *Gambling*.

Gambler's Fallacy – A belief that if a number is more dormant than statistically expected, its future is likely to be more active. Also known as *Monte Carlo Fallacy* or maturity of chances fallacy.

Gambling – The act of betting or wagering money, favors, rights, or anything else of value, with known or unknown unfavorable odds, with the hopes of winning or being right. In short, it requires a risk (taking a chance), with a certain amount (usually money), in the hopes of winning.

Game – A structured form of play undertaken by players to educate, have fun, or make money.

Game of Luck – A player's outcome in any game, heavily influenced by some randomized device, such as dice, a roulette wheel, playing cards, spinning tops, numbered balls, or RNGs.

Game of Luck/Game of Skill Debate – The ongoing discussion on whether gambling/poker playing is a game of luck or skill.

Game of Skill – A player's outcome in any game, as heavily influenced by expertise, adeptness, ability, and/or mastery.

Game Protection – The scrupulous watching of the game to ensure that players, other dealers, or equipment function doesn't cheat or do something dishonest that affects the integrity of the game. A few examples are: Verifying the cash brought to the table, accurate counting of cheques, counterfeit cash/cheques, proper payouts, collecting losing bets, paying winning bets, verifying fill orders, watching for stealing or cheating (such as dragging bets or dice switching/tampering), observing that all equipment functions properly, and much more. See also *Integrity*.

Game-Closing Card – An official document detailing the denomination amounts of cheques in a table's bank, completed by the closing supervisor and dealer. Also known as *Table Inventory Card*. See also *Rack Count*, definition 2.

Gaming Commission – Any of the different local, state, national, or tribal organizations that regulate, oversee, and enforce gaming laws within its jurisdiction. Their aim is to ensure the legality, fairness, and integrity of gaming establishments and to protect the interests of players and the public.

Gaming License – 1. The legal permit that a casino must obtain to own and operate a casino for profit. 2. The legal permit that employees must obtain to work or deal in a casino.

Gappers – Any unsuited hole cards in Holdem that are close in rank and could make a Straight with community cards but have one or more missing cards in between them, preventing them from being connectors. Examples: Jack of Spades and 9 of Clubs is a one gapper, 6 of Clubs and 3 of Hearts is a two gapper, and King of Diamonds and 9 of Clubs is a three gapper. See also *Connectors*.

Garbage Hand – A poor and often viewed upon losing hand. See also *Zip*.

George – (slang) A person who generously tips dealers and the casino staff well. Also known as *John*, definition 1. Opposite of *Stiff*, definition 1, and *Tom*.

Get Away – A player folding a strong hand against a perceived stronger hand. See also *Fold*.

Go All-In – To bet all of one's chips/cheques/money or any other wagered object. See *All-In*.

Go Bank – Players who assume the monetary role/risk/reward of being the banker of the house by paying the winning bets and collecting the losing bets out of their personal funds. They are essentially bank. Usually, the requirement is to be first on the signup list at the table and have sufficient funds to cover all player's wagers that win. Observing non-players may also share in this risk. Commonly offered in Baccarat and in Pai Gow Poker. See *Banker*, both definitions, and *Banque*.

Grand – 1. (slang) One thousand dollars. 2. Something magnificent, imposing, superb, or monumental. 3. Expressed as a "k" after a number, hence "three grand" can be written as 3k.

Gratuity – The gift of money as a tip or toke from a player to the dealer for winning a bet, providing good service, etc. See also *Cheque*, *Chip*, *Fiche*, *Hand-In*, *Jeton*, *Mil*, *Toke/Token*, and *Zuke*.

Graveyard – The overnight shift for workers. Also shortened to "Grave." See *Day* and *Swing*.

Gravy – (slang) A player's winnings.

Greek Bottom – A cheating method in which the dealer deals from the second card from the bottom. This is done so that if any player accidentally sees the bottom of the deck, he'll think that the dealer couldn't possibly have dealt from the bottom since the bottom card is still there. See also *Base Deal(ing)* and *Bottom Dealing*.

Green – 1. The standard green $25 cheque. 2. The color displayed on the Digital Display Board with a hand resulting in a Tie in Baccarat.

Grids – Also known as Baccarat roads or roadmap scorecards.

Griffin Book – See *Black Book*.

Grifter – A cheater or scammer. See *Cheater*.

Grind Down – A losing of player's money over time due to the mathematical house edge.

Grind Joint – Any casino advertising low betting limits on all of its table games. It is also the place where break-in dealers are often hired for their first dealing job to gain experience.

Grinder/Grinding – A player/his action to play conservatively over a long period of time with minimal risk and modest gains.

Guts – A player's bravery to bet, call, raise, go all-in, or make any large wager for most or all his chips on a suboptimal hand.

Gutshot – To draw to an inside Straight. A single "belly buster." See *Inside Straight (Draw)*.

Gutshot Straight – See *Inside Straight (Draw)*.

Hand – 1. The cards dealt to a specific player eligible to receive them. 2. The involvement of players, or their playing in a current pot. 3. The time between the dealer's first riffle to start a new round of card playing until the pot is pushed and just before a new riffle is started by the dealer. 4. The cards retained by a player. 5. The combination of cards for a player to win a pot.

Hand-In – A tip or gratuity handed to a dealer. See *Toke/Token*.

Handle – 1. The total amount of money wagered on a specific game. 2. The total gross revenue for a casino over a specific time period.

Hanger – When the bottom card of the dealer's deck sticks out beyond the others. Sometimes looked at to tell that a dealer is dealing off the bottom of the deck (cheating). Also known as *Base Deal(ing)*.

Heads-Up – 1. Only two players remain to contest/win a pot. 2. A type of poker tournament in which two players play against each other in a bracket-style, single elimination round. As players win, they play another player heads-up who has won his round of heads-up play. Play continues until there is one winner each round, culminating in a final round of the two players remaining in the tournament.

Head-to-Head – See *Heads-Up*.

Hearts ♥ – One of the four common suits in a deck of cards. Also known as valentine's day, all my hearts, heart breaker.

Heat – Any type of casino management attention (usually unwanted from the player) if the player is "too much" of a winner. This may lead to a player being told he can no longer play. See also *Back Off*.

Heater – A player's winning streak or run of good cards. See *Run*, definition 2.

Hedge – The act of placing two or more bets such that if one wins, the other loses. Players hedge/insure to lessen their risk.

Heeling – A specialized tilting of a chip/cheque stack so that chips are more exposed to viewing. A dealer will hold the entire stack of payout chips in his hand, drop one chip to the felt, and then balance the remaining chips on that chip's edge and the felt—almost to look like a woman's boot.

Help Card – A card that improves a player's hand.

Hero – During instructional or hand reviewing, it is the player whose hand is being reviewed or focused. Opposite of *Villain*.

Hidden Pair – Two cards of the same rank that no player can see because they are down cards, such as in Stud or Holdem.

High – 1. Cards or hands that rank on the upper or strongest, and usually most favorably. 2. In Pai Gow Poker, the highest 5-Card hand a player or dealer sets. See also *Low*.

High-Limit/High-Stakes Game – A special area or room in the casino that caters to high rollers, whales, or anyone who wants to wager larger amounts and often requires privacy to gamble. Table minimums and maximums are much larger, and sometimes even gaming rules can be amended to be more accommodating for the player upon request.

High Card Flush/I Love Suits – A Carnival Game variant focused exclusively on flushes.

High Pair – In Pai Gow Poker, any Pair of Jacks through Aces.

High Roller – A player who gambles with a large amount of money, usually found in a high-limit or high-stakes room. See also *Whale*.

High Society – The highest denomination of chips/cheques a casino or card room offers.

Hit and Run – The player's act of joining a poker cash game, winning one or more big pots, and leaving the game with the winnings shortly thereafter. This usually upsets other players as they figure they won't have another chance to win their money back from this player. However, the H&R player is acting well within the nature of cash game play—to play as short or as long as he likes. This term can also be used in any casino game or slot machine when a player starts playing, wins, cashes out, and leaves immediately, not allowing for the casino a chance to win that money back.

Hold – Percentage. The amount of the drop that the casino keeps for its operations.

Holdem – 1. The most common flop game. 2. The most popular poker game. Players receive two down cards and share five community cards to make their best poker hand from five of seven cards. 3. Several Carnival Games (Texas Hold'em Bonus Poker, Ultimate Texas Hold'em, and others) utilize the common Poker card game Texas Holdem community cards as the basis for playing, dealing, and reading hands.

Holdout Artist – A cheater who uses a holdout machine. See also *Jacob's Ladder* and *Vest Holdout*.

Holdout Machine – Any cheating device a player uses to hide certain card(s) only to reintroduce them later at a more opportune time. See *Jacob's Ladder* and *Vest Holdout*.

Hole Cards – A player's cards dealt face down that remain concealed in front of the player. See also *Down Card*.

Hollywood – 1. When a player acts, talks, or exaggerates in a way to encourage a reaction by another player. 2. When a player criticizes, overreacts, or takes too much time to decide on a hand when observed by others that the time-wasting show was unnecessary. Also known as Hollywooding.

Horse – A player who is financially backed by another to gamble and later split the profits as agreed.

Hot Deck – (slang) A deck that gives players several good winning/profitable hands. See also Hot Seat.

Hot Hands – Being dealt a series of high, good hands that win.

Hot Seat – (slang) A seat at a table that seems to win more often than other seats. Oftentimes, players will move to that seat once that seat becomes available.

Hot Streak – A series of good fortune or luck that enables a player to win more than average.

Hot Table – Any table where multiple players are winning repeatedly in a short time frame. Usually, their excitement and loud cheering draws the attention of other players.

House – 1. The casino, building establishment, poker room, or its owners/operators who offer gambling and/or poker. 2. The house's money in the form of gaming cheques in the cheque rack in front of a dealer. Also known as *Bank*.

House Edge – The mathematical advantage a casino has over the player in any given game or individual bet. This edge, expressed as a percentage, is what the casino can expect, on average, to make or keep in the long run. Casinos need every game they offer to favor the house to be profitable and to stay in business.

House Rules – Set of regulations by the casino/poker room governing conduct and normal customaries not required by any gaming rule.

House Way – 1. A casino's standard rules for dealers to follow to arrange (set) all possible poker hands. 2. The lammer "House Way" used when the dealer sets a player's hand in Pai Gow Poker.

Human Inspectors – Before video- and digital-recorded technologies, casinos had employees either on the floor or were watching behind one-way mirrors, on rafters and walkways above the ceiling, overlooking the gaming area. Many were former casino employees, retired employees, and yes, even cheaters themselves. They were there to watch for cheating from everyone on the floor. Also known as *Eye in the Sky*. See also *Security* and *Surveillance*.

Hustle – (slang) To encourage, persuade, beg, ask, or obtain something of someone else. Generally, with regards to casino tips/tokes, it is almost always frowned upon by casino management for a dealer to ask players to monetarily offer a gratuity at any time, most especially after a big win. See also *Rip and Tear*.

Image – How a player is perceived by other players. This can be an accurate or false perception that the one player demonstrates to all other players. Oftentimes a player remains one type of player, but on occasion, a player may temporarily or periodically take on a different persona.

Improve – To draw cards to make a better hand.

In – To remain or to stay in the hand/pot.

In a Row – 1. In a succession or line. 2. Any sequence or Straight.

In Action – The time during which a player plays his hand.

In the Hole – 1. The amount of money a player has lost (in the negative), either per session or during any other time period. 2. Hole cards. See *Hole Cards*.

Index – 1. The printed number or letter to signify the rank and suit of each card in a deck. 2. The edge marks a cheater puts on cards, also known as *Pegging*.

Indexing – See *Pegging*.

Inside Straight (Draw) – A hand that contains four of the five cards required for a Straight but is missing one of the three middle cards. Also known as single belly buster. See *Gutshot*.

Integrity – [Lat. *integritas* intact]. The quality of being honest and having strong moral principles. This is the single most important trait a casino employee can have. Casino gaming skills can be taught, but the desire, to be honest, comes from within each and every casino employee to run a fair and honest game while dealing. A scrupulous dealer is on the constant lookout for dishonest or unfair play. In every situation, a dealer should always "Do the right thing." See also *Game Protection*.

J, Jack – Any Jack. The lowest-ranking face card above a 10 but below a Queen. Also known as Jake, John, J-Boy, Knave, or Valet.

Jack Up – (slang) To Increase the bet. See *Raise*.

Jackpot – Any prize pool collected by a casino to reward a player or a group of players for achieving a certain promotional requirement while gambling.

Jacob's Ladder – Like the Kepplinger device, this is also an Old West, under-the-sleeve, cheating device to retract, hold, and extend certain value cards to help the cheater in any card game. This device was the forerunner of all long-sleeved card-hiding devices. Hence the phrase "Ace up the sleeve." See also *Ace Up the Sleeve* and *Vest Holdout*.

Jagging – See *Pegging*.

Jam – 1. A big bet, or an all-in by a player. 2. A pot raised by several players.

Jam (Up) – Table actions that slow the pace of the game considerably.

Jeton – [Fr.] A chip, token, or cheque. Also spelled Jetton. See also *Cheque, Chip, Fiche, Gratuity, Mil, Toke/Token,* and *Zuke*.

Jinx – A curse, bad luck.

Jog – An uneven deck that a cheater marked to show his accomplice where to cut the deck.

John – 1. (slang) See *George*. 2. The restroom, the toilets, or the WC (water closet).

Joker – An extra "wild," substitution, or trump card in a full deck of cards. Normally, two are found: a black/white version and a colorized one. This card is usually represented by a clown-like jester. Not every game employs its usage. When it is used, it most often has a very set, specific usage on how it can be played. Invented by Samuel Hart in the 1860s, who introduced it as a trump card for the Euchre card game. DJ Wild uses one Joker. Pai Gow Poker uses one joker used to complete a Straight, a Flush, a Straight Flush, or otherwise to represent an Ace. When used to complete a Flush, the Joker represents the highest value card not already part of the hand. Also known as mistigris.

Jonah – (slang) An unlucky player.

K, King – Any King. The highest-ranking face card above a Queen. Sometimes, it is the highest card if the Ace is low.

Kamikaze – A tilted player (or his action) who wildly bets or goes all-in, effectively throwing away much or all of his money on high-risk bets. This type of player has essentially given up. See *Steam*, and *Tilt*, both definitions.

Key Card – A card making/completing a player's hand or gives a player a draw to an improved hand.

Key Hand – In a playing session, whether cash or tournament, refers to a hand that is a turning point for the player, for better or worse. It is often said to be THE hand that starts the storytelling of how a player continued or even finished the rest of his poker playing for that day or the tournament.

Kibitzer – A cheering or commentating onlooker/spectator, usually from the rail. See *Railbird*.

Kick It – (slang) Another name for *Raise*.

Kicker – The highest unpaired "helping" card used in poker hands, such as Four of a Kind, Three of a Kind, Two Pair, One Pair, Or High Card to help determine the winning hand. For example, in Holdem, a player with A-Q beats a player with A-9 on a board showing A-A-K-8-3 because the Queen card "plays" or is used, and thus is a better kicker. A dealer might announce "Three of a Kind Aces, King Queen kicker" or "Three of a Kind Aces, Queen plays." Never underestimate the value of a kicker.

Killed Hand – Any mucked hand that the dealer puts into the muck pile or discard tray. These cards are now considered dead.

Knock – 1. To check. See *Check*, definition 1. 2. The action of a player tapping the table once or more to indicate a check action. 3. A variation of poker with elements of Gin Rummy. 4. The decline or refusal of a player to the dealer's right to cut the deck when offered during a home game.

Knot – (slang) A rolled-up wad of cash fastened by a rubber band.

Komodo Dragoned – A player's hand that lost to another hand that completed a Straight or Flush on any river card.

Lady – (rare) Pink £100 chip.

Lammer – 1. Any clear plastic, round disc (clear spacer) stored in chip trays that is used to separate full stacks of 20 chips/cheques for easier rack counting. Lammers are also used to separate bigger denominations when less than a full stack exists. Usually, green $25 cheques are separated by each $100. Black $100 cheques are separated by each $500. 2. Any of the other solid-colored discs a dealer uses to show everyone a certain table/player situation. Poker lammers: Big Blind, Small Blind, Absent, Reserved, (Deal) Out, Bomb Pot, Kill, Half-Kill, No Kill, Leg Up, Seat Change 1, Seat Change 2, All-In, Call, Third Man Walking, Open, No Player, Bounty, and Time (Bank). Craps lammers: Buy, Lay, On, Off, Buy Back, and Dealer Tokes. Blackjack or Carnival Games lammers: Ace-High, Banker, Player, Envy, Free Bet, House Way, Tie, Jackpot, Dealer Push 22, and Surrender. 3. Any numbered small, colored disc put onto the table by dealers and management to identify a marker or credit line. 4. A disc (usually oversized) with a printed value on it given to poker players for winning a satellite or other tournament to be used as a money waiver for another tournament. 5. A small, round disc used by dealers with an abacus way to track how many mixed game hands have been dealt/remaining for that mixed game. 6. Small, round discs with numbers on them signifying how much cash/cheques have been taken out by a chip runner to complete a fill order and replace the rack with proper and plentiful amounts to make change. These discs are placed next to the chip rack in full view of surveillance, floorman, chip runners, and the next dealer (if needed).

Last Call – The dealer's/supervisor's announcement to close the table after several more rounds.

Late Bets – Any bet—verbal, placed, or tossed—onto the layout that happens after the first card has been dealt. Normally, this bet is disallowed. Warnings should be issued to players who consistently place late bets. Alert the floor. Accepted late bets may be allowed with supervisor approval.

Lay Down – The act of a player folding his hand. See *Fold*.

Layout – The printed table felt with all the betting areas where a player can make wagers. Also known as *Betting Area*, and *Betting Stakes*, definition 1.

Leak – A player exposing one or more of his hole cards, sometimes unknowingly, divulging information to what he has. See *Exposed Cards* and *Flashed Card/Flashing*.

Let It Ride – 1. A player's choice to leave the previous winning bet and its winnings on the table for the next bet, rather than removing the winnings. 2. A Carnival Game variant focused on a player using his three cards with two community cards.

Lice and Mites – A poker hand consisting of twos and threes, either as Two Pairs or as a Full House.

Lid – 1. The top card of the deck. Sometimes, a burn card. 2. The cover for a Baccarat discard can.

Limit – The house-posted minimum/maximum amounts that a player may wager on a bet.

Liner – Any face card, because a line can be seen around the border of the image.

Little Cat – (rare) A five card hand ranking from 3 to 8 (or 9) with no Pair. Also known as little tiger.

Little Dog – (rare) A five card hand ranking from 2 to 7 with no Pair.

Live – 1. A physical B&M casino where people go to gamble. 2. Working bets that are at risk of winning or losing. See also *At Risk* and *Working Bet*.

Live Card(s) – 1. The current, active hand a player is trying to improve by getting/catching the right card(s) to win. 2. Any card still in play is considered live, as opposed to dead cards/dead hand.

Live Hand – See *Live Card(s)*, definition 1.

Live One – (slang) A pigeon. See *Pigeon*.

Lock – A bet or hand regarded as a guaranteed win for the player.

Lock It Up – 1. A directive to put all loose cheques into the house bank (or a dealer's working stack) because no one claims it, or it now belongs to the house. 2. (rare) No more bets. See *No More Bets*.

Lock Up – An object (clear spacer, chip, player's card, or some other type of marker) placed on the table to hold a seat for a player. See also *Reserved*.

Long Odds – A low probability that something that a player will win. Also called long shot.

Loose – A player who plays more than average.

Loss – The negative difference between a player's buy-in versus his cash out. Opposite of *Profit*.

Low – 1. Cards or hands that rank on the lower or weakest, and usually most unfavorably. 2. In Pai Gow Poker, the 2nd highest 2-Card hand a player/dealer sets after the High hand. See also *High*.

Low Card – The lowest card by rank and suit if needed.

Low Pair – In Pai Gow Poker, any Pair of twos through sixes.

Low-Limit/Low-Stakes Game – Any game during which low amounts of money are wagered.

Luck – Success (good luck) or failure (bad luck) brought on by chance rather than by one's own action, skill, or strategy. See *Lucky*, definition 1.

Lucky – 1. The act of having luck alter the course of a player winning or losing the hand. See *Luck*. 2. A player who has good fortune.

Lump/Lumpy – 1. A table that has noticeable imperfections such as uneven boards or foam under the felt, making a dealer's sliding of cheques across them more difficult and cause them to topple but does not affect the outcome of rolled numbers. 2. (slang) A dealer (often an inexperienced one) who has a difficult time managing heavy or complex betting action or payouts. See also *Break-In Dealer*.

Made Hand – Refers to a hand's value (such as a pocket Pair or higher) that is already superior to any high-card hand that needs to improve to win.

Make – (obsolete) To shuffle the deck. See *Shuffle*.

Make a Move – A player who takes action, places a bet, or makes a strategic gambling decision.

Making a Hand – Any hand that improved and has a better chance of winning.

Mark – A term applied to an inexperienced player (sucker) at the table who attracts attention due to his inexperience or lack of skill. Seasoned players often go after this type of player, thinking they can easily win money from them. Also known as *Donkey*, spot, and *Sucker*. See also *Pigeon*.

Marked Cards – 1. Any card that has any noticeable extra imprint or blemish of any kind (bend, fold, tear, fray, ink issues, wear and tear, stain, etc.) when compared to a card from the same manufacturer's new and unused deck. 2. Cards that have been illegally tampered with and purposely marked for a player's advantage. All marked cards should be brought to a floorman's attention, replaced, and not used again.

Marker – See *Casino Credit*.

Marry(ing) – Combining sections of cards from multiple deck piles to form a new pile to hand shuffle.

Martingale System – A progressive betting system in which the bettor doubles his wager every time the bet loses until he wins the bet. One win erases all previous losses. To prevent a full, unlimited execution of this strategy, casinos almost always have a table maximum wager posted. See also *Reverse Martingale System*.

Match Play – A free bonus bet (often given in the form of a ticket, voucher, or promotional chip to reward repeat players) a player can use to make a bigger wager by putting up usually only half the total bet. For example, if the match play is for $15, the player would need to wager $15 of his own money alongside the match play for a total bet of $30. If the bet wins, the bet would be paid $30, and the dealer would remove the match play instrument. Should the bet lose, the player would only lose his $15 wager plus the match play instrument. Restrictions apply. Similar to *Free Play*. See also *Promotional Chips*.

Maxi Baccarat – See *Big Baccarat*.

Mechanic – A cheating dealer who manipulates the deck or any casino equipment for his own or another player's advantage. Some examples are: False, incomplete, or shoddy shuffling; palming cards; dealing from any other location of the deck (such as a second card from the top or the bottom of the deck); creating a stacked deck; or any other unfair, unethical, nonstandard shuffle or dealing practice. See also *Artist*, and *Grifter*.

Meet – To call. See *Call*.

Middle Pair – 1. In Holdem, any of the middle-ranked Pairs that a player is dealt. Pair of eights through Pair of Jacks are examples. 2. In a flop game, a card in a player's hand that pairs with the middle-ranked card on the community board. 3. In Pai Gow Poker, any Pair of sevens through tens.

Middles Dealer – 1. A cheating dealer who deals cards from the middle of the deck. 2. A mechanic skilled in middles. See also *Cheat*, definition 1 and *Mechanic*.

Midi Baccarat – Baccarat played on a smaller semi-circular table than the Big Baccarat table and the player with the highest bet (on Banker or Player) has the privilege to handle the cards that match his bet. Generally, this table seats up to nine players. Banker wins may or may not impose a 5% commission. See also *Mini Baccarat* and *Big Baccarat*.

Mil – A large gratuity. See also *Cheque*, *Chip*, *Gratuity*, *Jeton*, *Toke/Token*, and *Zuke*.

Mini Baccarat – Baccarat played on a smaller, semi-circular table than the Big Baccarat table and the dealer handles all the cards. Generally, this table seats seven players, at most. Banker wins may or may not require a 5% commission to be paid. See also *Midi Baccarat* and *Big Baccarat*.

Mini-Fan – Some casinos provide a cooling fan on the table for the dealer. No longer common.

Miracle Card – One of a few rare cards that improves a player's hand from an almost sure losing hand to a winning hand.

Misdeal – Any hand dealt incorrectly, cannot be corrected, and requires the dealer to collect all cards, shuffle again, and re-deal. There are many reasons for a misdeal.

Miss – A player's hand that fails to improve after the final card is dealt.

Mississippi Stud – A Carnival Game variant focused on a player using his two cards with three community cards.

Mites and Lice – See *Lice and Mites*.

Modulo 10 – The modulo operation, often written as "mod," finds the remainder after the division of one number by another. When performing modulo 10, find the remainder after a number is divided by 10. For example, Baccarat games will only use the far digit on the right, the one's column. For example, if a hand contains a 7 and 8 ranked cards, it totals 15. Modulo 10 would divide it by 10 (1.5) and use the remainder and not the whole number, in this case, the number 5 for the hand total.

Money Plays – Refers to games where cash is accepted as part of a player's table stake and counts toward their wager. However, many casinos now prohibit this practice, requiring players to convert all cash into chips/cheques before play. This change reduces the risk of miscounting cash bundles, ensures accurate betting amounts, and helps prevent money laundering and misconduct. See also *Cash Plays/Cash Does Not Play*.

Monkey –1. (slang) Any face- or ten-value card. 2. Derived from an Asian legend where players reportedly mispronounced "monarchy" as "monkey," associating it with Kings, Queens, or any ten-value cards, leading to the term's adoption. See *Face Cards*.

Monotone Board – When the first three, four, or all five community cards are of one suit.

Monster – Anything big, such as a big bet, winning streak, chip/cheque stack, or win.

Monte Carlo Fallacy – See *Gambler's Fallacy*. Also known as maturity of chances fallacy.

Move-In – See *All-In*.

9, Nine – Any nine. The ranking numbered card above an eight but below a ten.

Nailing – Marks made by a cheater to the edge of cards to tell the cheater what cards other players have in later rounds of play. See *Peg*.

Natural – A hand without wild cards. In Baccarat, this refers to a hand totaling 8 or 9 with the first two cards dealt. In Pai Gow, it describes a hand formed without the use of a Joker.

New Game – The period of time allowed for players to bet and all previous hands have been settled. The dealer may announce "Place Your Bets." See also *Closed Game*, *No More Bets* and *Place Your Bets*.

Nice Catch –1. (slang) A phrase said in sincerity, praising the player's luck of getting the card(s) he had hoped to win the hand. 2. A phrase said sarcastically, shaming the other player's luck for getting the card(s) needed to win over an otherwise losing hand that perhaps "should" have lost.

Nickel – 1. (slang) Five dollars, usually denominated by a red casino cheque with $5 imprinted on it. 2. (vague) In higher stakes games, it can mean a $500 or $5000 cheque.

Nickel-Dime – Any small-stakes game.

Nits and Lice – 1. A Full House consisting of twos and threes. 2. A game in which twos and/or threes are wild cards.

No More Bets – A callout by the dealer that betting is closed, and players can no longer wager or place any bets. Opposite of *Place Your Bets*. See also *Closed Game* and *New Game*.

Non-Progressive Betting System – Any betting strategy based on maintaining the same or similar betting units from one bet to the next round of bets. Opposite of *Progressive Betting System*.

Nosebleed – Ultra high-stakes games during which players losing and winning a few million U.S. dollars is not a big deal.

Nucleus Players – (uncommon) Regular, dependable, and often local players who frequently play at the same location and/or game. See *Reg (Regular)*.

Nursing – To play conservatively when a player has been losing chips and has few chips left.

Nut – 1. A label given to a player to describe him or his playing as crazy, daring, or unorthodox. 2. Winnings a professional player needs to sustain his playing or profession. See also *Bankroll*. 3. The general cost/overhead of running and keeping a casino operational.

Nut Flush – The best possible flush available for the current hand.

Nut Flush Draw – A hand that has four cards of the same suit needs a fifth card of that same suit to make the best possible Flush.

Nut Low – The best possible low hand using the lowest-ranked cards. Opposite of *Nut*.

Nut Nut – A hand that is already the nuts, but still has a chance to improve to an even better hand.

Nuts – 1. An unbeatable hand. 2. The best possible hand at any given point during play. This ranking may change as additional cards are dealt. The term can also be used as "second nuts" or "third nuts" meaning second- or third-best hand, respectively. According to folklore, the term originated in the Old West when players would bet the nuts from their wagon wheels as collateral. This wager symbolized confidence in holding the strongest hand, as losing meant the player couldn't flee without repaying their debts. The phrase "stone cold nuts" emphasizes absolute certainty in having the best hand. These games were often played in the winter when the wagons were full of the fall harvest and during cold weather. Hence the expanded phrase, "stone cold nuts." Also known as World's Fair, cinch hand, immortal, iron duke, iron-clad hand, and lock.

Odds – The probability of a particular outcome (winning, losing, or tying).

Odds Against – The number of failures per success. For example, if the odds against a player are four to one, the player expects to lose/fail four times for every successful/winning outcome.

Odds For – The number of successes per failure. For example, if the odds for a player are two to one, the player expects to win twice as much for every losing outcome.

Offsetting Chips – The dealer practice of combining like-colored chips/cheques on a winning number/bet and then slightly grouping each color by five chips/cheques in a way that visually, can be counted quickly and accurately.

Off-Suit – Cards of different suits, or suits that do not match the desired suit.

On a Draw – A weak hand (or the player holding it) that hopes to catch one or more cards to improve to something far better. See also *Straight Draw* and *Flush Draw*.

On Call – Type of employment for which the dealer is not a full-time or part-time employee with a set schedule. At times, he may receive no scheduled hours to work for a week or two. Generally, these dealers are extra dealers the casino likes to keep on the active roster and, since they're already hired with a valid gaming license to that venue, these dealers can be called upon at the last minute to fill in for any staffing shortages. Also known as *Extra Board*.

On Tilt – A player's subpar, aggressive, and sometimes angry playing due to being emotionally upset. Also known as *Steam*. See *Tilt*.

One Pair – Two same-ranked cards.

One-End – In contrast to an open-ended straight, this refers to four consecutive cards that can only complete a Straight on one end. For example, a hand of A-K-Q-J requires a Ten to complete the Straight, while a hand of A-2-3-4 only needs a Five.

One-Gapper – See *Gappers*.

One-Outer – A losing hand that wins by drawing the remaining card in the deck that improves it to the best hand.

Open at Both Ends – See *Open End(ed)*.

Open Card – A card that is dealt face up.

Open End(ed) – Four consecutive cards to a Straight that can be completed on either end. For example, a player holding 5-6-7-8 is open-ended, as drawing either a 4 or a 9 completes the Straight.

Open Game – A game currently available to anyone who wants to play. Opposite of *Closed Game*.

Open Spot – A section of the table that is available to anyone who wants to play.

Open-Ended Straight Draw – A hand that hopes to draw one of the cards to complete a four-card open-ended Straight. See *Open End(ed)*.

Open-Ended Straight Flush Draw – A hand that hopes to draw one of the two cards to complete a four-card open-ended Straight Flush. See *Open End(ed)*.

Order for Credit – The supervisor request for the removal of one or more large denomination cheques from a table's cheque rack. The credit slip is similar to the Fill Order/Fill slip but states Credit instead of Fill. Instead of security bringing cheques to fill the bank, they arrive to remove the extra or high-value cheques that are not standardly kept on that particular table.

Out of Line – Out of order, rule breaking, or inappropriate behavior.

Outdraw – The good fortune of a player being dealt a card to make his previously inferior hand now better than his opponent's hand.

Outkicked – A hand that has a weaker kicker than the opponent holding a stronger hand. See also *Kicker*.

Outs – Any card(s) left in a deck that will improve a player's hand into a probable winning hand.

Outside-L Bet – A combination bet containing two splits and a corner. Pays 42.

Over – 1. A card value/rank that is higher than the one being compared. 2. Used when describing a Two-Pair hand, announced as the higher Pair "over" the lower Pair. (for example, "Two Pair, Kings over sevens.") 3. A lammer used to identify each remaining player who agreed to temporarily alter the betting from a structured fixed limit poker game to a higher fixed limit or even to an unstructured no-limit game during, and for the remainder of, that hand only.

Overcards – 1. Any card in a flop game in which one or more community cards ranks higher than a player's Pair. See also *Over*, definition 1. 2. As a pair in a flop game, a player holding a pocket Pair higher than any card rank on the community board. Also known as *Overpair*.

Overpair – Opposite of *Underpair*. See *Overcards*, definition 2.

Paddle – A flat, wide acrylic tool with a handle on it used to plunge currency and fill slips into the drop box below it.

Paint Cards/Paints – See *Face Card*.

Pai Gow Poker – A Carnival Game variant focused on players and the dealer separating their initial seven cards into the best 5-card High hand and the best 2-card Low Hand.

Pair – Two cards of the same rank, such as two nines (9-9) or two sevens (7-7).

Pair Plus – Optional bonus bet based solely on the strength of the player's three card hand. Any Pair or higher wins. Depending on house rule, a player may/may not be required to place an Ante bet hoping to achieve a qualifying hand of a Pair or better. Found primarily in *Three Card Poker*.

Paper Scorecards – Long, heavy cardstock paper displaying rows of empty squares where Baccarat players write on with the Red/Blue pen (also supplied) to track, by hand, the current game's result.

Parlay – 1. A progressive betting system wherein a player reinvests his winnings to his original bet for his next bet. See also *Let It Ride*, definition 1. 2. In sports betting, a group of individual bets to make one overall bet. If any part of the bet loses, the entire bet loses.

Past Posting – Any illegal bet that occurs when a player places chips/cheques on any winning betting spot on the layout any time after the dealer announces that the current game's bets are closed. Unlike capping a bet where a bet already exists, past posting simply makes any and all illegal late bets a winner. A supervisor should be informed anytime this happens. See also *Capping* and *Pinching*.

Pat – See *Check*, definition 1 and *Stand Pat*.

Payoff – A winning bet's payout. See *Payout*.

Payout – A winning bet's payment by the dealer. If a mistake is made, it should be promptly corrected.

Peg – Marks made by a cheater to cards to tell the cheater what cards other players have. Also known as punch or blister. See also *Pegging*.

Pegging – Any act by a card cheat to mark one or more cards using an object or his fingernail. Also known as *Blistering*, *Cosmetics*, daubing, *End Strippers*, *Indexing*, *Jagging*, *Pricking*, and *Punctuating*.

Penalty – A form of punishment for players who violate rules or engage in unfair, unsafe, or unprofessional behavior. Staff may issue warnings to address illegal, inappropriate, or disruptive conduct. Depending on the severity, penalties can range from verbal warnings and timed suspensions from the table to removal from play, bans from the casino, or, in extreme cases, civil or criminal penalties, including arrest. In severe cases, a player may be *Blacklisted*. See *Warning*.

Pencil/Pencil Person – A supervisor or manager responsible for scheduling dealers and supervisors to their table or string of tables on the casino floor. A short list includes opening/closing tables, working the EO list, and sending employees on a break or home for the shift. See also *Roadmap*.

Penny – (uncommon slang) A one-dollar cheque. See *Dollar*, definition 1.

Penny Ante – A very low-stakes game.

Picking – The act of using a thumb, index, and middle finger to remove one to five cheques from the top of a working stack without looking at the cheques or hands.

Picture Cards – Any face card: King, Queen, or Jack. Also known as *Court Card* or *Face Card*.

Pigeon – (derogatory, slang) Name-calling a player this term infers this player is inexperienced or foolish and may not fully understand the game. In poker, more experienced players target these types of players as easy money. Also known as *Donk*, *Donkey*, *Fish*, *Live One*, provider, and *Sausage*.

Pinching – A sleight-of-hand cheating technique used when a pincher/player swiftly and discreetly removes chip(s) from a losing bet after the outcome of a hand has been determined. The player hopes to reduce losses thinking the dealer is not looking and doesn't think surveillance won't catch this either. See *Cheat*, *Cheater*, *Dragging* and *Past Posting*.

Pips – 1. The dots on each die's side when tallied indicate that side's number. Hence four dots on a side is four pips and is the number four. A dice roll is always the sum of the top pips on both dice. 2. The spots or marks on a card, normally Aces up through tens. A 3 of Hearts will have three hearts in the middle of the card, while a 9 of Clubs will have nine clubs in the center of the card. Getting pipped is when another player's number of pips on a card beats a player's own number of pips.

Pit – One of several restricted areas on the casino floor inside a double row of gaming tables and its dealers facing out. Only casino employees are allowed in this area.

Pitch(ing) – The act of a dealer delivering cards either face up or face down one at a time to each player in the hand. See *Deal*, definition 1 (a).

Place Your Bets – A dealer's verbal invitation to all players at the table that betting is open, and players may begin wagering and posting/placing their bets on the layout. Opposite of *No More Bets*. See also *Closed Game* and *New Game*.

Plaque – Rectangular gaming plaques are often used for high-value chip or cheque denominations. They substitute for their much smaller, round chip or cheque counterpart. See also *Chip* or *Cheque*.

Play – The wager a player makes after deciding to go ahead and engage (play) the hand to compete against the dealer's hand.

Play it or Drop it – A player verbally offering a choice to the dealers what they'd like to do with the toke currently being given. Dealers can either play (and gamble) the toke to hopefully win more and risk losing it altogether, or they can drop it into the toke box face value without risk. Some casinos have strict rules that if a dealer is offered a choice, they must drop the toke into the toke box.

Play(ing) the Board – Any flop or poker-related game during which a player uses all five of the community cards as his best five-card poker hand.

Played Card – A card that has left a player's hand, whether it has been turned up or mucked face down.

Player – In Baccarat, the first hand to receive and usually to reveal the cards. A player will bet this bet if he thinks the Player's card total will be higher than the Banker's card total. Any tie with the Banker hand results in a push for this bet. This bet pays 1:1. See also *Banker*, definition 1.

Player's Card – Most every casino has a player's card/rewards program providing benefits for playing at that casino. These cards track all gaming activity, including which machine, table game, or poker game is played; dates, times, length of play; and wager amounts. Players can earn points, comps, free play, free parking, free food, free drinks, free or discounted hotel rooms, or travel consideration to other properties owned by the same company. Higher tier status levels earned from playing more earns players greater benefits or perks. Points and tier levels usually reset to zero at the end of a 6- or 12-month period.

Playover Box – A clear plastic box used to cover an absent player's chip stack. This may allow another temporary player to play in that seat until the absent player returns, and the box protects and separates the absent player's stack from the temporary player's stack.

Playing Blind – See *Blind*, definition 2.

Plucking – A professional (and eye-appealing) method to remove single cheques quickly from the rack. A dealer pinches, plucks, and snaps the chips/cheques from the rack into his fingers and thumb.

Pocket – The down or hole cards a player has that no one else is entitled to see. Frequently used in conjunction with Pairs. For example, Aces in the hole signify that the player has Pocket Rockets or Pocket Aces. See *Pocket Pair*.

Pocket Pair – Any two cards of the same rank, such as two Jacks, as a player's hole cards in Holdem.

Poker – Any of the card games that have its early ancient roots in Spain, France, Italy, or Germany and have been described in literature since at least 1526. It is a game that uses some, all, or even more than one standard 52-card playing deck (with or without Jokers). Players use strategy, deception, memory, and bully tactics to win money from other players. Players make wagers over which hand is best according to the hand ranking and other rules of the game being played. It is said to be a game of incomplete information because players would often play better/differently if they knew what cards other players were holding. There are well over 100 different poker games that have been invented. Poker is often used as a basic structure in many of the Carnival Games.

Poker Face – A person's face that shows no emotion or change in expression when a new situation, (card, betting action, table talk, etc.) is presented. Also known as *Zombie*.

Poker Game – 1. Any of the more than 100 different types of poker games people can play. 2. Any place, public or private, where players gather to play one or more types of poker.

Poker Room – The public or private space where games of poker are played. This space can be a standalone poker room (commonly called a card room), a room or designated area on a casino floor, or any private area, home, or elsewhere a game takes place.

Poker Rules – A standard list of explicit or understood regulations or principles governing poker game play, and players' responsibilities and conduct. Most poker rooms post some kind of rules list somewhere and it is made available to players who ask to see it.

Pony – (rare) Black £25 chip.

Position – Where a player is seated in relation to the dealer, the dealer button, and/or other players.

Post – To place a bet. See *Place Your Bets*.

Post-Mortem – The discussion or analysis of a hand(s). spin, dice roll, or game after it is over.

Pre-Flop – Any action, betting, or situation that occurs before the flop in a flop game such as Holdem or Omaha.

Premium Hands – The best hands a player can start with or be dealt. For example, Pocket Kings for games requiring 2 cards, or a 7-Card Straight Flush in Pai Gow Poker.

Press – To increase/raise the bet from a previous bet size. The primary reason is to take advantage of any favorable situation such as a "hot" table, to recover from previous losses, or for excitement.

Pressure – To double any bet, usually after it had just won. See also *Parlay*, definition 1, and *Press*.

Pricking – See *Pegging*.

Private Poker – A poker game that is not generally made available to the public and is often by invitation only to a select group of players. Home games are one example. Opposite *Public Poker*.

Probability – The likelihood of a player's bet or hand to win or lose.

Profit – The positive difference between a player's buy-in versus his cash out. Opposite of *Loss*.

Progressive Betting System – Any betting strategy based on gradually increasing (or decreasing) the initial betting unit from one bet to the next bet. Opposite of *Non-Progressive Betting System*.

Promotional Chips – Free chips given to players to wager as a bet and win real money in its place. Payouts and use differ with each casino. See also *Free Bet*.

Prop – Short for "proposition player." A player paid by the house but uses his own money to help start and maintain casino games, so that the tables look full. See also *Pumper*, *Ringer*, and *Shill*.

Prop (Proposing) Bets – Side bets made between/among players that do not affect the outcome of the hand being played. See also *Last Longer*.

Proposition Player – See *Prop*.

Protection – Also known as *Game Protection*. See *Integrity*.

Prove – A dealer's act of verifying an accurate count of chips/cheques for himself, the player, any member of management, and surveillance before making an exchange for money or cheques, or to pay the player a winning bet. See also *Run it Down*.

Pumper – A player, often employed by the casino, who places large bets to create an illusion of big betting action on the table with the goal of attracting players. Casinos use this method to create excitement and get people to bet on an otherwise slow or dead table. See also *Prop* and *Shill*.

Punctuating – See *Pegging*.

Punter – (slang) A British and Australian term for bettor or gambler, especially in horse racing.

Purple – The lavender-colored $500 cheques. Also known as lavender.

Purse – The total prize pool in a tournament that goes to the players.

Push – 1. In Poker, the act of a dealer awarding and physically moving the cheques to the winning player(s) at the end of each game. 2. Dealer term for the time or the act to rotate to another or next table. Short for "pushing the line." 3. A tie, or an equal outcome. See *Tie*.

Push(ing) Chip Stacks – The process of a dealer skillfully sliding multi-columned cheques (usually one-handed) to a player.

Put Down – See *Fold*.

Q, Queen – Any Queen. The second highest ranking face card, above a Jack but below a King.

Quadruplets – (slang) Four of a Kind. See *Four of a Kind*.

Quads – (slang) Four of a Kind. Short for "quadruplets."

Qualifier – 1. In Carnival Games, a requirement a dealer's hand must meet to be eligible to play against the players. 2. In Poker, a requirement a hand must meet to be eligible to win a certain pot. For example, a hand "eight or better" needs all cards that are eight or lower to qualify.

Quarter – (slang) Twenty-five dollars ($25), usually a green casino cheque. See also *Greens* and *Pony*.

Quint – (slang) A *Straight Flush*.

Quint Major – (slang) A *Royal Flush*.

Quitting Time – A curfew. Usually, a previously agreed-upon time to end a gambling game/session.

Rabbit Hunting – The curious act of seeing all the next cards that would have been dealt (cards to come) if the hand had continued further. This is usually asked of the dealer when the hand is over. Similar to *Fox Hunting*.

Racetrack – The wooden/granite or other hard surface that surrounds the casino table's edge outside the felt but just inside the table rail/armrest.

Rack – Located in front of a dealer, it is the cheque holder installed into the table to store cheques, lammers, and any other items needed to organize and run a casino table game. If racks store cheques overnight, they have locking covers.

Rack Count – 1. The periodic act of verifying the cheques in the table rack. 2. The table closing counting of cheques of each denomination by management to report on the *Game-Closing Card*.

Radio Frequency ID (RFID) – Chips/Cheques of higher denominations may have an embedded computer chip or be stamped with a blue-light marking known as RFID. Chips/Cheques marked in this way allow the casino to track them, providing an extra level of security.

Ragged – A community board in Holdem that doesn't seem to help any player.

Rags – 1. Any hand dealt to a player that is considered bad, very low quality, unplayable from a large consensus of skilled players, who can agree players should fold these hands and not play them. Holdem pocket cards examples are: J-3, 9-4, 7-2. 2. Can also be used singularly, rag, such as Ace-rag for hands like A-3, A-6, when a poker player pairing an Ace could present kicker problems.

Rail – 1. A barrier of some sort to keep *Railbirds* at a safe yet observing distance from the players at the table. 2. The soft outer perimeter of the table where players can rest their arms and elbows.

Railbird – Non-players who watch casino or poker game(s) from the rail. They may cheer one or more players, or they may scope out a game as part of game and/or table selection. See *Kibitzer*.

Rainbow – In Holdem or Omaha, when either: 1. The flop contains three different suits, meaning a Flush cannot be completed on the turn card. Also known as rainbow flop. 2. The five-card community board contains no more than two cards of the same suit, meaning no Flush is possible.

Raise – To increase the bet, implying a call plus an added amount of at least the previous single bet.

Raise Blind – See *Blind Raise*.

Random Number Generator (RNG) – This component of the computer processing unit (CPU) produces randomness and fairness in a required number or sequence of numbers. See also *Computer Processing Unit (CPU)*.

Rank – 1. The numerical or lettered face card value from High to Low. 2. The 10 poker hands hierarchy from Royal Flush to High Card.

Rap – (slang) When a player knocks the top of the table to indicate a Check. See *Check*, definition 2.

Reading – The analysis of a dealer or anyone stating the value of a player's hand at showdown, which may or may not be correct or binding. See also *Cards Speak*.

Re-Buy – A player adding money to increase/replenish the cheques he has available to play.

Red – 1. The color associated with the Banker in Baccarat. 2. The common $5 cheque used in casinos.

Red/Blue Pen – In Baccarat, a double-ended pen comprising red ink on one end and blue ink on the opposite end allowing players to track, by hand, the current game's results on paper scorecards. Red marks Banker wins. Blue marks Player wins. See also *Scorecards*.

Re-Deal – A new deal that takes place after a misdeal nullifies the previous hand. See also *Misdeal*.

Re-Draw – Extra outs that allow for a hand (such as a made Straight) to draw to a bigger hand (Flush or Straight Flush).

Reg (Regular) – A player found at the tables fairly often, either daily or several times weekly. This can be either a professional or a recreational player or any player in between. See *Nucleus Players*.

Reserved – A table restricted to certain players, such as close friends, and not open to the public. Opposite of *Open Game*.

Response Call – Same as Approval Call. See *Approval Call*.

Reverse Martingale System – A modified progressive Martingale betting system that differs as the player doubles (or increases somewhat) the bet amount after each win and decreases the bet amount after each loss to the table minimum. This popular system looks to extend winning streaks by adding the player's current winnings to the next bet until he loses. See also *Martingale System*.

Ribbon Clerk – A low-stakes or small-scale gambler.

Riffle – One of the repeated steps to mix the cards professionally in a dealer's hand. See *Shuffle*.

Ringer – A player who is brought in to play at a higher "skill" level than the other players (such as at a poker game) with an "unfair advantage." Wise players will know if they are outmatched and will simply not play against such a person. See also *Prop* and *Shill*.

Rip and Tear – The overly enthusiastic and aggressive way dealers hustle tips. This is severely frowned upon by management. See also *Hustle*.

Rivered – (slang) To obtain the last card on a flop game to beat an opponent's hand. Example, "Joe caught a Seven of Clubs on the river to make a Full House and rivered Bill's Straight."

RNG – See *Random Number Generator (RNG)*. See also *CPU*.

Roadmap – A detailed daily or shift itinerary for dealers, specifying their table assignments, break periods, and other critical tasks for their shift. This structured plan ensures the casino runs smoothly and efficiently, with dealers clearly understanding their duties and locations.

Robusto – A player who has increased his chip stack or bankroll by winning a lot.

ROI – Acronym for "Return on Investment." See *Return on Investment (ROI)*.

Rotation – 1. Clockwise movement of the deal. 2. The counterclockwise movement in the direction of payouts.

Rounders – 1. Poker players who hustle and play for a living in a lot of poker games. 2. The name of a popular poker movie starring Matt Damon and Ed Norton as a pair of rounders, aptly titled.

Royal Flush – A one-suited Ace-High Straight. A-K-Q-J-T all the same suit. The best high hand in poker. Also known as *Quint Major*.

Run – 1. See *Straight*. 2. Several successful winning hands in a short time period. Also known as, *Heater*, *Running Good*, *Rush*, and *Winning Streak*.

Run it Down – To verify or prove a column of chips by separating them into smaller, easier-to-count, piles of 4 or 5 chips each. Also known as *Prove*.

Runner-Runner – See *Backdoor*.

Running Bad – A consistently losing player or losing streak. Opposite of *Running Good*.

Running Good – A consistently winning player or winning streak. Opposite of *Running Bad*.

Running Pair – The appearance of the last two cards on a community board to be a Pair.

Rush – See *Run*, definition 2.

6 Card Bonus – The side bet in certain Carnival Games that pays out after combining the player's cards with specific dealer's cards to achieve a six-card winning card combination.

6, Six – Any six. The ranking numbered card above a five but below a seven.

7, Seven – Any seven. The ranking numbered card above a six but below an eight.

Sausage – (slang) A player who plays substandard, often making poor and costly decisions. See *Pigeon*.

Scared Money – Any amount of money that a player cannot afford to lose.

Scorecards – Long, thick strips of paper used by Baccarat players to keep track of the current game's results when there is no digital display board to store this information electronically. Players are also normally supplied with a double-ended red/blue pen. Blue circles on the scorecards represent Player wins, while red circles represent Banker wins. See also *Digital Display Board* and *Red/Blue Pen*.

Scramble – The process of a dealer spreading the deck(s) face down on the felt and mixing the cards in a two-handed circular motion to ensure randomness, either after verifying both sides of a new setup or between dealing hands before the next shuffle. During this process, the dealer should check for boxed cards that flipped over and for damaged cards to replace. Also known as *Wash*.

Second Pair – Pairing the second-highest card in a flop game's community board with the same-ranked card in a player's hand.

Security – Team of trained individuals who protect the casino's money, property, staff, and patrons from violent crime, theft, cheating, inappropriate behavior, and trespassers. Escorts people off the premises and can detain people who have committed a crime until police arrive. Also oversees the count team while on the floor collecting money from the table drop boxes and slot machines. Bring fill orders to tables.

See – (slang) To call. See *Call*.

Sequence – Consecutively ranked cards, as found in a *Straight*. For example, 9-T-J-Q-K.

Session – Any time period a player gambles/plays poker in a casino.

Set – 1. (slang) Three of a Kind. In Holdem and Omaha, refers to a Three of a Kind hand with the player holding a pocket Pair of the three cards matching a third card on the community board. See also *Trips*. 2. The way a player organizes a hand. 3. In Pai Gow Poker, the House Way of setting a hand.

Set Mining – In Holdem, the act of a player holding a pocket Pair, usually a low or medium Pair, hoping to get a third card of the same rank (Three of a Kind). The hope is usually for it to happen on the flop, but the term still applies if the player hopes for this improvement on the turn or even the river. See also *Set*, definition 1.

Set the Deck – Directive term to dealers to sort the deck back to successive order by suit and rank. This is typically done when new cards are introduced, the table closes, or during a poker tournament break to ensure that all 52 cards are accounted for.

Set-Over-Set – An instance when two hands each have Three of a Kind (also known as *Set*). Thus, one hand's set is ranked higher (over) than the other hand's set.

Shift – A specific time period when a casino employee works (or is scheduled to work) throughout the day. See also *Day*, *Graveyard*, *Roadmap*, and *Swing*.

Shill – A player paid by the house and who uses house money to help start and maintain a casino game, so the table doesn't look empty. See also *Pumper*, *Ringer*, and *Prop*.

Short Stack – A player's small number of chips, or his stack value is small relative to other players.

Shove – See *All-In*.

Show – To intentionally expose one or more cards to other players. See also *Exposed Cards*.

Showdown – The act of comparing a player's hand face-up hand to compare to the dealer's hand after the last betting round to determine the winner of the hand. Also called *Table(d) Cards*.

Shuffle – The dealer's action of mixing (riffling) cards to randomize the deck before a new hand is to begin. In poker, this signifies the start of a new hand, and card rooms often have rules that once a new dealer shuffle begins, players can no longer dispute the previous hand. In Carnival Games or Blackjack, it ends the current deck's usage and indicates a new round of play. The dealer must always look for any obvious boxed cards and/or damaged cards. See also *Box*, *Make*, *Riffle*, and *Strip*.

Shuffle Machine – A rectangular machine (attached to the table) that shuffles cards quickly in 30 seconds. This eliminates the time a dealer must manually shuffle in between hands. While one deck is being dealt to the players, a second deck is being shuffled, ready to go by the end of the current hand. These auto-shuffling machines can also sort the deck by suit and rank. They do break down and need repairing/servicing every few weeks. Most casinos have extra machines to swap out.

Side Bet – 1. Any private bet made outside the current poker hand or pot. 2. Any of the optional wagers a player can make on the Blackjack or Carnival Games layouts. These bets normally carry a higher house edge than the main bets on the same game. But they offer larger payouts, including Jackpots when a certain hand type is achieved.

Sitting Out – Usually a voluntary act by a player to remove himself from table play temporarily, such as a restroom or smoke break. House rules vary widely, but usually after being away for some time (15 minutes to more than an hour), the dealer calls the floorman to count, rack up this player's cheques, turned into security for safekeeping, and make the space available for another new player.

Sizing-In – The process of professionally and evenly aligning cheques on the table by using the remaining cheques in the dealer's hand, employing the finger-hook technique to integrate them with the existing stack.

Slow Roll/Slow Rolling – The act of deliberately or unintentionally delaying the reveal of a player's hand, often the winning hand during Showdown. This can give other players false hope that they have won, until the "slow roller" reveals their superior hand. It is widely considered poor etiquette. If a player is unsure of their hand's value, they should promptly turn it face-up for the dealer to read.

Small Pair – See *Baby Pairs*.

Snapped Off – To get a good hand beat, or to beat a good hand.

Soft money – Any readily accessible funds that are available for immediate betting, such as cash, credit markers, and casino cheques.

Soft Seat – A seat or game that is desirable to play because of a perceived lack of skill and chance for easy money.

Solid – A term to describe a tight or exceptionally good player.

Spades ♠ – One of the four common suits in a deck of cards. Also known as digging deep, in the hole, and laborers.

Speech Play – See *Coffee Housing*.

Speed Cloth/Suited Speed Cloth – The professional-grade felt found on casino tables. The extra smoothness of this Teflon-coated, stain-resistant cloth surface eliminates surface drag.

Splash Around – Ill-advised aggressive gambling and usually without regard to consequences.

Split – See *Tie*.

Squaring the Deck – The process of neatly aligning and stacking the deck into a single, even pile after shuffling or riffling, but before cutting the deck.

Stack – The pile of chips/cheques in front of a player. Short for chip stack.

Stacked Deck – A deck that has been pre-arranged to give a player a big advantage. See also *Cheat*, definition 1 and *Mechanic*.

Stake – 1. The amount of money a player buys into or brings to gamble for that session. See also *Table Stakes*. 2. A backer who bankrolls/finances (stakes) another individual to play poker. See *Backer*.

Stand – To remain in the same position and not draw any further cards or place any additional wagers. See also *Check*, *Pat*, and *Stand Pat*.

Stand Pat – See *Stand*. Also known as *Pat*.

Starting Hand – Any number of hole cards dealt face down to all players at the beginning of the hand.

Steal – 1. Theft. A felony if caught in a casino and punishable by jail time and being blacklisted. 2. In Poker, to win a pot with a raise and a mediocre hand is said to steal the pot.

Steam – Tilt. See also *On Tilt* and *Tilt*.

Steel Wheel – An Ace to Five Straight Flush.

Stiff – 1. (slang) Any player/patron of the casino who does not or fails to toke/tip, especially when the player just won a decent-sized amount of money and/or the dealer gave great service. Also known as *Tom*. Opposite of *George*. 2. (Stiffed) The failure to receive a toke/tip from a player when generally appropriate. 3. A card that is the only one of its suit in a hand (not matching the other cards).

Stone Cold Nuts – The nuts. See also *Nuts*, definition 2.

Store – (non-standard) Informal reference to the casino or tables. Also known as church. See *Casino*.

Straight – Five consecutively ranked cards having at least two different suits. Also known as *Run*, and *Sequence*.

Straight Draw – A player having four of the five consecutive cards needed to make a Straight.

Straight Flush – A one-suited Straight. Also known as *Quint*. See *Straight* and *Flush*.

Stranger – Any card that does not belong in a player's hand and could be replaced with a better card.

Strategy – A deliberate plan designed to achieve a specific goal, especially in situations involving uncertainty or risk, such as gambling. It incorporates decision-making, adaptability, and calculated actions to optimize outcomes despite unpredictable conditions. Similar to *System*.

Streak – A player's run of winning or losing games or playing sessions. See also *Breaking Streaks* and *Following Streaks*.

Street – A card that is dealt on a particular round. For example, a fourth community card in Holdem is known as fourth street, and a player's fifth card in Seven-Card Stud is fifth street.

Streets (3rd, 4th, 5th) – A card that is dealt on a particular round.

Strip – A step in the shuffling process when the dealer takes top sections of the deck and stacks them on top of each other on the table several times. Sometimes known as *Box*. See also *Shuffle*.

Stub – The unused and undealt portion of the deck. At the conclusion of dealing a hand, a poker dealer having any cards remaining will spread this pile of cards in front of him and place the cut card on top to protect the stub in case a hand reversal is needed, and the top card needs to be dealt. Carnival Games dealers will put these cards in a discard tray.

Stuck – The amount of money a player is losing or has lost in a casino. Applies to any time period.

Suck Out – (slang) Refers to catching a crucial card that drastically improves a losing hand, often referred to as a "miracle" card. This term is commonly used when an underdog player's hand unexpectedly takes the lead. For example, in Hold'em, a player holding K-K goes all-in against a player with Q-Q. The Kings are favored to win unless a Straight or Flush is possible for either hand. However, on the river, one of the two remaining Queens appears, giving the player with Q-Q Three of a Kind Queens and the winning hand.

Sucker – Also known as *Mark*.

Sucker Bet – (slang) Any of the high-risk proposition bets that heavily favor the house.

Suit – One of four distinct groupings of playing cards. In a standard deck of cards, they are: Spades ♠, Hearts ♥, Diamonds ♦, and Clubs ♣.

Suited Connectors – Any starting Holdem hand that is consecutive in rank and of the same suit. For example, 8-7 of Hearts. See also *Connectors*.

Suited Gappers – Any same-suited hole cards in Holdem that are close in rank and could make a straight with community cards but have one or more missing cards in between the hole cards. Examples: J-9 of Spades is a suited one gapper, 7-4 of Clubs is a suited two gapper, and Q-8 of Diamonds is a suited three gapper. See also *Suited Connectors*.

Super Bonus – A required side bet that must match the Ante bet to be dealt cards. Found on Crazy 4 Poker.

Supervisor – See *Floorman*.

Surveillance – 1. Video cameras constantly record nearly every square inch of the casino property, except where prohibited by law (restrooms, inside hotel rooms). 2. The highly trained technical (IT) team to watch, monitor, suspect, flag, and investigate any problem, individual, or situation. Works with Security. See also *Security*.

Sweat the Money – The visible concern/worry/anxiety shown by supervisors or higher level management that players are winning large amounts or consistently winning during a *Hot Streak*.

Swing – The late afternoon/evening shift for casino workers. See *Day* and *Graveyard*.

System – A structured, organized set of components or methods designed to work together to accomplish a goal. Similar to *Strategy*.

2, Two – Any two. The lowest ranked card in the deck below a three, and at times, the second lowest card above an Ace when the Ace is low. Also known as deuce.

2-Way – Any bet that is placed for the player and dealer.

3, Three – Any three. The ranking numbered card above a two but below a four. Also known as trey, tree.

3-Card Bonus – An optional bonus bet based solely on a player's three specific cards, with rules and payouts varying by game.

10, T, Ten – Any ten. The highest-ranking numbered card above a nine but below a Jack. T is a substitute letter for 10.

3 Shot Poker – A Carnival Game variant focused on players making three- and five-card hands using their two cards with community cards.

T.I.T.O. – Acronym for Ticket In, Ticket Out. Used in place for cash and allows players to move quickly from one slot or gaming machine to another. Printed paper tickets always include the date, time, bar code, serial number, establishment's name, expiration date, and value amount.

Table – The horizontal surface upon which Carnival Games are played. Each game has specific requirements regarding the table's size, height, the number of players it can accommodate, and whether the dealer is standing or seated. A fully operational table includes a cheque bank, a betting layout, cards, various lammers, a slit and paddle for the drop box, an armrest around the perimeter, and a drink rail near the armrest.

Table Inspector – European term for *Floorman* or *Supervisor*.

Table Inventory Card – See *Game-Closing Card*.

Table Selection – A player's scouting/examining of any number of available games in which to sit down and play. This potential player can observe a few hands at several tables to determine player action, loose/tight players, amount of money on the table, pace of the game, and available seat position relevant to certain players who are conducive, favorable, or promising to his style of play.

Table Sign – A sign on the table stating the minimum/maximum wagers and oftentimes a few rules and payouts.

Table(d) Cards – At the end of the final betting round, all remaining players turn their cards face up for hand evaluation to determine the winner. To officially win, the backs of all the players' cards must lie flat on the table, ensuring that surveillance can verify the winning hand. See *Showdown*.

Take a Walk/Take a Hike – (slang) A rude verbal comment from one player to another to leave the table area, either temporarily or permanently. Usually said to an upset player.

Take it Down – (slang) An encouragement to a player to win.

Take Out/Tapped Out – 1. The end of a dealer's shift or time at the table. Another dealer will step in to take over the table and relieve the current one. 2. A player who has lost his entire bankroll, either in general or what was in his pocket.

Tank/Tanking/In the Tank – A player taking an unusually long time to think and decide to act.

Tap – 1. To wager an all-in bet or bet big enough to force another player to go all-in. 2. A dealer's hand physically tapping a dealer on the shoulder to initiate a dealer change and push the dealer out of that table. This "tap" can also be a verbal "Last Hand" command. See also *Dealer Change* and *Take Out/Tapped Out*, definition 1.

Tap In/Tap Out – See *Dealer Change*.

Tap Out – See *Dealer Change*.

Tapped Out – Out of money. Either in general or in a player's pocket.

Tapping the Aquarium – Unsolicited advice from a know-it-all player telling another player what he is doing wrong or how to play better.

Texas Hold'em – Complete name for Holdem. See *Holdem*.

Texas Hold'em Bonus Poker – A Carnival Game variant focused on players using hole and community cards to beat the dealer. Similar to *Ultimate Texas Hold'em*.

Texture – In flop games, the relatedness of community cards to each other and the potential for completing draws.

The Expert at the Card Table – The first "How To" book written on card cheating, published in 1902 by S. W. Erdnase, a pseudonymous author whose identity has remained a mystery.

Third Card Rule – Baccarat's set of rules that governs whether a third card is dealt to the Player or Banker hands, based on the initial two-card totals and specific game criteria.

Third Street – 1. In stud games, it is the third card (first face-up card) dealt to a player. 2. In Mississippi Stud, it is the first community card to be dealt.

Three Card Poker – A Carnival Game variant focused on players using their three cards.

Three Flush – Three cards of the same suit.

Three Gapper – See *Gappers*.

Three of a Kind – Three same-ranked cards. Also known as *Set*, *Triplets*, *Trips*, and trio.

Thumb-Cut (ting) Cheques – An unprofessional dealer method of cutting cheques by using the thumb to separate and count a stack of cheques outwardly to the side. While players often use this method, a dealer should remain professional and avoid it. The proper way is to drop cut by hooking the index finger and sizing-in. See *Drop Cut(ting)* and *Sizing-In*.

Ticket – A card. See *Card*.

Tie – 1. In Baccarat, both the Player and Banker cards' final point values are equal. A player will bet this bet if he thinks both Player and Banker hands are equal in value, thus resulting in a push for those hands, while the Tie bet will pay 8:1. If the result is not a tie, this bet loses. Usually noted in either green or with a "T" on scorecards. 2. In Pai Gow Poker, a hand that the player and dealer have equaled. This generally results in the player losing that High or Low Hand. 3. Two or more hands of equal value at showdown. Also known as *Split*. 4. To push bets. Also known as *Push*.

Tied On – Any hand worthy of playing until showdown.

Tiger – A little cat. See *Little Cat*.

Tilt – 1. Negative behavior because of losing. 2. An upset player, usually following a single or a string of losing hands, who uses this negative energy and, as a result, plays less than optimal in the hopes of recapturing some or all his losses. Also known as *Steam*.

Timid Player – A shy/inexperienced player who makes less than or loses more than he should.

Title 31 – In the U.S., the Bank Secrecy Act (BSA) establishes regulations for financial institutions, including casinos, aimed at preventing money laundering and other financial crimes. Management staff and dealers/croupiers receive specialized training to identify irregularities at the tables.

To – A house designation of what the bet will pay out. For example, 15 to 1 (15:1) means for every unit wagered, the winning bet will receive fifteen. See also *For*.

Toke Box – A container attached to the gaming table to store tips/tokes/gratuities given by players to the dealer. See also *Drop Box*.

Toke Committee – For shared or pooled tokes, a small group of elected dealers responsible for collecting all tokes across the entire casino floor on a daily basis. They then rack up the cheques, count them, report and turn in the total amount to the employee cage. This can happen each shift or, more commonly, every 24-hour period. The previous day's toke rate (total) is posted for the dealers to see, and they can get a fairly good idea what their paycheck will be. Committee members are compensated for their extra time and responsibility before or after their scheduled shift.

Toke/Token – A tip or gratuity given to dealers to show appreciation. Many casino table games pool tokes together and every dealer on that shift, or 24-hour period, earns the same toke rate. Poker and KYO dealers keep their own tokes. Tips represent a substantial amount of a dealer's income. Tipping is considered good etiquette in some countries, but banned, frowned upon, or discouraged in others. Short for "token of appreciation." Also known as *Fiche, Gratuity, Jeton, Mil, Pourboire* and *Zuke*.

Tom – See *Stiff*, definition 1.

Top Pair – The highest possible Pair a player can have using a hole and community card.

Top Pair Top Kicker – The best Pair and best kicker a player can have.

Top Two Pairs – In any flop game, Two Pairs made with both of a player's hole cards and the highest two cards on the board. Similar examples can include bottom Two Pairs, middle Two Pairs, top and bottom Pairs, top and middle Pairs, and middle and bottom Pairs.

Towel – 1. A request by or for the player that an actual towel, or cover, such as a playover box is needed to cover his cheques while he steps away from the table. It also serves to mark and protect his spot at the table until he returns. 2. An urgent request to a supervisor that an actual towel is needed to wipe up any food or drinks that spilled onto any part of the craps table.

Tray – A stackable tray holding 100 (five rows of 20 each) standard casino or poker chips/cheques.

Triple Up – Any bet that gets paid twice the amount that is wagered. For example, a $10 bet pays $20 and is now worth $30 total.

Triplets – (nonstandard) Three of a Kind. See *Three of a Kind*.

Trips – Any wager that requires *Three of a Kind* or better to receive a payout.

Turn/River – The remaining set of community cards revealed by the dealer for everyone's use to make or complete a full poker hand. See also *Flop*.

Two Flush – Any two cards that are same-suited.

Two Pair – Two same-ranked cards plus two more same-ranked cards.

Two-Gapper – See *Gappers*.

Ultimate Texas Hold'em – A Carnival Game variant focused on players using hole plus community cards to beat the dealer. Similar to *Texas Hold'em Bonus Poker*.

Undercards – 1. In a flop game, one or more community cards that rank lower than a player's Pair. 2. In a flop game, a pocket Pair held by a player that is lower than any card rank on the community board. Also known as underpair.

Undercut – 1. A cheating shuffling technique to prepare a stacked deck. See also *Mechanic*. 2. The final down card in low-hole stud turns out to be the lowest hole card.

Underdog – A player who is not mathematically favored to win or be right.

Underfull – The worst and smaller Full House in poker. Opposite of *Big Full*. See *Full House*.

Underground Casino – Any illegal gambling business, operation, or activity secretly operating without the proper permits or licenses.

Underpair – See *Undercards*, definition 2. Opposite of *Overpair*.

Uniform – The attire that dealers wear. Shirts, vests, aprons, name tags, and jackets are issued by the casino. Dealers are often expected to provide their own black pants and comfortable black shoes.

Up Card – The dealer's revealed card, face up for the players to see while acting on their hands. This card often determines what action, if any, players take before it is the dealer's turn to act. It is usually the first card dealt to the dealer and is place on top of the Down Card. Opposite of *Down Card*.

Upswing – A series of wins by a player during a session or a time period. Opposite of *Downswing*.

Value – The strength of a hand according to that game being played and its perceived expectation to win that hand.

Vest Holdout – An invented cheating device worn under the vest or coat and the long sleeve of a cheater. Simple by design, this "breastplate" metal gadget was able to take card(s), conceal them out of play under the cheater's clothing, and allow the user to reintroduce the card(s) at a more opportune time. The Kepplinger Machine was the most famous of all these devices from the late 1880s to early 1920s and used primarily in the Old West. See also *Holdout Machine* and *Jacob's Ladder*.

Victory Rip – 1. The triumphant spreading of a player's hand at showdown either with the player winning or thinking he's won the hand. 2. Any poker or table games dealer's spreading of the entire deck of cards on the table in front of him for inspection (by the dealer, players, management, and the eye in the sky) that all cards are accounted for.

Villain – During instructional or hand reviewing, it is the player's opponent whose hand is being reviewed or focused. Opposite of *Hero*.

Visible Cards – Anytime a card is correctly dealt face up for all players to see, and if a community card, to use to complete their poker hands. See *Up Card*.

Wager – A Bet. See *Bet*.

War – See *Casino War*.

Warning – A verbal (or written) disciplinary measure during which management speaks to a player regarding his behavior, play, or conduct. Depending on the seriousness of the infraction, this step may be skipped, and a player can be issued a direct penalty. See *Penalty*.

Wash – See *Scramble*.

Waving – The act of coiling or crimping cards by a cheater to easily identify the wavy card in another player's hand or within the deck. However, this is acceptable in Midi-Baccarat games.

Weak – A type of player who folds many hands.

Wedges – Tapered or shaved-edged cards easily retrieved from a deck by a cheater when needed.

Welch/Welcher – The failure of/or the player who fails to pay a debt or avoids paying it.

Wet Board – Connected or suited cards that give a lot of possibilities to drawing hands. For example, a Holdem board of 6d-7s-8s-8h-9s has many possibilities for hands to complete Straight Flushes, Four of a Kind eights, many Full Houses, Flushes, and Straights. Also known as *Coordinated*.

Whack – The proper bet stacking of cheques from the largest denominations on the bottom to the smallest denominations on the top of the stack.

Whale – An extreme high roller. A player is designated when $5 million is risked in a gaming weekend.

Wheel – A hand consisting of the five lowest cards in which Ace is low, hence A-2-3-4-5. Also known as *Bicycle/Bike*.

Whiff(ed) – A hand (or a player) that missed the draw to improve the hand. See *Draw*, definition 6.

White Chip – (slang) One dollar, usually denominated by a white casino cheque with $1 imprinted on it. The lowest chip denomination generally a player can use.

Window – In a flop game, the first card (after the burn) that the dealer snaps onto the table and turns over before spreading these three cards in the center of the table.

Winning Hand – Any hand that receives payment from the dealer or a Banker.

Winning Streak – See *Run*, definition 2.

Wired – Back-to-back or consecutive. Any hand that improves with each street. For example, a Pair improves to Three of a Kind, then improves to Four of a Kind.

Wired Pair – In Holdem or Seven-Card Stud, a pocket Pair. In Five-Card Stud, the door card pairing the hole card.

Wooden Hand – A hand that cannot improve to win. See *Drawing Dead*.

Woppitzer – Usually an onlooker but could be a player, it is anyone who smells of body odor and/or bad breath who is near any other player at any casino table. These people can make matters worse as they often offer unsolicited advice/comments, and at times are obnoxious.

Work the Broads – To cheat at cards. See also *Cheater*.

Working the Telegraph – – A cheating method where players exchange pre-arranged signals—physical, verbal, or emotional—to share hidden information. These signals resemble sign language or use unique words or cues understood only by the cheaters. Other methods include embedding keywords or pitch variations in casual conversations, often unnoticed except by vigilant observers.

Worst of It – To be in the least advantageous position. Opposite of *Best of It*.

Yard – Short for $100 or a $100 bill. See also *Benjamin (Franklin)* and *C-Note*.

Yellow – A $1000 cheque. Also known as *Biscuit*, *Canary*, and *Dime*.

YO – 1. Abbreviation for "yoleven." 2. Expression to greet someone or get his attention.

Z-Game – The lowest stakes game in the house. Opposite of *A-Game*, definition 2.

Zip – Nothing.

Zuke – (slang) Dealer term for toke. See *Toke/Token*.

FOOTNOTES

The following sources were referenced in this work:

[1] "3 Shot Poker Opens at Two Las Vegas Casinos." *Vegas Advantage*. Accessed March 11, 2025. https://vegasadvantage.com/3-shot-poker-opens-at-two-las-vegas-casinos/.

[2] Caroline Richardson. "Baccarat History." Reviewed by Jack Cooper. *Baccarat Online*. Accessed October 2, 2024. https://www.Baccarat.net/history/.

[3] Whiting, T. (2010). "The History of Baccarat." In D. Schwartz (Ed.), *Center for Gaming Research Occasional Paper Series: Paper 03*, 1–8. Accessed October 3, 2024. https://digitalscholarship.unlv.edu/cgi/viewcontent.cgi?article=1019&context=occ_papers/.

[4] "Big Six Wheel." *Showmen's Museum*. Accessed October 22, 2024. https://showmensmuseum.org/concessions/a-beautifully-preserved-big-6-gaming-wheel/.

[5] "Source for the History of the Big Six Wheel." *Casino Blog*. Accessed October 22, 2024. https://www.casino.com/blog/2024/10/22/big-six-wheel-casino-game/.

[6] David Sklansky. "I Invented Caribbean Stud." *Two Plus Two Forum*. Accessed December 13, 2024. https://forumserver.twoplustwo.com/74/special-sklansky-forum/i-invened-caribbean-stud-641/.

[7] "Complete Guide to Caribbean Stud Poker." *Medium – Unshuffled*. Accessed December 13, 2024. https://medium.com/unshuffled/complete-guide-to-caribbean-stud-poker-28b14876789.

[8] "Casino War: A Basic History." *Casino777 Blog*. Accessed October 28, 2024. https://blog.casino777.ch/en/a-basic-history-of-casino-war/.

[9] "Crazy 4 Poker." *Wizard of Odds*. Accessed October 28, 2024. https://wizardofodds.com/games/crazy-4-poker/.

[10] "DJ Wild: How to Play." *Wagers*. Accessed December 9, 2024. https://wagers.com/staging/4285/how-to-play/dj-wild/.

[11] Brian Jeacoma. "High Card Flush." Accessed November 12, 2024. https://playslots4realmoney.com/online-casino-games/table/high-card-flush/.

[12] "Shuffle Master Inc. Places Winning Bet." *Chicago Tribune*. October 8, 1995. Accessed October 10, 2024. https://www.chicagotribune.com/1995/10/08/shuffle-master-inc-places-winning-bet/.

[13] "Understanding Mississippi Stud Strategy." *Casino.org*. Accessed September 29, 2024. https://www.casino.org/blog/understanding-mississippi-stud-strategy/.

[14] "Pai Gow Poker." *Los Angeles Times*. Accessed December 3, 2024. https://www.latimes.com/archives/la-xpm-2002-nov-03-me-poker3-story.html.

[15] "Texas Hold'em Bonus Poker." *Wizard of Odds*. Accessed December 2, 2024. https://wizardofodds.com/games/texas-hold-em-bonus/.

[16] "Three Card Brag." Accessed October 13, 2024. https://gambiter.com/poker/Three-card_brag.html.

[17] "History of Three Card Poker." *Rainbow Casino Blog*. Accessed October 10, 2024. https://rainbowcasino.co.uk/blog/history-three-card-poker.

[18] "CasinoReviews Interviews Stephen Au-Yeung: Creator of Casino Hold'em." *CasinoReviews Blog*. Accessed October 31, 2024. https://casinoreviews.com/blog/casinoreviews-interviews-stephen-au-yeung-creator-of-casino-hold-em.

[19] "An Introduction to Ultimate Texas Hold'em." *Plaza Royal News*. Accessed November 1, 2024. https://www.plazaroyal.com/news/an-introduction-to-ultimate-texas-holdem.

NOTES

INDEX

3 Shot Poker 30, 130
accepting employment and starting 72-74
age verification/check for identification 12-13
amenities 21
application 72
armrest (rail) 15, 18
audition 72-73
Baccarat 31-45, 130
    bets
        Player/Banker 31-45
        side bets 41-42
        Tie 40
    burning cards 38
    commission 17-18, 31, 32, 40, 41, 45
    commission boxes 18, 37, 38, 40, 41
    dealing procedures
        adding point totals/card values 39
        cutting the cards 38
        dealing cards from the shoe 39
        end of shoe 41
        third card (drawing/standing) rule 40-41
        tie hands 40
    equipment 34-38
        baton/dealer paddle 38
        discard can and lid/tray 37
        lammer rack 18, 38
        Player/Banker buttons 37
        shoes 37
        tables/layout 34-36
    grids/scorecards 37, 43-44
    types of
        Baccarat Banque 31, 33, 45
        Chemin de Fer 31, 32, 33, 38, 45
        Punto Banco 31-32, 40, 45
            Mini-Baccarat 32, 34-35, 37, 39, 41
            Midi-Baccarat 32, 34-35, 37-38, 41
bank
    cover 10, 14
    house 7, 11, 15-16, 25, 36
bet types
    ①, ②, and $ 56-57
    3 Card Bonus 56-57, 58-59
    3rd, 4th, 5th Streets 51, 58-59
    6 Card Bonus 66-67
    Ante 48, 50-51, 52-53, 54-55, 58-59, 65, 66-67, 68-69
    Bet 7-13, 30-70
    Blind 30, 48, 52-53, 65, 66-67, 68-69
    Check 56-57, 58-59, 65, 68-69
    Flush/Flush Rush 54-55
    Fold 30, 48, 50-51, 52-53, 54-55, 58-59, 64, 65, 66-67, 68-69
    Fortune Bonus 61, 64
    Pair Plus 66-67
    Play 23, 50-51, 52-53, 66-67, 68-69
    Progressive 18, 42, 48, 49, 50-51, 52-53, 54-55, 56-57, 58-59, 60, 64, 65, 66-67, 68-69
    Queens Up 50-51

    Raise 51, 54-55, 68-69
    Straight Flush/Straight Flush Rush 54-55
    Super Bonus 50-51
    Trips 52-53, 68-69
Big Wheel 45-46, 130
black and whites 72
breaking a table/broken games 14
breaks versus brushes 74
burn(ing) cards 8, 38, 51, 57, 59
callouts (alert/approval) 7, 11, 13, 22, 25, 71
Caribbean Stud Poker 48, 130
cash handling 11
cash/money plays 22
casino personnel/hierarchy of staff 9
Casino War 49, 130
chairs 18, 21, 71
change only 71
changing cash for cheques 21, 71
cheating 7, 13, 14, 70, 71
cheques 15-16, 24-25
    cheque change 25, 71
    chunking 25
    cutting cheques/chips 11, 24-25
    pinching 25
    plucking 25
    rack maintenance 25
    sizing-in 11, 24-25
chip 15
chips versus cheques, colors/values 15
clap/clear hands 7, 10
clarifications 14
collusion 7, 13, 69
color up 16, 19, 70, 71
community cards 30, 56-57, 58-59, 65, 68-69
controlling the game 13, 70
counting cash/bill layering 11, 36
Crazy 4 Poker 50-51, 130
credit/marker 9, 17, 19, 23, 71
criminal background check 73
dead spread/closing the table 14
dealer
    expectations/conduct (do's/don'ts) 6-8
    game procedures 7-8, 11, 22-23, 30, 38, 41, 47, 48, 49, 51, 53, 55, 57, 59, 64, 65, 67, 69
    push/rotation 6, 10-11, 74, 76-77
    qualifying hand 30, 48, 50, 52, 54, 56, 58, 61, 65, 66, 68
    responsibilities 6, 9, 10-14, 25, 73-74, 77
discrepancies 11
DJ Wild 16, 52-53, 130
drug testing 73
dual rate 74
education/training 10, 70, 72
equipment 13, 15-21, 30, 34-38, 46, 48, 49, 50, 52, 54, 56, 58, 60-61, 65, 66, 68, 70, 72
    armrest rail 15, 18
    bank cover 10, 14

126 CARNIVAL GAMES

brush 18
cards
    deck inspections/spreading 26, 29
    dropping the stub 16, 59, 61
    hand/finger placement 24-25, 27-29
    joker 16, 36, 39, 52-53, 60, 62, 63, 64
    scrambling 26, 29
    shuffle/riffle/sequence 26-29
        box 29
        butterfly 29, 86
        cut card placement/cutting 8, 14, 16, 29, 31, 38, 41, 44, 51, 53, 55, 57, 59, 69
        marry 29, 105
        strip 29
    squaring up the deck 26-27, 29
    turning cards 27
chairs 18, 21, 71
cheque bank 10, 11, 15-16, 18
chip carrying case 19
chip tray 11-12, 17, 19
cup and dice (Pai Gow Poker) 60, 64
cup holder 15, 21
cut cards 8, 14, 16, 29, 31, 38, 41, 51, 53, 55, 57, 59, 69
digital display board 18, 43, 44, 60, 64
discard tray 17, 30, 37, 48, 49, 50, 51, 52, 54, 56, 58, 60, 64, 65, 66, 68
drop box/slit/paddle 11, 12, 19, 22, 25, 71
fill order (slip)/credit order 11, 13, 19-20, 74
game closing card 20
lammers 10-11, 13-15, 17-18, 23, 38, 49, 60, 61, 63
layout 14
machine shuffler 17, 26, 76, 130
minimum/maximum sign 13, 16, 32, 70
mini-fan 17
playover box/cover 19
shoe access plate 18
table
    assignment 10, 14
    closing 9, 14, 20
    layouts and types of 15, 30, 34-36, 46, 48, 49, 50, 52, 54, 56, 58, 60-61, 65, 66, 68
    opening 9, 10
    stakes 22, 32, 33, 34, 45
toke box 19, 22, 23
errors, mistakes, and problems 7, 8, 9, 10, 14, 17, 22, 25, 26, 70, 74, 75, 77
etiquette (player) 45, 70
fanning the deck 26
financial transactions 11, 22-23
fingerprinting 73
floorman (see *supervisor*)
Flop/Turn/River 65, 68-69
Footnotes 124
foreign cheques 22, 71
full-time/part-time work 73-74

gambling addiction 75
game protection 13
game-closing card 20
gaming licensure 73-74
glossary 80-123
High Card Flush – I Love Suits 54-55, 130
history (see *Footnotes*)
illegal 70
integrity 7-9, 13, 77
job searching 72
know the game(s) being dealt 10, 70
Let It Ride 56-57, 130
lighting/atmosphere 21, 45
logging in/out of dealers and players 12
making change for the player 6, 70
marker (credit) (see *credit/marker*)
Mississippi Stud 57-58, 130
No More Bets 47, 70, 71
No Roll 64
on call/extra board/temporary work 73-74
Pai Gow Poker 60-64, 130
    Ace-High 60, 63, 64
    commission 41, 64
    Envy 17, 60, 61, 64
    Face Up Pai Gow Poker 60, 61
    High hand 60-64
    House way to setting hands 17, 60, 61, 62, 63
    Low Hand 60-64
    Main bet 60-64
    player spot number 60-61
    RNG 17, 61, 64
payout
    correct hand 7, 8, 10, 25, 39
    correct order (see *dealer, game procedures*)
pencil/pencil person 9, 14
promotional chips 15, 23
proposition players 74
qualifying hand (see *dealer, qualifying hand*)
rack
    count 17, 20
    maintenance 11, 25
re-buy 22
RFID 15
shills 74
squaring up the deck 26-29
starting/ending the shift 10, 14
supervisor 6, 8, 9, 10, 12-14, 19-20, 23, 26, 34, 71, 74
surveillance 9, 22, 24, 51, 57, 59
Texas Hold'em Bonus Poker 65, 130
theft 9, 13, 14, 71
Three Card Poker 30, 66-67, 130
tokes/tips 22-23
    committee 23
    keep your own (KYO) 23
    shared 23
Ultimate Texas Hold'em (UTH) 68-69, 130

POKER HAND RANKINGS and PAYOUTS

Standard Rankings:

Royal Flush	A♥ K♥ Q♥ J♥ 10♥	Any one-suited Ace-High straight
Straight Flush	9♥ 8♥ 7♥ 6♥ 5♥	Any one-suited straight
Four of a Kind	7♥ 7♠ 7♦ 7♣ 8♥	Four same-ranked cards
Full House	4♥ 4♠ 4♣ 7♥ 7♣	Three same-ranked cards plus two same-ranked cards
Flush	J♥ 8♥ 7♥ 4♥ 2♥	Any five one-suited cards
Straight	9♣ 8♥ 7♠ 6♣ 5♦	Five consecutively ranked cards
Three of a Kind	9♠ 9♣ 9♦ Q♣ 3♥	Three same-ranked cards
Two Pair	7♥ 7♠ 4♠ 4♣ K♣	Two same-ranked cards plus two same-ranked cards
One Pair	3♥ 3♠ A♠ K♥ 6♣	Two same-ranked cards
High Card	A♠ Q♣ 9♦ 6♣ 2♥	Five unmatched cards
♠ ♥ ♦ ♣		Highest to lowest suit ranking: Spades, Hearts, Diamonds, Clubs

3 Shot Poker (3 Cards)
Royal Flush	50:1
Straight Flush	30:1
Three of a Kind	20:1
Straight	4:1
Flush	2:1
Pair	1:1

3 Shot Poker (5 Cards)
Royal Flush	500:1
Straight Flush	200:1
Four of a Kind	50:1
Full House	40:1
Flush	30:1
Straight	20:1
Three of a Kind	10:1

Caribbean Stud Progressive
Royal Flush	100% of Jackpot
Straight Flush	10% of Jackpot
Four of a Kind	$500
Full House	$100
Flush	$50

Caribbean Stud (Bet)
Royal Flush	100:1
Straight Flush	50:1
Four of a Kind	20:1
Full House	7:1
Flush	5:1
Straight	4:1
Three of a Kind	3:1
Two Pair	2:1
All other hands	1:1

Crazy 4 Poker (Queens Up)
Four of a Kind	50:1
Straight Flush	40:1
Three of a Kind	7:1
Flush	4:1
Straight	3:1
Two Pairs	2:1
Queens or Better	1:1

Crazy 4 Poker (Super Bonus)
Four Aces	200:1
Four of a Kind	30:1
Straight Flush	15:1
Flush	3:2
Straight	1:1

DJ Wild Progressive
Royal Flush	100% of Jackpot
Straight Flush	10% of Jackpot
Four of a Kind	$500
Full House	$100
Flush	$50

DJ Wild (Bet)
Royal Flush	100:1
Straight Flush	50:1
Four of a Kind	20:1
Full House	7:1
Flush	5:1
Straight	4:1
Three of a Kind	3:1
Two Pair	2:1
All other hands	1:1

High Card Flush (Flush/Flush Rush)
7-Card Flush	300:1
6-Card Flush	100:1
5-Card Flush	10:1
4-Card Flush	1:1

High Card Flush (Straight Flush/Super Flush Rush)

7-Card Straight Flush 8000:1
6-Card Straight Flush 1000:1
5-Card Straight Flush 100:1
4-Card Straight Flush 60:1
3-Card Straight Flush 7:1

High Card Flush Progressive

7-Card Straight Flush 100% of Jackpot
6-Card Straight Flush 10% of Jackpot
5-Card Straight Flush 300 for 1
4-Card Straight Flush 50 for 1
3-Card Straight Flush 3 for 1

Let It Ride Payouts

Royal Flush 1000:1
Straight Flush 200:1
Four of a Kind 50:1
Full House 11:1
Flush 8:1
Straight 5:1
Three of a Kind 3:1
Two Pair 2:1
Pair of 10s or Better 1:1

Let It Ride (3 Card Bonus)

Straight Flush 40:1
Three of a Kind 30:1
Straight 6:1
Flush 3:1
Pair 1:1

Mississippi Stud (Ante and Streets)

Royal Flush 500:1
Straight Flush 100:1
Four of a Kind 40:1
Full House 10:1
Flush 6:1
Straight 4:1
Three of a Kind 3:1
Two Pair 2:1
Pair of Jacks or Better 1:1
Pair of 6s – 10s Push

Mississippi Stud (3 Card Bonus)

Straight Flush 40:1
Three of a Kind 30:1
Straight 6:1
Flush 3:1
Pair 1:1

Pai Gow Poker 5-Card High Hand Ranking

Royal Flush
Straight Flush
Four of a Kind
Full House
Flush
Ace-High Straight
A-5 Wheel Straight
Remaining Straights
Three of a Kind
Two Pairs
One Pair
High Card

Pai Gow Poker 2-Card Low Hand Ranking

Pair
Highest Card

Pai Gow Poker Fortune Bet

7-Card Straight Flush – No Joker 8000:1
Royal Flush Plus Royal Match 2000:1
7-Card Straight Flush – with Joker 1000:1
Five Aces 400:1
Royal Flush 150:1
Straight Flush 50:1
Four of a Kind 25:1
Full House 5:1
Flush 4:1
Three of a Kind 3:1
Straight 2:1

Pai Gow Poker Insurance

9-High 100:1
10-High 25:1
Jack-High 15:1
Queen-High 6:1
King-High 5:1
Ace-High 3:1

Pai Gow Poker Ace-High

Dealer and Player Ace High 40:1
Dealer Ace-High with Joker 15:1
Dealer Ace-High No Joker 5:1

Three Card Poker (Ante Bonus)

Straight Flush 5:1
Three of a Kind 4:1
Straight 1:1

Three Card Poker (Pair Plus)

Straight Flush 40:1
Three of a Kind 30:1
Straight 6:1
Flush 3:1
Pair 1:1

Three Card Poker (6 Card Bonus)

6-Card Royal Flush $100,000
5-Card Royal Flush 1000:1
5-Card Straight Flush 200:1
Four of a Kind 50:1
Full House 20:1
5-Card Flush 15:1
5-Card Straight 10:1
Three of a Kind 5:1 (or 7:1)

Ultimate Texas Holdem Blinds

Royal Flush 500:1
Straight Flush 50:1
Four of a Kind 10:1
Full House 3:1
Flush 3:2
Straight 1:1
Other Hands/Tie Push* (must beat the dealer)

Ultimate Texas Holdem Trips

Royal Flush 50:1
Straight Flush 40:1
Four of a Kind 30:1
Full House 8:1
Flush 7:1
Straight 4:1
Three of a Kind 3:1

CARNIVAL GAMES QUICK REFERENCE

GAME	OBJECTIVE	DECK USAGE	PLAY AGAINST	DEALER QUALIFY	BONUS BETS
3 SHOT	To form the best possible three-card and five-card poker hands by combining the player's two hole cards with one and three community cards, respectively	1 Deck*	Players play to achieve a hand	—	YES
BACCARAT	To wager on the Player or Banker hand closer to 9 points	2 to 8 Decks	Bettors chose Player hand or Banker hand will be higher	—	YES
BIG WHEEL	To win by having the Wheel's pointer align with the number the player selects	NO	Non-winning slots on the wheel	—	NO
CARIBBEAN STUD POKER	To achieve a payable 5-card hand higher than the Dealer's hand	1 Deck*	Player vs. Dealer	Ace-King or higher	YES
CASINO WAR	To secure a higher single card than the Dealer's, or, in the event of a tie, to wager in pursuit of higher secondary cards	1 to 6 Decks	Player vs. Dealer	—	YES
CRAZY 4 POKER	To form a higher-ranked hand than the Dealer's by selecting the best 4 out of 5 cards	1 Deck*	Player vs. Dealer	King High	YES
DJ WILD	To achieve a higher-ranking five-card hand than the Dealer's five-card hand	1 Deck with 1 Joker*	Player vs. Dealer	Always	YES
HIGH CARD FLUSH / I LOVE SUITS	To achieve a payable higher flush-only hand than the Dealer's hand	1 Deck*	Player vs. Dealer	3-Card Flush, 9 High	YES
LET IT RIDE	To achieve a payable five-card hand by combining both community cards with three hole cards	1 Deck*	Players play to achieve a hand	—	YES
MISSISSIPPI STUD	To achieve a payable five-card hand by combining three community cards with two hole cards	1 Deck*	Players play to achieve a hand	—	YES
PAI GOW POKER	To create two poker hands—a five-card hand and a two-card hand—that both rank higher than the Dealer's corresponding hands	1 Deck with 1 Joker*	Player vs. Dealer	Always, unless Ace-High rule is used	YES
TEXAS HOLD'EM BONUS POKER	To achieve a higher-ranking five-card poker hand than the Dealer's by combining two hole cards with the five community cards	1 Deck*	Player vs. Dealer	Always	YES
THREE CARD POKER	To form a higher-ranking three-card hand than the Dealer's	1 Deck*	Player vs. Dealer	Queen High	YES
ULTIMATE TEXAS HOLD'EM	To achieve a higher-ranking five-card poker hand than the Dealer's by combining two hole cards with the five community cards	1 Deck*	Player vs. Dealer	Any Pair	YES

* When a single deck is used, it is common to have two decks in rotation: one being dealt while the other is in the shuffle machine.

Made in the USA
Las Vegas, NV
06 April 2025